Fundamentals of Machine Learning

Fundamentals of Machine Learning

Mia Williams

WILLFORD PRESS
www.willfordpress.com

Published by Willford Press,
118-35 Queens Blvd., Suite 400,
Forest Hills, NY 11375, USA

ISBN: 978-1-64728-028-4

Cataloging-in-Publication Data

Fundamentals of machine learning / Mia Williams.
p. cm.
Includes bibliographical references and index.
ISBN 978-1-64728-028-4
1. Machine learning. 2. Artificial intelligence. 3. Machine theory. I. Williams, Mia.
Q325.5 .F86 2022
006.31--dc23

For information on all Willford Press publications
visit our website at www.willfordpress.com

TABLE OF CONTENTS

PREFACE

This book is a culmination of my many years of practice in this field. I attribute the success of this book to my support group. I would like to thank my parents who have showered me with unconditional love and support and my peers and professors for their constant guidance.

The scientific study of statistical models and algorithms that computer systems use in order to perform a specific task without any explicit instructions is referred to as machine learning. It relies on patterns and inference. Machine learning is a subset of artificial intelligence. The study of mathematical optimization contributes significantly to the methods, applications and theory of machine learning. Some of the different models, which are used within this field are artificial neural networks, decision trees and Bayesian networks. Machine learning is applied in various other fields such as in machine perception, agriculture, adaptive websites, bioinformatics, optimization, sentiment analysis, etc. The topics included in this book on machine learning are of utmost significance and bound to provide incredible insights to readers. It unfolds the innovative aspects of this field, which will be crucial for the progress of this field in the future. Those in search of information to further their knowledge will be greatly assisted by this book.

The details of chapters are provided below for a progressive learning:

Chapter – What is Machine Learning?

Machine learning falls under artificial intelligence to study algorithms and statistical models used by computer systems for performing certain computing operations and processes. Computational statistics, mathematical optimization and data mining fall under its domain. This is an introductory chapter which will briefly introduce about machine learning and its uses.

Chapter – Supervised Learning and Algorithms

Supervised learning refers to the task of learning a function that maps an input to output. Some of the algorithms of machine learning include decision tree, linear regression, logistic regression, random forests, linear discriminant analysis, etc. The topics elaborated in this chapter will help in gaining a better perspective about supervised learning and these machine learning algorithms.

Chapter – Unsupervised Learning and Algorithms

Unsupervised learning deals with the use of unlabeled data for its working and modeling without supervision. It includes cluster analysis, hidden Markov model, Gaussian mixture model, etc. This chapter closely examines about unsupervised learning and these related algorithms to provide an extensive understanding of the subject.

Chapter – Reinforcement Learning and Algorithms

Reinforcement learning is one of the basic machine paradigms of machine learning which uses dynamic programming techniques for maximizing notions of cumulative reward in an environment. It involves value function, Monte Carlo method, brute-force search, etc. This chapter has been carefully written to provide an easy understanding of reinforcement learning and its algorithms.

Chapter – Applications

There are a wide range of applications of machine learning which include price optimization and dynamic pricing, heart disease diagnosis, diabetes and liver disease prediction, robotic surgery, cancer detection, drug discovery, etc. All these applications of machine learning have been carefully analyzed in this chapter.

Mia Williams

Machine learning falls under artificial intelligence to study algorithms and statistical models used by computer systems for performing certain computing operations and processes. Computational statistics, mathematical optimization and data mining fall under its domain. This is an introductory chapter which will briefly introduce about machine learning and its uses.

Machine Learning (ML) is a category of algorithm that allows software applications to become more accurate in predicting outcomes without being explicitly programmed. The basic premise of machine learning is to build algorithms that can receive input data and use statistical analysis to predict an output while updating outputs as new data becomes available.

The processes involved in machine learning are similar to that of data mining and predictive modeling. Both require searching through data to look for patterns and adjusting program actions accordingly. Many people are familiar with machine learning from shopping on the internet and being served ads related to their purchase. This happens because recommendation engines use machine learning to personalize online ad delivery in almost real time. Beyond personalized marketing, other common machine learning use cases include fraud detection, spam filtering, network security threat detection, predictive maintenance and building news feeds.

Working of Machine Learning

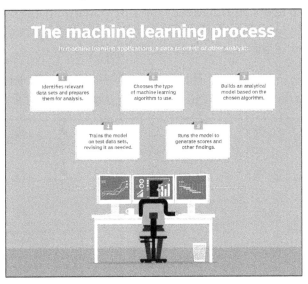

Machine learning algorithms are often categorized as supervised or unsupervised. Supervised algorithms require a data scientist or data analyst with machine learning skills to provide both input and desired output, in addition to furnishing feedback about the accuracy of predictions during algorithm training. Data scientists determine which variables, or features, the model should analyze and use to develop predictions. Once training is complete, the algorithm will apply what was learned to new data.

Unsupervised algorithms do not need to be trained with desired outcome data. Instead, they use an iterative approach called deep learning to review data and arrive at conclusions. Unsupervised learning algorithms -- also called neural networks -- are used for more complex processing tasks than supervised learning systems, including image recognition, speech-to-text and natural language generation. These neural networks work by combing through millions of examples of training data and automatically identifying often subtle correlations between many variables. Once trained, the algorithm can use its bank of associations to interpret new data. These algorithms have only become feasible in the age of big data, as they require massive amounts of training data.

Examples of Machine Learning

Machine learning is being used in a wide range of applications today. One of the most well-known examples is Facebook's News Feed. The News Feed uses machine learning to personalize each member's feed. If a member frequently stops scrolling to read or like a particular friend's posts, the News Feed will start to show more of that friend's activity earlier in the feed. Behind the scenes, the software is simply using statistical analysis and predictive analytics to identify patterns in the user's data and use those patterns to populate the News Feed. Should the member no longer stop to read, like or comment on the friend's posts, that new data will be included in the data set and the News Feed will adjust accordingly.

Machine learning is also entering an array of enterprise applications. Customer relationship management (CRM) systems use learning models to analyze email and prompt sales team members to respond to the most important messages first. More advanced systems can even recommend potentially effective responses. Business intelligence (BI) and analytics vendors use machine learning in their software to help users automatically identify potentially important data points. Human resource (HR) systems use learning models to identify characteristics of effective employees and rely on this knowledge to find the best applicants for open positions.

Machine learning also plays an important role inself-driving cars. Deep learning neural networks are used to identify objects and determine optimal actions for safely steering a vehicle down the road.

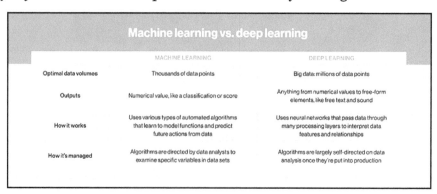

Machine learning vs. deep learning		
	MACHINE LEARNING	DEEP LEARNING
Optimal data volumes	Thousands of data points	Big data: millions of data points
Outputs	Numerical value, like a classification or score	Anything from numerical values to free-form elements, like free text and sound
How it works	Uses various types of automated algorithms that learn to model functions and predict future actions from data	Uses neural networks that pass data through many processing layers to interpret data features and relationships
How it's managed	Algorithms are directed by data analysts to examine specific variables in data sets	Algorithms are largely self-directed on data analysis once they're put into production

Virtual assistant technology is also powered through machine learning. Smart assistants combine several deep learning models to interpret natural speech, bring in relevant context -- like a user's personal schedule or previously defined preferences -- and take an action, like booking a flight or pulling up driving directions.

MACHINE LEARNING ALGORITHM

Machine learning algorithms are programs (math and logic) that adjust themselves to perform better as they are exposed to more data. The "learning" part of machine learning means that those programs change how they process data over time, much as humans change how they process data by learning. So a machine-learning algorithm is a program with a specific way to adjusting its own parameters, given feedback on its previous performance making predictions about a dataset.

Linear Regression

Linear regression is simple, which makes it a great place to start thinking about algorithms more generally. Here it is:

```
ŷ = a * x + b
```

Read aloud, you'd say "y-hat equals a times x plus b".

- y-hat is the output, or guess made by the algorithm, the dependent variable.

- a is the coefficient. It's also the slope of the line that expresses the relationship between x and y-hat.

- x is the input, the given or independent variable.

- b is the intercept, where the line crosses the y axis.

Linear regression expresses a linear relationship between the input x and the output y; that is, for every change in x, y-hat will change by the same amount no matter how far along the line you are. The x is transformed by the same a and b at every point.

Linear regression with only one input variable is called Simple Linear Regression. With more than one input variable, it is called Multiple Linear Regression. An example of Simple Linear Regression would be attempting to predict a house price based on the square footage of the house and nothing more.

```
house_price_estimate = a * square_footage + b
```

Multiple Linear Regression would take other variables into account, such as the distance between the house and a good public school, the age of the house, etc.

The reason why we're dealing with y-hat, an estimate about the real value of y, is because linear regression is a formula used to estimate real values, and error is inevitable. Linear regression is often used to "fit" a scatter plot of given x-y pairs. A good fit minimizes the error between y-hat and the actual y; that is, choosing the right a and b will minimize the sum of the differences between each y and its respective y-hat.

That scatter plot of data points may look like a baguette – long in one direction and short in another – in which case linear regression may achieve a fit. (If the data points look like a meandering river, a straight line is probably not the right function to use to make predictions.)

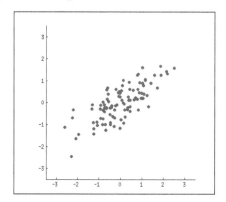

Testing one line after another against the data points of the scatter plot, and automatically correcting it in order to minimize the sum of differences between the line and the points, could be thought of as machine learning in its simplest form.

Logistic Regression

Let's analyze the name first.Logistic regressionis not really regression, not in the sense of linear regression, which predicts continuous numerical values. (And it has nothing to do with logistics. ;)

Logistic regression does not do that. It's actually a binomial classifier that acts like a light switch. A light switch essentially has two states, on and off. Logistic regression takes input data and classifies it ascategoryornot_category, on or off expressed as 1 or 0, based on the strength of the input's signal. So it's a light switch for signal that you find in the data. If you want to mix the metaphor, it's actually more like a transistor, since it both amplifies and gates the signal.

Logistic regression takes input data and*squishes*it, so that no matter what the range of the input is, it will be compressed into the space between 1 and 0. Notice, in the image below, no matter how large the input$x$becomes, the output$y$cannot exceed 1, which it asymptotically approaches, and no matter low$x$is,$y$cannot fall below 0. That's how logistic regression compresses input data into a range between 0 and 1, through this s-shaped, sigmoidal transform.

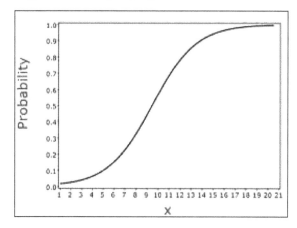

Decision Tree

Decision is about the cutting off of possibilities. Decision trees can be used to classify data, and they cut off possibilities of what a given instance of data might be by examining a data point's features. Is it bigger than a bread box? Well, then it's not a marble. Is it alive? Well, then it's not a bicycle. Think of a decision as a game of 20 questions that an algorithm is asking about the data point under examination.

A decision tree is a series of nodes, a directional graph that starts at the base with a single node and extends to the many leaf nodes that represent the categories that the tree can classify. Another way to think of a decision tree is as a flow chart, where the flow starts at the root node and ends with a decision made at the leaves. It is a decision-support tool. It uses a tree-like graph to show the predictions that result from a series of feature-based splits.

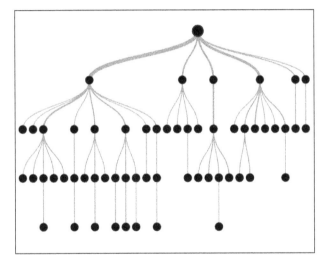

Here are some useful terms for describing a decision tree:

- Root Node: A root node is at the beginning of a tree. It represents entire population being analyzed. From the root node, the population is divided according to various features, and those sub-groups are split in turn at each decision node under the root node.

- Splitting: It is a process of dividing a node into two or more sub-nodes.

- Decision Node: When a sub-node splits into further sub-nodes, it's a decision node.

- Leaf Node or Terminal Node: Nodes that do not split are called leaf or terminal nodes.

- Pruning: Removing the sub-nodes of a parent node is called pruning. A tree is grown through splitting and shrunk through pruning.

- Branch or Sub-tree: A sub-section of decision tree is called branch or a sub-tree, just as a portion of a graph is called a sub-graph.

- Parent Node and Child Node: These are relative terms. Any node that falls under another node is a child node or sub-node, and any node which precedes those child nodes is called a parent node.

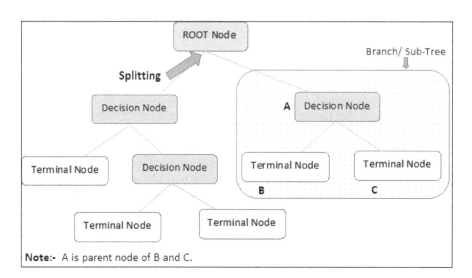

Decision trees are a popular algorithm for several reasons:

- Explanatory power: The output of decision trees is interpretable. It can be understood by people without analytical or mathematical backgrounds. It does not require any statistical knowledge to interpret them.

- Exploratory data analysis: Decision trees can enable analysts to identify significant variables and important relations between two or more variables, helping to surface the signal contained by many input variables.

- Minimal data cleaning: Because decision trees are resilient to outliers and missing values, they require less data cleaning than some other algorithms.

- Any data type: Decision trees can make classifications based on both numerical and categorical variables.

- Non-parametric: A decision tree is a non-parametric algorithm, as opposed to neural networks, which process input data transformed into a tensor, via tensor multiplication using large number of coefficients, known as parameters.

Random Forest

Random forests are made of many decision trees. They are ensembles of decision trees, each decision tree created by using a subset of the attributes used to classify a given population (they are sub-trees. Those decision trees vote on how to classify a given instance of input data, and the random forest bootstraps those votes to choose the best prediction. This is done to prevent overfitting, a common flaw of decision trees.

A random forest is a supervised classification algorithm. It creates a forest (many decision trees) and orders their nodes and splits randomly. The more trees in the forest, the better the results it can produce.

If you input a training dataset with targets and features into the decision tree, it will formulate some set of rules that can be used to perform predictions.

Example: You want to predict whether a visitor to your e-commerce website will enjoy a mystery novel. First, collect information about past books they've read and liked. Metadata about the novels will be the input; e.g. number of pages, author, publication date, which series it's part of if any. The decision tree contains rules that apply to those features; for example, some readers like very long books and some don't. Inputting metadata about new novels will result in a prediction regarding whether or not the Web site visitor in question would like that novel. Arranging the nodes and defining the rules relies on information gain and Gini-index calculations. With random forests, finding the root node and splitting the feature nodes is done randomly.

TYPES OF MACHINE LEARNING ALGORITHMS

- Supervised machine learning algorithmscan apply what has been learned in the past to new data using labeled examples to predict future events. Starting from the analysis of a known training dataset, the learning algorithm produces an inferred function to make predictions about the output values. The system is able to provide targets for any new input after sufficient training. The learning algorithm can also compare its output with the correct, intended output and find errors in order to modify the model accordingly.

- In contrast,unsupervised machine learning algorithmsare used when the information used to train is neither classified nor labeled. Unsupervised learning studies how systems can infer a function to describe a hidden structure from unlabeled data. The system doesn't figure out the right output, but it explores the data and can draw inferences from datasets to describe hidden structures from unlabeled data.

- Semi-supervised machine learning algorithms fall somewhere in between supervised and unsupervised learning, since they use both labeled and unlabeled data for training – typically a small amount of labeled data and a large amount of unlabeled data. The systems that use this method are able to considerably improve learning accuracy. Usually, semi-supervised learning is chosen when the acquired labeled data requires skilled and relevant resources in order to train it / learn from it. Otherwise, acquiring unlabeled data generally doesn't require additional resources.

- Reinforcement machine learning algorithmsis a learning method that interacts with its environment by producing actions and discovers errors or rewards. Trial and error search and delayed reward are the most relevant characteristics of reinforcement learning. This method allows machines and software agents to automatically determine the ideal behavior within a specific context in order to maximize its performance. Simple reward feedback is required for the agent to learn which action is best; this is known as the reinforcement signal.

Machine learning enables analysis of massive quantities of data. While it generally delivers faster, more accurate results in order to identify profitable opportunities or dangerous risks, it may also require additional time and resources to train it properly. Combining machine learning with AI and cognitive technologies can make it even more effective in processing large volumes of information.

IMPORTANCE AND USES
OF MACHINE LEARNING

To better understand the uses of Machine Learning, consider some instances where Machine Learning is applied: the self-driving Google car; cyber fraud detection; and, online recommendation engines from Facebook, Netflix, and Amazon. Machines can enable all of these things by filtering useful pieces of information and piecing them together based on patterns to get accurate results.

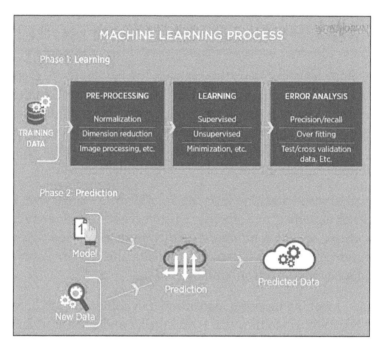

The rapid evolution in Machine Learning has caused a subsequent rise in the use cases, demands—and, the sheer importance of ML in modern life. Big Data has also become a well-used buzzword in the last few years. This is, in part, due to the increased sophistication of Machine Learning, which enables the analysis of large chunks of Big Data. Machine Learning has also changed the way data extraction and interpretations are done by automating generic methods/algorithms, thereby replacing traditional statistical techniques.

Uses of Machine Learning

Typical results fromMachine Learning applicationswe either see or don't regularly include web search results, real-time ads on web pages and mobile devices, email spam filtering, network intrusion detection, and pattern and image recognition. All these are by-products of using Machine Learning to analyze massive volumes of data.

Traditionally, data analysis was trial and error-based, an approach that becomes impossible when data sets are large and heterogeneous. Machine Learning provides smart alternatives to analyzing vast volumes of data. By developing fast and efficient algorithms and data-driven models for real-time processing of data, Machine Learning can produce accurate results and analysis.

References

- Machine-learning-ML: searchenterpriseai.techtarget.com, Retrieved 14 August, 2019

- Machine-learning-algorithms: skymind.ai, Retrieved 19 April, 2019

- Machine-learning-definition: expertsystem.com, Retrieved 25 May, 2019

- What-is-machine-learning-and-why-it-matters-article: simplilearn.com, Retrieved 26 July, 2019

Supervised Learning and Algorithms

Supervised learning refers to the task of learning a function that maps an input to output. Some of the algorithms of machine learning include decision tree, linear regression, logistic regression, random forests, linear discriminant analysis, etc. The topics elaborated in this chapter will help in gaining a better perspective about supervised learning and these machine learning algorithms.

Supervised learning, in the context of artificial intelligence (AI) and machine learning, is a type of system in which both input and desired output data are provided. Input and output data are labelled for classification to provide a learning basis for future data processing. The term supervised learning comes from the idea that an algorithm is learning from a training dataset, which can be thought of as the teacher.

Supervised machine learning systems provide the learning algorithms with known quantities to support future judgments. Chatbots, self-driving cars, facial recognition programs, expert systems and robots are among the systems that may use either supervised or unsupervised learning. Supervised learning systems are mostly associated with retrieval-based AI but they may also be capable of using a generative learning model.

In general, supervised learning occurs when a system is given input and output variables with the intentions of learning how they are mapped together, or related. The goal is to produce an accurate enough mapping function that when new input is given, the algorithm can predict the output. This is an iterative process, and each time the algorithm makes a prediction, it is corrected or given feedback until it achieves an acceptable level of performance.

Training data for supervised learning includes a set of examples with paired input subjects and desired output (which is also referred to as the supervisory signal). For example, in an application of supervised learning for image processing, an AI system might be provided with labeled pictures of vehicles in categories such as cars or trucks. After a sufficient amount of observation, the system should be able to distinguish between and categorize unlabeled images, at which time the training is complete.

Applications of supervised learning are typically broken down into two categories, classification and regression. Classification is similar to the example above, when the output value is a category such as car or truck and true or false. A regression problem is when the output is a real, computed value such as the price or weight.

A wide range of supervised learning algorithms are available, each with its strengths and weaknesses. There is no single learning algorithm that works best on all supervised learning problems.

There are four major issues to consider in supervised learning:

Bias-variance Tradeoff

A first issue is the tradeoff between *bias* and *variance*. Imagine that we have available several different, but equally good, training data sets. A learning algorithm is biased for a particular input x if, when trained on each of these data sets, it is systematically incorrect when predicting the correct output for x. A learning algorithm has high variance for a particular input x if it predicts different output values when trained on different training sets. The prediction error of a learned classifier is related to the sum of the bias and the variance of the learning algorithm. Generally, there is a tradeoff between bias and variance. A learning algorithm with low bias must be "flexible" so that it can fit the data well. But if the learning algorithm is too flexible, it will fit each training data set differently, and hence have high variance. A key aspect of many supervised learning methods is that they are able to adjust this tradeoff between bias and variance (either automatically or by providing a bias/variance parameter that the user can adjust).

Function Complexity and Amount of Training Data

The second issue is the amount of training data available relative to the complexity of the "true" function (classifier or regression function). If the true function is simple, then an "inflexible" learning algorithm with high bias and low variance will be able to learn it from a small amount of data. But if the true function is highly complex (e.g., because it involves complex interactions among many different input features and behaves differently in different parts of the input space), then the function will only be able to learn from a very large amount of training data and using a "flexible" learning algorithm with low bias and high variance.

Dimensionality of the Input Space

A third issue is the dimensionality of the input space. If the input feature vectors have very high dimension, the learning problem can be difficult even if the true function only depends on a small number of those features. This is because the many "extra" dimensions can confuse the learning algorithm and cause it to have high variance. Hence, high input dimensional typically requires tuning the classifier to have low variance and high bias. In practice, if the engineer can manually remove irrelevant features from the input data, this is likely to improve the accuracy of the learned function. In addition, there are many algorithms for feature selection that seek to identify the relevant features and discard the irrelevant ones. This is an instance of the more general strategy of dimensionality reduction, which seeks to map the input data into a lower-dimensional space prior to running the supervised learning algorithm.

Noise in the Output Values

A fourth issue is the degree of noise in the desired output values (the supervisory target variables). If the desired output values are often incorrect (because of human error or sensor errors), then the learning algorithm should not attempt to find a function that exactly matches the training examples. Attempting to fit the data too carefully leads to overfitting. You can overfit even when there are no measurement errors (stochastic noise) if the function you are trying to learn is too complex for your learning model. In such a situation, the part of the target function that cannot be modeled "corrupts" your training data - this phenomenon has been called deterministic noise. When either type of noise is present, it is better to go with a higher bias, lower variance estimator.

In practice, there are several approaches to alleviate noise in the output values such as early stopping to prevent overfitting as well as detecting and removing the noisy training examples prior to training the supervised learning algorithm. There are several algorithms that identify noisy training examples and removing the suspected noisy training examples prior to training has decreased generalization error with statistical significance.

Other Factors

Other factors to consider when choosing and applying a learning algorithm include the following:

- Heterogeneity of the data: If the feature vectors include features of many different kinds (discrete, discrete ordered, counts, continuous values), some algorithms are easier to apply than others. Many algorithms, including Support Vector Machines, linear regression, logistic regression, neural networks, and nearest neighbor methods, require that the input features be numerical and scaled to similar ranges (e.g., to the [-1,1] interval). Methods that employ a distance function, such as nearest neighbor methods and support vector machines with Gaussian kernels, are particularly sensitive to this. An advantage of decision trees is that they easily handle heterogeneous data.

- Redundancy in the data: If the input features contain redundant information (e.g., highly correlated features), some learning algorithms (e.g., linear regression, logistic regression, and distance based methods) will perform poorly because of numerical instabilities. These problems can often be solved by imposing some form of regularization.

- Presence of interactions and non-linearities: If each of the features makes an independent contribution to the output, then algorithms based on linear functions (e.g., linear regression, logistic regression, Support Vector Machines, naive Bayes) and distance functions (e.g., nearest neighbor methods, support vector machines with Gaussian kernels) generally perform well. However, if there are complex interactions among features, then algorithms such as decision trees and neural networks work better, because they are specifically designed to discover these interactions. Linear methods can also be applied, but the engineer must manually specify the interactions when using them.

When considering a new application, the engineer can compare multiple learning algorithms and experimentally determine which one works best on the problem at hand. Tuning the performance of a learning algorithm can be very time-consuming. Given fixed resources, it is often better to spend more time collecting additional training data and more informative features than it is to spend extra time tuning the learning algorithms.

DECISION TREE

A decision tree is a flowchart-like structure in which each internal node represents a `test` on a feature (e.g. whether a coin flip comes up heads or tails) , each leaf node represents a `class label` (decision taken after computing all features) and branches represent conjunctions of features that lead to those class labels. The paths from root to leaf represent classification rules. Below diagram illustrate the basic flow of decision tree for decision making with labels (Rain(Yes), No Rain(No)).

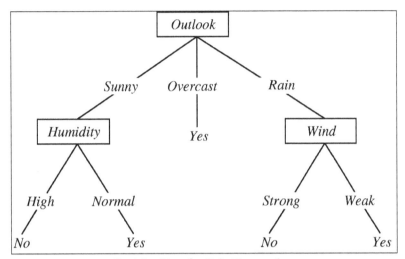

Decision Tree for Rain Forecasting.

Decision tree is one of the predictive modelling approaches used in statistics, data mining and machine learning.

Decision trees are constructed via an algorithmic approach that identifies ways to split a data set based on different conditions. It is one of the most widely used and practical methods for supervised learning. Decision Trees are a non-parametric supervised learning method used for both classification and regression tasks.

Tree models where the target variable can take a discrete set of values are called classification trees. Decision trees where the target variable can take continuous values (typically real numbers) are called regression trees. Classification and Regression Tree (CART) is general term for this.

Data Format Data comes in Records of Forms

```
(x,Y)=(x1,x2,x3,....,xk,Y)
```

The dependent variable, Y, is the target variable that we are trying to understand, classify or generalize. The vector x is composed of the features, x1, x2, x3 etc., that are used for that task.

Example:

```
training_data = [
                ['Green', 3, 'Apple'],
                ['Yellow', 3, 'Apple'],
                ['Red', 1, 'Grape'],
                ['Red', 1, 'Grape'],
```

```
                    ['Yellow', 3, 'Lemon'],

                    ]
```

```
# Header = ["Color", "diameter", "Label"]

# The last column is the label.

# The first two columns are features.
```

Approach to make Decision Tree

While making decision tree, at each node of tree we ask different type of questions. Based on the asked question we will calculate the information gain corresponding to it.

Information Gain

Information gain is used to decide which feature to split on at each step in building the tree. Simplicity is best, so we want to keep our tree small. To do so, at each step we should choose the split that results in the purest daughter nodes. A commonly used measure of purity is called information. For each node of the tree, the information value measures how much information a feature gives us about the class. The split with the highest information gain will be taken as the first split and the process will continue until all children nodes are pure, or until the information gain is 0.

Example:

```
class Question:

    """A Question is used to partition a dataset.

This class just records a 'column number' (e.g., 0 for Color) and a

'column value' (e.g., Green). The 'match' method is used to compare

the feature value in an example to the feature value stored in the

question. See the demo below.

"""

def __init__(self, column, value):

        self.column = column

        self.value = value

def match(self, example):

        # Compare the feature value in an example to the

        # feature value in this question.

        val = example[self.column]

        if is_numeric(val):

            return val >= self.value
```

```
        else:

                return val == self.value

def __repr__(self):

# This is just a helper method to print

# the question in a readable format.

condition = "=="

if is_numeric(self.value):

        condition = ">="

return "Is %s %s %s?" % (

        header[self.column], condition, str(self.value))
```

Let's try querying questions and its outputs.

```
Question(1, 3) ## Is diameter >= 3?

Question(0, "Green") ## Is color == Green?
```

Now we will try to Partition the dataset based on asked question. Data will be divided into two classes at each steps.

```
def partition(rows, question):

    """Partitions a dataset.

        For each row in the dataset, check if it matches the question. If

        so, add it to 'true rows', otherwise, add it to 'false rows'.

        """

        true_rows, false_rows = [], []

        for row in rows:

                if question.match(row):

                true_rows.append(row)

        else:

                false_rows.append(row)

return true_rows, false_rows

# Let's partition the training data based on whether rows are Red.

true_rows, false_rows = partition(training_data, Question(0, 'Red'))

# This will contain all the 'Red' rows.

true_rows ## [['Red', 1, 'Grape'], ['Red', 1, 'Grape']]
```

```
false_rows ## [['Green', 3, 'Apple'], ['Yellow', 3,
'Apple'], ['Yellow', 3, 'Lemon']]
```

Algorithm for constructing decision tree usually works top-down, by choosing a variable at each step that best splits the set of items. Different algorithms use different metrices for measuring best.

Gini Impurity

First let's understand the meaning of Pure and Impure.

Pure

Pure means, in a selected sample of dataset all data belongs to same class (PURE).

Impure

Impure means, data is mixture of different classes.

Definition of Gini Impurity

Gini Impurity is a measurement of the likelihood of an incorrect classification of a new instance of a random variable, if that new instance were randomly classified according to the distribution of class labels from the data set.

If our dataset is Pure then likelihood of incorrect classification is 0. If our sample is mixture of different classes then likelihood of incorrect classification will be high.

Calculating Gini Impurity

```
def gini(rows):

"""Calculate the Gini Impurity for a list of rows.

There are a few different ways to do this, I thought this one was

the most concise. See:

https://en.wikipedia.org/wiki/Decision_tree_learning#Gini_impurity

"""

counts = class_counts(rows)

impurity = 1

for lbl in counts:

prob_of_lbl = counts[lbl] / float(len(rows))

impurity -= prob_of_lbl**2

return impurity
```

Example:

```
# Demo 1:

# Let's look at some example to understand how Gini Impurity works.

#

# First, we'll look at a dataset with no mixing.

no_mixing = [['Apple'],

            ['Apple']]

# this will return 0

gini(no_mixing) ## output=0

## Demo 2:

# Now, we'll look at dataset with a 50:50

apples:oranges ratio

some_mixing = [['Apple'],

              ['Orange']]

# this will return 0.5 - meaning, there's a 50% chance of misclassifying

# a random example we draw from the dataset.

gini(some_mixing) ##output=0.5

## Demo 3:

# Now, we'll look at a dataset with many different labels

lots_of_mixing = [['Apple'],

                 ['Orange'],

                 ['Grape'],

                 ['Grapefruit'],

                 ['Blueberry']]

# This will return 0.8

gini(lots_of_mixing) ##output=0.8

#######
```

Steps for making Decision Tree

- Get list of rows (dataset) which are taken into consideration for making decision tree (recursively at each nodes).

- Calculate uncertainty of our dataset or Gini impurity or how much our data is mixed up etc.

- Generate list of all question which needs to be asked at that node.

- Partition rows into True rows and False rows based on each question asked.

- Calculate information gain based on gini impurity and partition of data from previous step.

- Update highest information gain based on each question asked.

- Update best question based on information gain (higher information gain).

- Divide the node on best question. Repeat again from step 1 again until we get pure node (leaf nodes).

Code for above Steps

```
def find_best_split(rows):
    """Find the best question to ask by iterating over every feature / value
and calculating the information gain."""
best_gain = 0 # keep track of the best information gain
best_question = None # keep train of the feature / value that produced it
current_uncertainty = gini(rows)
n_features = len(rows[0]) - 1 # number of columns
for col in range(n_features): # for each feature
values = set([row[col] for row in rows]) # unique values in the column
for val in values: # for each value

    question = Question(col, val)

    # try splitting the dataset

    true_rows, false_rows = partition(rows,
question)

    # Skip this split if it doesn't divide the

    # dataset.

    if len(true_rows) == 0 or len(false_rows) == 0:

    # Calculate the information gain from this
Split

    gain = info_gain(true_rows, false_rows, current_uncertainty)

    # You actually can use '>' instead of '>=' here
```

```
# but I wanted the tree to look a certain way for our
# toy dataset.
    if gain >= best_gain:
        best_gain, best_question = gain, question
return best_gain, best_question
#######
# Demo:
# Find the best question to ask first for our toy dataset.
    best_gain, best_question =
find_best_split(training_data)
best_question
  ## output - Is diameter >= 3?
```

Now build the Decision tree based on step recursively at each node.

```
def build_tree(rows):
"""Builds the tree.
Rules of recursion: 1) Believe that it works. 2) Start by checking
for the base case (no further information gain). 3) Prepare for
giant stack traces.
"""
  # Try partitioning the dataset on each of the unique attribute,
  # calculate the information gain,
  # and return the question that produces the highest gain.
  gain, question = find_best_split(rows)
  # Base case: no further info gain
  # Since we can ask no further questions,
  # we'll return a leaf.
  if gain == 0:
      return Leaf(rows)
# If we reach here, we have found a useful feature / value
  # to partition on.
```

```
 true_rows, false_rows = partition(rows, question)

 # Recursively build the true branch.

 true_branch = build_tree(true_rows)

 # Recursively build the false branch.

 false_branch = build_tree(false_rows)

 # Return a Question node.

 # This records the best feature / value to ask at this point,

 # as well as the branches to follow

 # dependingo on the answer.

return Decision_Node(question, true_branch, false_branch)
```

Building Decision Tree

Let's build decision tree based on training data.

```
training_data = [

                 ['Green', 3, 'Apple'],

                 ['Yellow', 3, 'Apple'],

                 ['Red', 1, 'Grape'],

                 ['Red', 1, 'Grape'],

                 ['Yellow', 3, 'Lemon'],

                 ]

# Header = ["Color", "diameter", "Label"]

# The last column is the label.

# The first two columns are features.

my_tree = build_tree(training_data)

print_tree(my_tree)
```

Output

```
Is diameter >= 3?

 --> True:

   Is color == Yellow?

   --> True:

       Predict {'Lemon': 1, 'Apple': 1}
```

```
--> False:

    Predict {'Apple': 1}
--> False:

  Predict {'Grape': 2}
```

From above output we can see that at each steps data is divided into Trueand False rows. This process keep repeated until we reach leaf node where information gain is 0 and further split of data is not possible as nodes are Pure.

Advantage of Decision Tree

- Easy to use and understand.

- Can handle both categorical and numerical data.

- Resistant to outliers, hence require little data preprocessing.

Disadvantage of Decision Tree

- Prone to overfitting.

- Require some kind of measurement as to how well they are doing.

- Need to be careful with parameter tuning.

- Can create biased learned trees if some classes dominate.

How to Avoid Overfitting the Decision Tree Model

Overfitting is one of the major problem for every model in machine learning. If model is overfitted it will poorly generalized to new samples. To avoid decision tree from overfitting we remove the branches that make use of features having low importance. This method is called as Pruning or post-pruning. This way we will reduce the complexity of tree, and hence imroves predictive accuracy by the reduction of overfitting.

Pruning should reduce the size of a learning tree without reducing predictive accuracy as measured by a cross-validation set. There are 2 major Pruning techniques:

- Minimum Error: The tree is pruned back to the point where the cross-validated error is a minimum.

- Smallest Tree: The tree is pruned back slightly further than the minimum error. Technically the pruning creates a decision tree with cross-validation error within 1 standard error of the minimum error.

Early Stop or Pre-pruning

An alternative method to prevent overfitting is to try and stop the tree-building process early, before it produces leaves with very small samples. This heuristic is known as *early stopping* but is also sometimes known as pre-pruning decision trees.

At each stage of splitting the tree, we check the cross-validation error. If the error does not decrease significantly enough then we stop. Early stopping may underfit by stopping too early. The current split may be of little benefit, but having made it, subsequent splits more significantly reduce the error.

Early stopping and pruning can be used together, separately, or not at all. Post pruning decision trees is more mathematically rigorous, finding a tree at least as good as early stopping. Early stopping is a quick fix heuristic. If used together with pruning, early stopping may save time. After all, why build a tree only to prune it back again?

Decision Tree in Real Life

- Selecting a Flight to Travel.

Suppose you need to select a flight for your next travel. How do we go about it? We check first if the flight is available on that day or not. If it is not available, we will look for some other date but if it is available then we look for may be the duration of the flight. If we want to have only direct flights then we look whether the price of that flight is in your pre-defined budget or not. If it is too expensive, we look at some other flights else we book it!

- Handling Late Night Cravings.

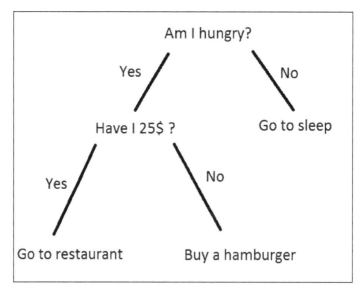

NAIVE BAYES CLASSIFIER

In machine learning, naïve Bayes classifiers are a family of simple "probabilistic classifiers" based on applying Bayes' theorem with strong (naïve) independence assumptions between the features. They are among the simplest Bayesian network models.

Naïve Bayes has been studied extensively since the 1960s. It was introduced (though not under that name) into the text retrieval community in the early 1960s, and remains a popular (baseline) method for text categorization, the problem of judging documents as belonging to one category or the other (such as spam or legitimate, sports or politics, etc.) with word frequencies as the features. With appropriate pre-processing, it is competitive in this domain with more advanced methods including support vector machines. It also finds application in automatic medical diagnosis.

Naïve Bayes classifiers are highly scalable, requiring a number of parameters linear in the number of variables (features/predictors) in a learning problem. Maximum-likelihood training can be done by evaluating a closed-form expression, which takes linear time, rather than by expensive iterative approximation as used for many other types of classifiers.

Naive Bayes is a simple technique for constructing classifiers: models that assign class labels to problem instances, represented as vectors of feature values, where the class labels are drawn from some finite set. There is not a single algorithm for training such classifiers, but a family of algorithms based on a common principle: all naive Bayes classifiers assume that the value of a particular feature is independent of the value of any other feature, given the class variable. For example, a fruit may be considered to be an apple if it is red, round, and about 10 cm in diameter. A naive Bayes classifier considers each of these features to contribute independently to the probability that this fruit is an apple, regardless of any possible correlations between the color, roundness, and diameter features.

For some types of probability models, naive Bayes classifiers can be trained very efficiently in a supervised learning setting. In many practical applications, parameter estimation for naive Bayes models uses the method of maximum likelihood; in other words, one can work with the naive Bayes model without accepting Bayesian probability or using any Bayesian methods.

Despite their naive design and apparently oversimplified assumptions, naive Bayes classifiers have worked quite well in many complex real-world situations. In 2004, an analysis of the Bayesian classification problem showed that there are sound theoretical reasons for the apparently implausible efficacy of naive Bayes classifiers. Still, a comprehensive comparison with other classification algorithms in 2006 showed that Bayes classification is outperformed by other approaches, such as boosted trees or random forests.

An advantage of naive Bayes is that it only requires a small number of training data to estimate the parameters necessary for classification.

Probabilistic Model

Abstractly, naive Bayes is a conditional probability model: given a problem instance to be classified, represented by a vector $\mathbf{x} = (x_1, \ldots, x_n)$ representing some n features (independent variables), it assigns to this instance probabilities.

$$p(C_k \mid x_1, \ldots, x_n)$$

for each of K possible outcomes or *classes* C_k.

The problem with the above formulation is that if the number of features n is large or if a feature can take on a large number of values, then basing such a model on probability tables is infeasible.

We therefore reformulate the model to make it more tractable. Using Bayes' theorem, the conditional probability can be decomposed as:

$$p(C_k \mid \mathbf{x}) = \frac{p(C_k)\,p(\mathbf{x} \mid C_k)}{p(\mathbf{x})}$$

In plain English, using Bayesian probability terminology, the above equation can be written as:

$$posterior = \frac{prior \times likelihood}{evidence}$$

In practice, there is interest only in the numerator of that fraction, because the denominator does not depend on C and the values of the features x_i are given, so that the denominator is effectively constant. The numerator is equivalent to the joint probability model:

$$p(C_k, x_1, \ldots, x_n)$$

which can be rewritten as follows, using the chain rule for repeated applications of the definition of conditional probability:

$$
\begin{aligned}
p(C_k, x_1, \ldots, x_n) &= p(x_1, \ldots, x_n, C_k) \\
&= p(x_1 \mid x_2, \ldots, x_n, C_k)\, p(x_2, \ldots, x_n, C_k) \\
&= p(x_1 \mid x_2, \ldots, x_n, C_k)\, p(x_2 x_3, \ldots, x_n, C_k)\, p(x_3, \ldots, x_n, C_k) \\
&= \ldots \\
&= p(x_1 \mid x_2, \ldots, x_n, C_k)\, p(x_2 \mid x_3, \ldots, x_n, C_k) \ldots p(x_{n-1} \mid x_n, C_k)\, p(x_n \mid C_k)\, p(C_k)
\end{aligned}
$$

Now the "naive" conditional independence assumptions come into play: assume that all features in $\mathbf{x}$ are mutually independent, conditional on the category C_k. Under this assumption,

$$p(x_i \mid x_{i+1}, \ldots, x_n, C_k) = p(x_i \mid C_k).$$

Thus, the joint model can be expressed as:

$$
\begin{aligned}
p(C_k \mid x_1, \ldots, x_n) &\propto p(C_k, x_1, \ldots, x_n) \\
&= p(C_k)\, p(x_1 \mid C_k)\, p(x_2 \mid C_k)\, p(x_3 \mid C_k) \cdots \\
&= p(C_k) \prod_{i=1}^{n} p(x_i \mid C_k),
\end{aligned}
$$

where $\propto$ denotes proportionality.

This means that under the above independence assumptions, the conditional distribution over the class variable C is:

$$p(C_k \mid x_1, \ldots, x_n) = \frac{1}{Z} p(C_k) \prod_{i=1}^{n} p(x_i \mid C_k)$$

where the evidence $Z = p(\mathbf{x}) = \sum_k p(C_k)p(\mathbf{x}|C_k)$ is a scaling factor dependent only on $x_1, \ldots, x_n$, that is, a constant if the values of the feature variables are known.

Constructing a Classifier from the Probability Model

The discussion so far has derived the independent feature model, that is, the naive Bayes probability model. The naive Bayes classifier combines this model with a decision rule. One common rule is to pick the hypothesis that is most probable; this is known as the *maximum a posteriori* or *MAP* decision rule. The corresponding classifier, a Bayes classifier, is the function that assigns a class label $\hat{y} = C_k$ for some k as follows:

$$\hat{y} = \underset{k \in \{1, \ldots, K\}}{\mathrm{argmax}} \; p(C_k) \prod_{i=1}^{n} p(x_i | C_k).$$

Parameter Estimation and Event Models

A class's prior may be calculated by assuming equiprobable classes (i.e., priors = 1 / (number of classes)), or by calculating an estimate for the class probability from the training set (i.e., (prior for a given class) = (number of samples in the class) / (total number of samples)). To estimate the parameters for a feature's distribution, one must assume a distribution or generate nonparametric models for the features from the training set.

The assumptions on distributions of features are called the *event model* of the Naive Bayes classifier. For discrete features like the ones encountered in document classification (include spam filtering), multinomial and Bernoulli distributions are popular. These assumptions lead to two distinct models, which are often confused.

Gaussian Naive Bayes

When dealing with continuous data, a typical assumption is that the continuous values associated with each class are distributed according to a normal (or Gaussian) distribution. For example, suppose the training data contains a continuous attribute, x. We first segment the data by the class, and then compute the mean and variance of x in each class. Let μ_k be the mean of the values in x associated with class C_k, and let σ_k^2 be the Bessel corrected variance of the values in x associated with class C_k. Suppose we have collected some observation value v. Then, the probability *distribution* of v given a class C_k, $p(x = v | C_k)$, can be computed by plugging v into the equation for a normal distribution parameterized by μ_k and σ_k^2. That is,

$$p(x = v | C_k) = \frac{1}{\sqrt{2\pi\sigma_k^2}} e^{-\frac{(v - \mu_k)^2}{2\sigma_k^2}}$$

Another common technique for handling continuous values is to use binning to discretize the feature values, to obtain a new set of Bernoulli-distributed features; some literature in fact suggests that this is necessary to apply naive Bayes, but it is not, and the discretization may throw away discriminative information.

Multinomial Naive Bayes

With a multinomial event model, samples (feature vectors) represent the frequencies with which certain events have been generated by a multinomial $(p_1, \ldots, p_n)$ where p_i is the probability that event i occurs (or K such multinomials in the multiclass case). A feature vector $\mathbf{x} = (x_1, \ldots, x_n)$ is then a histogram, with x_i counting the number of times event i was observed in a particular instance. This is the event model typically used for document classification, with events representing the occurrence of a word in a single document. The likelihood of observing a histogram $\mathbf{x}$ is given by:

$$p(\mathbf{x}|C_k) = \frac{(\sum_i x_i)!}{\prod_i x_i!} \prod_i p_{ki}^{x_i}$$

The multinomial naive Bayes classifier becomes a linear classifier when expressed in log-space:

$$\log p(C_k|\mathbf{x}) \propto \log\left(p(C_k) \prod_{i=1}^{n} p_{ki}^{x_i} \right)$$

$$= \log p(C_k) + \sum_{i=1}^{n} x_i \cdot \log p_{ki}$$

$$= b + \mathbf{w}_k^\top \mathbf{x}$$

where $b = \log p(C_k)$ and $w_{ki} = \log p_{ki}$.

If a given class and feature value never occur together in the training data, then the frequency-based probability estimate will be zero, because the probability estimate is directly proportional to the number of occurrences of a feature's value. This is problematic because it will wipe out all information in the other probabilities when they are multiplied. Therefore, it is often desirable to incorporate a small-sample correction, called pseudocount, in all probability estimates such that no probability is ever set to be exactly zero. This way of regularizing naive Bayes is called Laplace smoothing when the pseudocount is one, and Lidstone smoothing in the general case.

Rennie *et al.* discuss problems with the multinomial assumption in the context of document classification and possible ways to alleviate those problems, including the use of tf–idf weights instead of raw term frequencies and document length normalization, to produce a naive Bayes classifier that is competitive with support vector machines.

Bernoulli Naive Bayes

In the multivariate Bernoulli event model, features are independent booleans (binary variables) describing inputs. Like the multinomial model, this model is popular for document classification tasks, where binary term occurrence features are used rather than term frequencies. If x_i is a boolean expressing the occurrence or absence of the i'th term from the vocabulary, then the likelihood of a document given a class C_k is given by,

$$p(\mathbf{x}|C_k) = \prod_{i=1}^{n} p_{ki}^{x_i}(1 - p_{ki})^{(1-x_i)}$$

where p_{ki} is the probability of class C_k generating the term x_i. This event model is especially popular for classifying short texts. It has the benefit of explicitly modelling the absence of terms. Note that a naive Bayes classifier with a Bernoulli event model is not the same as a multinomial NB classifier with frequency counts truncated to one.

Semi-supervised Parameter Estimation

Given a way to train a naive Bayes classifier from labeled data, it's possible to construct a semi-supervised training algorithm that can learn from a combination of labeled and unlabeled data by running the supervised learning algorithm in a loop:

- Given a collection $D = L \uplus U$ of labeled samples L and unlabeled samples U, start by training a naive Bayes classifier on L.

Until convergence, do:

- Predict class probabilities $P(C|x)$ for all examples x in D.

- Re-train the model based on the *probabilities* (not the labels) predicted in the previous step.

Convergence is determined based on improvement to the model likelihood $P(D|\theta)$, where θ θ denotes the parameters of the naive Bayes model.

This training algorithm is an instance of the more general expectation–maximization algorithm (EM): the prediction step inside the loop is the E-step of EM, while the re-training of naive Bayes is the M-step. The algorithm is formally justified by the assumption that the data are generated by a mixture model, and the components of this mixture model are exactly the classes of the classification problem.

Discussion

Despite the fact that the far-reaching independence assumptions are often inaccurate, the naive Bayes classifier has several properties that make it surprisingly useful in practice. In particular, the decoupling of the class conditional feature distributions means that each distribution can be independently estimated as a one-dimensional distribution. This helps alleviate problems stemming from the curse of dimensionality, such as the need for data sets that scale exponentially with the number of features. While naive Bayes often fails to produce a good estimate for the correct class probabilities, this may not be a requirement for many applications. For example, the naive Bayes classifier will make the correct MAP decision rule classification so long as the correct class is more probable than any other class. This is true regardless of whether the probability estimate is slightly, or even grossly inaccurate. In this manner, the overall classifier can be robust enough to ignore serious deficiencies in its underlying naive probability model. Other reasons for the observed success of the naive Bayes classifier are discussed in the literature cited below.

Relation to Logistic Regression

In the case of discrete inputs (indicator or frequency features for discrete events), naive Bayes classifiers form a *generative-discriminative* pair with (multinomial) logistic regression classifiers: each naive Bayes classifier can be considered a way of fitting a probability model that optimizes the joint likelihood $p(C, \mathbf{x})$, while logistic regression fits the same probability model to optimize the conditional $p(C|\mathbf{x})..$

The link between the two can be seen by observing that the decision function for naive Bayes (in the binary case) can be rewritten as "predict class C_1 if the odds of $p(C_1|\mathbf{x})$ exceed those of $p(C_2|\mathbf{x})$". Expressing this in log-space gives:

$$\log \frac{p(C_1|\mathbf{x})}{p(C_2|\mathbf{x})} = \log p(C_1|\mathbf{x}) - \log p(C_2|\mathbf{x}) > 0$$

The left-hand side of this equation is the log-odds, or *logit*, the quantity predicted by the linear model that underlies logistic regression. Since naive Bayes is also a linear model for the two "discrete" event models, it can be reparametrised as a linear function $b + \mathbf{w}^\top x > 0$. Obtaining the probabilities is then a matter of applying the logistic function to $b + \mathbf{w}^\top x$, or in the multiclass case, the softmax function.

Discriminative classifiers have lower asymptotic error than generative ones; however, research by Ng and Jordan has shown that in some practical cases naive Bayes can outperform logistic regression because it reaches its asymptotic error faster.

Examples:

Sex Classification

Problem: classify whether a given person is a male or a female based on the measured features. The features include height, weight, and foot size.

Training

Table: Example training set below.

Person	height (feet)	weight (lbs)	foot size(inches)
male	6	180	12
male	5.92 (5'11")	190	11
male	5.58 (5'7")	170	12
male	5.92 (5'11")	165	10
female	5	100	6
female	5.5 (5'6")	150	8

female	5.42 (5'5")	130	7
female	5.75 (5'9")	150	9

The classifier created from the training set using a Gaussian distribution assumption would be (given variances are *unbiased* sample variances):

Person	mean (height)	variance (height)	mean (weight)	variance (weight)	mean (foot size)	variance (foot size)
male	5.855	$3.5033*10^{-2}$	176.25	$1.2292*10^2$	11.25	$9.1667*10^{-1}$
female	5.4175	$9.7225*10^{-2}$	132.5	$5.5833*10^2$	7.5	1.6667

Let's say we have equiprobable classes so P(male)= P(female) = 0.5. This prior probability distribution might be based on our knowledge of frequencies in the larger population, or on frequency in the training set.

Testing

Table: Below is a sample to be classified as male or female.

Person	height (feet)	weight (lbs)	foot size(inches)
sample	6	130	8

We wish to determine which posterior is greater, male or female. For the classification as male the posterior is given by,

$$\text{posterior (male)} = \frac{P(\text{male})\,p(\text{height}|\text{male})\,p(\text{weight}|\text{male})\,p(\text{foot size}|\text{male})}{evidence}$$

For the classification as female the posterior is given by,

$$\text{posterior (female)} = \frac{P(\text{female})\,p(\text{height}|\text{female})\,p(\text{weight}|\text{female})\,p(\text{foot size}|\text{female})}{evidence}$$

The evidence (also termed normalizing constant) may be calculated:

$$evidence = P(\text{male})\,p(\text{height}|\text{male})\,p(\text{weight}|\text{male})\,p(\text{foot size}|\text{male})$$
$$+P(\text{female})\,p(\text{height}|\text{female})\,p(\text{weight}|\text{female})\,p(\text{foot size}|\text{female})$$

However, given the sample, the evidence is a constant and thus scales both posteriors equally. It therefore does not affect classification and can be ignored. We now determine the probability distribution for the sex of the sample.

$$P(\text{male}) = 0.5$$

$$p(\text{height} | \text{male}) = \frac{1}{\sqrt{2\pi\sigma^2}} \exp\left(\frac{-(6-\mu)^2}{2\sigma^2}\right) \approx 1.5789,$$

where $\mu = 5.855$ and $\sigma^2 = 3.5033 \cdot 10^{-2}$ are the parameters of normal distribution which have been previously determined from the training set. Note that a value greater than 1 is OK here – it is a probability density rather than a probability, because *height* is a continuous variable.

$$p(\text{weight}|\text{male}) = \frac{1}{\sqrt{2\pi\sigma^2}} \exp\left(\frac{-(130-\mu)^2}{2\sigma^2}\right) = 5.9881 \cdot 10^{-6}$$

$$p(\text{foot size}|\text{male}) = \frac{1}{\sqrt{2\pi\sigma^2}} \exp\left(\frac{-(8-\mu)^2}{2\sigma^2}\right) = 1.3112 \cdot 10^{-3}$$

posterior numerator (male) = their product = $6.1984 \cdot 10^{-9}$

$P(\text{female}) = 0.5$

$p(\text{height}|\text{female}) = 2.2346 \cdot 10^{-1}$

$p(\text{weight}|\text{female}) = 1.6789 \cdot 10^{-2}$

$p(\text{foot size}|\text{female}) = 2.8669 \cdot 10^{-1}$

posterior numerator (female) = their product = $5.3778 \cdot 10^{-4}$

Since posterior numerator is greater in the female case, we predict the sample is female.

Document Classification

Here is a worked example of naive Bayesian classification to the document classification problem. Consider the problem of classifying documents by their content, for example into spam and non-spam e-mails. Imagine that documents are drawn from a number of classes of documents which can be modeled as sets of words where the (independent) probability that the i-th word of a given document occurs in a document from class C can be written as

$$p(w_i|C)$$

(For this treatment, we simplify things further by assuming that words are randomly distributed in the document - that is, words are not dependent on the length of the document, position within the document with relation to other words, or other document-context.)

Then the probability that a given document D contains all of the words w_i, given a class C, is

$$p(D|C) = \prod_i p(w_i|C)$$

The question that we desire to answer is: "what is the probability that a given document D belongs to a given class C?" In other words, what is $p(C|D)$?

Now by definition,

$$p(D|C) = \frac{p(D \cap C)}{p(C)}$$

and

$$p(C|D) = \frac{p(D \cap C)}{p(D)}$$

Bayes' theorem manipulates these into a statement of probability in terms of likelihood.

$$p(C|D) = \frac{p(C)p(D|C)}{p(D)}$$

Assume for the moment that there are only two mutually exclusive classes, S and $\neg S$ (e.g. spam and not spam), such that every element (email) is in either one or the other:

$$p(D|S) = \prod_i p(w_i|S)$$

and

$$p(D|\neg S) = \prod_i p(w_i|\neg S)$$

Using the Bayesian result above, we can write:

$$p(S|D) = \frac{p(S)}{p(D)} \prod_i p(w_i|S)$$

$$p(\neg S|D) = \frac{p(\neg S)}{p(D)} \prod_i p(w_i|\neg S)$$

Dividing one by the other gives:

$$\frac{p(S|D)}{p(\neg S|D)} = \frac{p(S) \prod_i p(w_i|S)}{p(\neg S) \prod_i p(w_i|\neg S)}$$

Which can be re-factored as:

$$\frac{p(S|D)}{p(\neg S|D)} = \frac{p(S)}{p(\neg S)} \prod_i \frac{p(w_i|S)}{p(w_i|\neg S)}$$

Thus, the probability ratio p(S | D) / p($\neg S$ | D) can be expressed in terms of a series of likelihood ratios. The actual probability p(S | D) can be easily computed from log (p(S | D) / p($\neg S$ | D)) based on the observation that p(S | D) + p($\neg S$ | D) = 1.

Taking the logarithm of all these ratios, we have:

$$\ln \frac{p(S|D)}{p(\neg S|D)} = \ln \frac{p(S)}{p(\neg S)} + \sum_i \ln \frac{p(w_i|S)}{p(w_i|\neg S)}$$

(This technique of "log-likelihood ratios" is a common technique in statistics. In the case of two mutually exclusive alternatives (such as this example), the conversion of a log-likelihood ratio to a probability takes the form of a sigmoid curve.)

Finally, the document can be classified as follows. It is spam if $p(S|D) > p(\neg S|D)$ (i. e.,

$\ln \dfrac{p(S|D)}{p(\neg S|D)} > 0$), otherwise it is not spam.

K-NEAREST NEIGHBORS

In pattern recognition, the k-nearest neighbors algorithm (k-NN) is a non-parametric method used for classification and regression. In both cases, the input consists of the k closest training examples in the feature space. The output depends on whether k-NN is used for classification or regression:

- In k-NN classification, the output is a class membership. An object is classified by a plurality vote of its neighbors, with the object being assigned to the class most common among its k nearest neighbors (k is a positive integer, typically small). If k = 1, then the object is simply assigned to the class of that single nearest neighbor.

- In k-NN regression, the output is the property value for the object. This value is the average of the values of k nearest neighbors.

k-NN is a type of instance-based learning, or lazy learning, where the function is only approximated locally and all computation is deferred until classification.

Both for classification and regression, a useful technique can be to assign weights to the contributions of the neighbors, so that the nearer neighbors contribute more to the average than the more distant ones. For example, a common weighting scheme consists in giving each neighbor a weight of $1/d$, where d is the distance to the neighbor.

The neighbors are taken from a set of objects for which the class (for k-NN classification) or the object property value (for k-NN regression) is known. This can be thought of as the training set for the algorithm, though no explicit training step is required.

A peculiarity of the k-NN algorithm is that it is sensitive to the local structure of the data.

Statistical Setting

Suppose we have pairs $(X_1, Y_1), (X_2, Y_2), \ldots, (X_n, Y_n)$ taking values in $\mathbb{R}^d \times \{1, 2\}$, where Y is the class label of X, so that $X \mid Y = r \sim P_r$ for $r = 1, 2$ (and probability distributions P_r). Given some norm $\|\cdot\|$ on $\mathbb{R}^d$ and a point $x \in \mathbb{R}^d$, let $(X_{(1)}, Y_{(1)}), \ldots, (X_{(n)}, Y_{(n)})$ be a reordering of the training data such that $\|X_{(1)} - x\| \leq \ldots \leq \|X_{(n)} - x\|$.

Algorithm

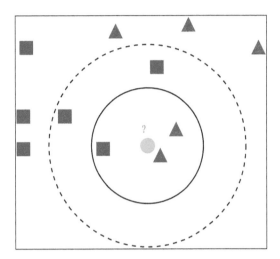

Example of k-NN classification. The test sample (green dot) should be classified either to blue squares or to red triangles. If $k = 3$ (solid line circle) it is assigned to the red triangles because there are 2 triangles and only 1 square inside the inner circle. If $k = 5$ (dashed line circle) it is assigned to the blue squares (3 squares vs. 2 triangles inside the outer circle).

The training examples are vectors in a multidimensional feature space, each with a class label. The training phase of the algorithm consists only of storing the feature vectors and class labels of the training samples.

In the classification phase, k is a user-defined constant, and an unlabeled vector (a query or test point) is classified by assigning the label which is most frequent among the k training samples nearest to that query point.

A commonly used distance metric for continuous variables is Euclidean distance. For discrete variables, such as for text classification, another metric can be used, such as the overlap metric (or Hamming distance). In the context of gene expression microarray data, for example, k-NN has been employed with correlation coefficients, such as Pearson and Spearman, as a metric. Often, the classification accuracy of k-NN can be improved significantly if the distance metric is learned with specialized algorithms such as Large Margin Nearest Neighbor or Neighbourhood components analysis.

A drawback of the basic "majority voting" classification occurs when the class distribution is skewed. That is, examples of a more frequent class tend to dominate the prediction of the new example, because they tend to be common among the k nearest neighbors due to their large number. One way to overcome this problem is to weight the classification, taking into account the distance from the test point to each of its k nearest neighbors. The class (or value, in regression problems) of each of the k nearest points is multiplied by a weight proportional to the inverse of the distance from that point to the test point. Another way to overcome skew is by abstraction in data representation. For example, in a self-organizing map (SOM), each node is a representative (a center) of a cluster of similar points, regardless of their density in the original training data. K-NN can then be applied to the SOM.

Parameter Selection

The best choice of k depends upon the data; generally, larger values of k reduces effect of the noise on the classification, but make boundaries between classes less distinct. A good k can be selected by various heuristic techniques. The special case where the class is predicted to be the class of the closest training sample (i.e. when $k = 1$) is called the nearest neighbor algorithm.

The accuracy of the k-NN algorithm can be severely degraded by the presence of noisy or irrelevant features, or if the feature scales are not consistent with their importance. Much research effort has been put into selecting or scaling features to improve classification. A particularly popular approach is the use of evolutionary algorithms to optimize feature scaling. Another popular approach is to scale features by the mutual information of the training data with the training classes.

In binary (two class) classification problems, it is helpful to choose k to be an odd number as this avoids tied votes. One popular way of choosing the empirically optimal k in this setting is via bootstrap method.

The 1-Nearest Neighbor Classifier

The most intuitive nearest neighbour type classifier is the one nearest neighbour classifier that assigns a point x to the class of its closest neighbour in the feature space, that is $C_n^{1nn}(x) = Y_{(1)}$.

As the size of training data set approaches infinity, the one nearest neighbour classifier guarantees an error rate of no worse than twice the Bayes error rate (the minimum achievable error rate given the distribution of the data).

The Weighted Nearest Neighbour Classifier

The k-nearest neighbour classifier can be viewed as assigning the k nearest neighbours a weight $1/k$ and all others o weight. This can be generalised to weighted nearest neighbour classifiers. That is, where the ith nearest neighbour is assigned a weight w_{ni}, with $\sum_{i=1}^{n} w_{ni} = 1$. An analogous result on the strong consistency of weighted nearest neighbour classifiers also holds.

Let C_n^{wnn} denote the weighted nearest classifier with weights $\{w_{ni}\}_{i=1}^{n}$. Subject to regularity conditions on the class distributions the excess risk has the following asymptotic expansion

$$\mathcal{R}_{\mathcal{R}}(C_n^{wnn}) - \mathcal{R}_{\mathcal{R}}(C^{Bayes}) = \left(B_1 s_n^2 + B_2 t_n^2\right)\{1 + o(1)\},$$

for constants B_1 and B_2 where $s_n^2 = \sum_{i=1}^{n} w_{ni}^2$ and $t_n = n^{-2/d} \sum_{i=1}^{n} w_{ni}\{i^{1+2/d} - (i-1)^{1+2/d}\}$.

The optimal weighting scheme $\{w_{ni}^*\}_{i=1}^n$, that balances the two terms in the display above, is given as follows: set $k^* = \left\lfloor Bn^{\frac{4}{d+4}} \right\rfloor$,

$$w_{ni}^* = \frac{1}{k^*}\left[1 + \frac{d}{2} - \frac{d}{2k^{*2/d}}\{i^{1+2/d} - (i-1)^{1+2/d}\}\right] \text{ for } i = 1, 2, \ldots, k^*$$

and,

$$w_{ni}^* = 0 \text{ for } i = k^* + 1, \ldots, n.$$

With optimal weights the dominant term in the asymptotic expansion of the excess risk is $\mathcal{O}(n^{-\frac{4}{d+4}})$. Similar results are true when using a bagged nearest neighbour classifier.

Properties

k-NN is a special case of a variable-bandwidth, kernel density "balloon" estimator with a uniform kernel.

The naive version of the algorithm is easy to implement by computing the distances from the test example to all stored examples, but it is computationally intensive for large training sets. Using an approximate nearest neighbor search algorithm makes k-NN computationally tractable even for large data sets. Many nearest neighbor search algorithms have been proposed over the years; these generally seek to reduce the number of distance evaluations actually performed.

k-NN has some strong consistency results. As the amount of data approaches infinity, the two-class k-NN algorithm is guaranteed to yield an error rate no worse than twice the Bayes error rate (the minimum achievable error rate given the distribution of the data). Various improvements to the k-NN speed are possible by using proximity graphs.

For multi-class k-NN classification, Cover and Hart prove an upper bound error rate of:

$$R^* \leq R_{k\text{NN}} \leq R^*\left(2 - \frac{MR^*}{M-1}\right)$$

where R^* is the Bayes error rate (which is the minimal error rate possible), R_{kNN} is the k-NN error rate, and M is the number of classes in the problem. For $M = 2$ and as the Bayesian error rate R^* approaches zero, this limit reduces to "not more than twice the Bayesian error rate".

Error Rates

There are many results on the error rate of the k nearest neighbour classifiers. The k-nearest neighbour classifier is strongly (that is for any joint distribution on (X,Y)) consistent provided $k := k_n$ diverges and k_n/n converges to zero as $n \to \infty$.

Let C_n^{knn} denote the k nearest neighbour classifier based on a training set of size n. Under certain regularity conditions, the excess risk yields the following asymptotic expansion.

$$\mathcal{R}_\mathcal{R}(C_n^{knn}) - \mathcal{R}_\mathcal{R}(C^{Bayes}) = \left\{ B_1 \frac{1}{k} + B_2 \left(\frac{k}{n} \right)^{4/d} \right\} \{1 + o(1)\},$$

for some constants B_1 and B_2.

The choice $k^* = \left\lfloor Bn^{\frac{4}{d+4}} \right\rfloor$ offers a trade off between the two terms in the above display, for which the k^*-nearest neighbour error converges to the Bayes error at the optimal (minimax) rate $\mathcal{O}(n^{-\frac{4}{d+4}})$.

Metric Learning

The K-nearest neighbor classification performance can often be significantly improved through (supervised) metric learning. Popular algorithms are neighbourhood components analysis and large margin nearest neighbor. Supervised metric learning algorithms use the label information to learn a new metric or pseudo-metric.

Feature Extraction

When the input data to an algorithm is too large to be processed and it is suspected to be redundant (e.g. the same measurement in both feet and meters) then the input data will be transformed into a reduced representation set of features (also named features vector). Transforming the input data into the set of features is called feature extraction. If the features extracted are carefully chosen it is expected that the features set will extract the relevant information from the input data in order to perform the desired task using this reduced representation instead of the full size input. Feature extraction is performed on raw data prior to applying k-NN algorithm on the transformed data in feature space.

An example of a typical computer vision computation pipeline for face recognition using k-NN including feature extraction and dimension reduction pre-processing steps (usually implemented with OpenCV):

- Haar face detection.

- Mean-shift tracking analysis.

- PCA or Fisher LDA projection into feature space, followed by k-NN classification.

Dimension Reduction

For high-dimensional data (e.g., with number of dimensions more than 10) dimension reduction is usually performed prior to applying the k-NN algorithm in order to avoid the effects of the curse of dimensionality.

The curse of dimensionality in the k-NN context basically means that Euclidean distance is unhelpful in high dimensions because all vectors are almost equidistant to the search query vector (imagine multiple points lying more or less on a circle with the query point at the center; the distance from the query to all data points in the search space is almost the same).

Feature extraction and dimension reduction can be combined in one step using principal component analysis (PCA), linear discriminant analysis (LDA), or canonical correlation analysis (CCA) techniques as a pre-processing step, followed by clustering by k-NN on feature vectors in reduced-dimension space. In machine learning this process is also called low-dimensional embedding.

For very-high-dimensional datasets (e.g. when performing a similarity search on live video streams, DNA data or high-dimensional time series) running a fast approximate k-NN search using locality sensitive hashing, "random projections", "sketches" or other high-dimensional similarity search techniques from the VLDB toolbox might be the only feasible option.

Decision Boundary

Nearest neighbor rules in effect implicitly compute the decision boundary. It is also possible to compute the decision boundary explicitly, and to do so efficiently, so that the computational complexity is a function of the boundary complexity.

Data Reduction

Data reduction is one of the most important problems for work with huge data sets. Usually, only some of the data points are needed for accurate classification. Those data are called the *prototypes* and can be found as follows:

- Select the *class-outliers*, that is, training data that are classified incorrectly by k-NN (for a given k).

- Separate the rest of the data into two sets: (i) the prototypes that are used for the classification decisions and (ii) the *absorbed points* that can be correctly classified by k-NN using prototypes. The absorbed points can then be removed from the training set.

Selection of Class-outliers

A training example surrounded by examples of other classes is called a class outlier. Causes of class outliers include:

- Random error.

- Insufficient training examples of this class (an isolated example appears instead of a cluster).

- Missing important features (the classes are separated in other dimensions which we do not know).

- Too many training examples of other classes (unbalanced classes) that create a "hostile" background for the given small class.

Class outliers with k-NN produce noise. They can be detected and separated for future analysis.

Given two natural numbers, $k>r>0$, a training example is called a *(k,r)*NN class-outlier if its k nearest neighbors include more than r examples of other classes.

CNN for Data Reduction

Condensed nearest neighbor (CNN, the *Hart algorithm*) is an algorithm designed to reduce the data set for k-NN classification. It selects the set of prototypes U from the training data, such that 1NN with U can classify the examples almost as accurately as 1NN does with the whole data set.

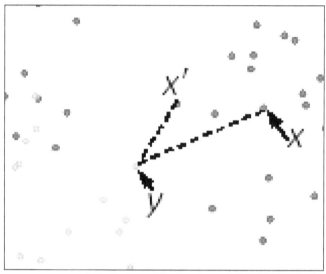

Calculation of the border ratio.

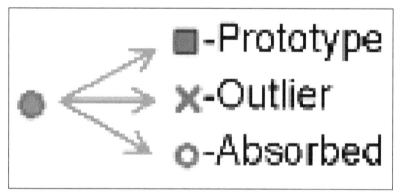

Three types of points: prototypes, class-outliers, and absorbed points.

Given a training set X, CNN works iteratively:

- Scan all elements of X, looking for an element x whose nearest prototype from U has a different label than x.

- Remove x from X and add it to U.

- Repeat the scan until no more prototypes are added to U.

Use U instead of X for classification. The examples that are not prototypes are called "absorbed" points.

It is efficient to scan the training examples in order of decreasing border ratio. The border ratio of a training example x is defined as:

$$a(x) = \frac{\|x'-y\|}{\|x-y\|}$$

where $\|x-y\|$ is the distance to the closest example y having a different color than x, and $\|x'-y\|$ is the distance from y to its closest example x' with the same label as x.

The border ratio is in the interval [0,1] because $\|x'-y\|$ never exceeds $\|x-y\|$. This ordering gives preference to the borders of the classes for inclusion in the set of prototypes U. A point of a different label than x is called external to x. The calculation of the border ratio is illustrated by the figure on the right. The data points are labeled by colors: the initial point is x and its label is red. External points are blue and green. The closest to x external point is y. The closest to y red point is x'. The border ratio $a(x) = \|x'-y\| / \|x-y\|$ is the attribute of the initial point x.

Below is an illustration of CNN in a series of figures. There are three classes (red, green and blue). Figure initially there are 60 points in each class. Figure shows the 1NN classification map: each pixel is classified by 1NN using all the data. Figure shows the 5NN classification map. White areas correspond to the unclassified regions, where 5NN voting is tied (for example, if there are two green, two red and one blue points among 5 nearest neighbors). Figure shows the reduced data set. The crosses are the class-outliers selected by the (3,2)NN rule (all the three nearest neighbors of these instances belong to other classes); the squares are the prototypes, and the empty circles are the absorbed points. The left bottom corner shows the numbers of the class-outliers, prototypes and absorbed points for all three classes. The number of prototypes varies from 15% to 20% for different classes in this example. Figure shows that the 1NN classification map with the prototypes is very similar to that with the initial data set. The figures were produced using the Mirkes applet.

CNN Model Reduction for k-NN Classifiers

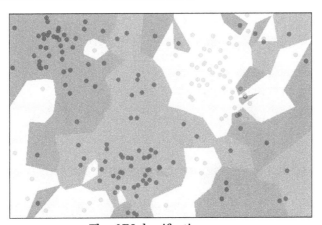

The 1NN classification map.

FCNN (for Fast Condensed Nearest Neighbor) is a variant of CNN, which turns out to be one of the fastest data set reduction algorithms for k-NN classification.

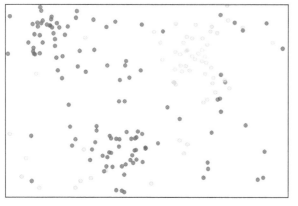

The dataset.

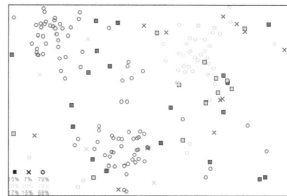

The CNN reduced dataset.

The 5NN classification map.

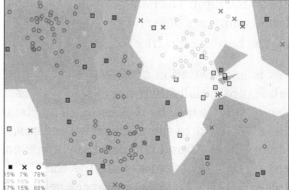

The 1NN classification map based on the CNN extracted prototypes.

k-NN Regression

In *k*-NN regression, the *k*-NN algorithm is used for estimating continuous variables. One such algorithm uses a weighted average of the *k* nearest neighbors, weighted by the inverse of their distance. This algorithm works as follows:

- Compute the Euclidean or Mahalanobis distance from the query example to the labeled examples.

- Order the labeled examples by increasing distance.

- Find a heuristically optimal number *k* of nearest neighbors, based on RMSE. This is done using cross validation.

- Calculate an inverse distance weighted average with the *k*-nearest multivariate neighbors.

k-NN Outlier

The distance to the *k*th nearest neighbor can also be seen as a local density estimate and thus is also a popular outlier score in anomaly detection. The larger the distance to the *k*-NN, the lower the local density, the more likely the query point is an outlier. To take into account the whole neighborhood of the query point, the average distance to the k-NN can be used. Although quite simple, this outlier model, along with another classic data mining method, local outlier factor, works quite well also in comparison to more recent and more complex approaches, according to a large scale experimental analysis.

Validation of Results

A confusion matrix or "matching matrix" is often used as a tool to validate the accuracy of k-NN classification. More robust statistical methods such as likelihood-ratio test can also be applied.

SUPPORT-VECTOR MACHINE

In machine learning, support-vector machines (SVMs, also support-vector networks) are supervised learning models with associated learning algorithms that analyze data used for classification and regression analysis. Given a set of training examples, each marked as belonging to one or the other of two categories, an SVM training algorithm builds a model that assigns new examples to one category or the other, making it a non-probabilistic binary linear classifier (although methods such as Platt scaling exist to use SVM in a probabilistic classification setting). An SVM model is a representation of the examples as points in space, mapped so that the examples of the separate categories are divided by a clear gap that is as wide as possible. New examples are then mapped into that same space and predicted to belong to a category based on the side of the gap on which they fall.

In addition to performing linear classification, SVMs can efficiently perform a non-linear classification using what is called the kernel trick, implicitly mapping their inputs into high-dimensional feature spaces.

When data are unlabelled, supervised learning is not possible, and an unsupervised learning approach is required, which attempts to find natural clustering of the data to groups, and then map new data to these formed groups. The support-vector clustering algorithm, created by Hava Siegelmann and Vladimir Vapnik, applies the statistics of support vectors, developed in the support vector machines algorithm, to categorize unlabeled data, and is one of the most widely used clustering algorithms in industrial applications.

Motivation

Classifying data is a common task in machine learning. Suppose some given data points each belong to one of two classes, and the goal is to decide which class a new data point will be in. In the case of support-vector machines, a data point is viewed as a p-dimensional vector (a list of p numbers), and we want to know whether we can separate such points with a $(p-1)$-dimensional hyperplane. This is called a linear classifier. There are many hyperplanes that might classify the data. One reasonable choice as the best hyperplane is the one that represents the largest separation, or margin, between the two classes. So we choose the hyperplane so that the distance from it to the nearest data point on each side is maximized. If such a hyperplane exists, it is known as the maximum-margin hyperplane and the linear classifier it defines is known as a maximum-margin classifier; or equivalently, the perceptron of optimal stability.

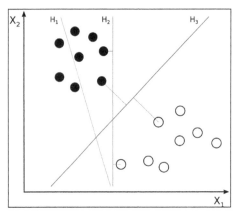

H_1 does not separate the classes. H_2 does, but only with a small margin. H_3 separates them with the maximal margin.

More formally, a support-vector machine constructs a hyperplane or set of hyperplanes in a high- or infinite-dimensional space, which can be used for classification, regression, or other tasks like outliers detection. Intuitively, a good separation is achieved by the hyperplane that has the largest distance to the nearest training-data point of any class (so-called functional margin), since in general the larger the margin, the lower the generalization error of the classifier.

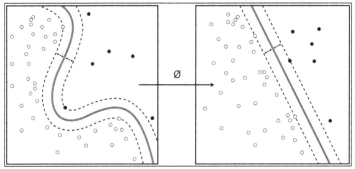

Kernel Machine.

Whereas the original problem may be stated in a finite-dimensional space, it often happens that the sets to discriminate are not linearly separable in that space. For this reason, it was proposed that the original finite-dimensional space be mapped into a much higher-dimensional space, presumably making the separation easier in that space. To keep the computational load reasonable, the mappings used by SVM schemes are designed to ensure that dot products of pairs of input data vectors may be computed easily in terms of the variables in the original space, by defining them in terms of a kernel function $k(x, y)$ selected to suit the problem. The hyperplanes in the higher-dimensional space are defined as the set of points whose dot product with a vector in that space is constant, where such a set of vectors is an orthogonal (and thus minimal) set of vectors that defines a hyperplane. The vectors defining the hyperplanes can be chosen to be linear combinations with parameters α_i of images of feature vectors x_i that occur in the data base. With this choice of a hyperplane, the points x in the feature space that are mapped into the hyperplane are defined by the relation $\sum_i \alpha_i k(x_i, x) = \text{Constant}$. Note that if $k(x, y)$ becomes small as y grows further away from x, each term in the sum measures the degree of closeness of the test point x to the corresponding data base point x_i. In this way, the sum of kernels above can be used to measure the relative nearness of each test point to the data points originating in one or the other of the sets to be discriminated. Note the fact that the set of points x mapped into any hyperplane can be quite convoluted as a result, allowing much more complex discrimination between sets that are not convex at all in the original space.

Applications

SVMs can be used to solve various real-world problems:

- SVMs are helpful in text and hypertext categorization, as their application can significantly reduce the need for labeled training instances in both the standard inductive and transductive settings. Some methods for shallow semantic parsing are based on support vector machines.

- Classification of images can also be performed using SVMs. Experimental results show that SVMs achieve significantly higher search accuracy than traditional query refinement schemes after just three to four rounds of relevance feedback. This is also true for image segmentation systems, including those using a modified version SVM that uses the privileged approach as suggested by Vapnik.

- Hand-written characters can be recognized using SVM.

- The SVM algorithm has been widely applied in the biological and other sciences. They have been used to classify proteins with up to 90% of the compounds classified correctly. Permutation tests based on SVM weights have been suggested as a mechanism for interpretation of SVM models. Support-vector machine weights have also been used to interpret SVM models in the past. Posthoc interpretation of support-vector machine models in order to identify features used by the model to make predictions is a relatively new area of research with special significance in the biological sciences.

The original SVM algorithm was invented by Vladimir N. Vapnik and Alexey Ya. Chervonenkis in 1963. In 1992, Bernhard E. Boser, Isabelle M. Guyon and Vladimir N. Vapnik suggested a way to create nonlinear classifiers by applying the kernel trick to maximum-margin hyperplanes. The current standard incarnation (soft margin) was proposed by Corinna Cortes and Vapnik in 1993 and published in 1995.

Linear SVM

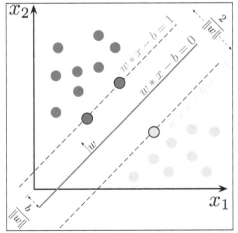

Maximum-margin hyperplane and margins for an SVM trained with samples
from two classes. Samples on the margin are called the support vectors.

We are given a training dataset of n points of the form:

$$(\vec{x}_1, y_1), \ldots, (\vec{x}_n, y_n),$$

where the y_i are either 1 or −1, each indicating the class to which the point $\vec{x}_i$ belongs. Each $\vec{x}_i$ is a p -dimensional real vector. We want to find the "maximum-margin hyperplane" that divides the group of points $\vec{x}_i$ for which $y_i = 1$ from the group of points for which $y_i = -1$, which is defined so that the distance between the hyperplane and the nearest point $\vec{x}_i$ from either group is maximized.

Any hyperplane can be written as the set of points $\vec{x}$ satisfying:

$$\vec{w} \cdot \vec{x} - b = 0,$$

where $\vec{w}$ is the (not necessarily normalized) normal vector to the hyperplane. This is much like Hesse normal form, except that $\vec{w}$ is not necessarily a unit vector. The parameter $\dfrac{b}{\|\vec{w}\|}$ determines the offset of the hyperplane from the origin along the normal vector $\vec{w}$.

Hard-margin

If the training data is linearly separable, we can select two parallel hyperplanes that separate the two classes of data, so that the distance between them is as large as possible. The region bounded by these two hyperplanes is called the "margin", and the maximum-margin hyperplane is the hyperplane that lies halfway between them. With a normalized or standardized dataset, these hyperplanes can be described by the equations.

$$\vec{w} \cdot \vec{x} - b = 1 \text{ (anything on or above this boundary is of one class, with label 1)}$$

and

$$\vec{w} \cdot \vec{x} - b = -1 \text{ (anything on or below this boundary is of the other class, with label −1)}.$$

Geometrically, the distance between these two hyperplanes is $\dfrac{2}{\|\vec{w}\|}$,so to maximize the distance between the planes we want to minimize $\|\vec{w}\|$. The distance is computed using the distance from a point to a plane equation. We also have to prevent data points from falling into the margin, we add the following constraint: for each i either.

$$\vec{w} \cdot \vec{x}_i - b \geq 1 \text{ , if } y_i = 1,$$

or

$$\vec{w} \cdot \vec{x}_i - b \leq -1, \text{ if } y_i = -1.$$

These constraints state that each data point must lie on the correct side of the margin.

This can be rewritten as

$$y_i(\vec{w} \cdot \vec{x}_i - b) \geq 1, \quad \text{for all } 1 \leq i \leq n.$$

We can put this together to get the optimization problem:

"Minimize $\|\vec{w}\|$ subject to $y_i(\vec{w}\cdot\vec{x}_i - b) \geq 1$ for $i = 1,\ldots,n$."

The $\vec{w}$ and b that solve this problem determine our classifier, $\vec{x} \mapsto \operatorname{sgn}(\vec{w}\cdot\vec{x} - b)$.

An important consequence of this geometric description is that the max-margin hyperplane is completely determined by those $\vec{x}_i$ that lie nearest to it. These $\vec{x}_i$ are called *support vectors*.

Soft-margin

To extend SVM to cases in which the data are not linearly separable, we introduce the *hinge loss* function,

$$\max\left(0, 1 - y_i(\vec{w}\cdot\vec{x}_i - b)\right).$$

Note that y_i is the i-th target (i.e., in this case, 1 or −1), and $\vec{w}\cdot\vec{x}_i - b$ is the current output.

This function is zero if the constraint in (1) is satisfied, in other words, if $\vec{x}$ lies on the correct side of the margin. For data on the wrong side of the margin, the function's value is proportional to the distance from the margin.

We then wish to minimize:

$$\left[\frac{1}{n}\sum_{i=1}^{n}\max\left(0, 1 - y_i(\vec{w}\cdot\vec{x}_i - b)\right)\right] + \lambda \|\vec{w}\|^2,$$

where the parameter λ determines the trade-off between increasing the margin size and ensuring that the $\vec{x}$ lie on the correct side of the margin. Thus, for sufficiently small values of λ, the second term in the loss function will become negligible, hence, it will behave similar to the hard-margin SVM, if the input data are linearly classifiable, but will still learn if a classification rule is viable or not.

Nonlinear Classification

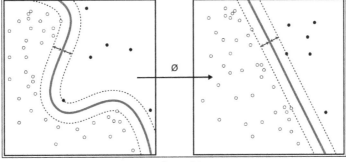

Kernel machine.

The original maximum-margin hyperplane algorithm proposed by Vapnik in 1963 constructed a linear classifier. However, in 1992, Bernhard E. Boser, Isabelle M. Guyon and Vladimir N. Vapnik suggested a way to create nonlinear classifiers by applying the kernel trick (originally proposed by Aizerman et al.) to maximum-margin hyperplanes.The resulting algorithm is formally similar, except that every dot product is replaced by a nonlinear kernel function. This allows the algorithm to fit the maximum-margin hyperplane in a transformed feature space. The transformation may be nonlinear and the transformed space high-dimensional; although the classifier is a hyperplane in the transformed feature space, it may be nonlinear in the original input space.

It is noteworthy that working in a higher-dimensional feature space increases the generalization error of support-vector machines, although given enough samples the algorithm still performs well.

Some common kernels include:

- Polynomial (homogeneous): $k(\vec{x_i}, \vec{x_j}) = (\vec{x_i} \cdot \vec{x_j})^d$.

- Polynomial (inhomogeneous): $k(\vec{x_i}, \vec{x_j}) = (\vec{x_i} \cdot \vec{x_j} + 1)^d$.

- Gaussian radial basis function: $k(\vec{x_i}, \vec{x_j}) = \exp(-\gamma \; \backslash \vec{x_i} - \vec{x_j} \; \backslash^2)$ for $\gamma > 0$. Sometimes parametrized using $\gamma = 1/(2\sigma^2)$.

- Hyperbolic tangent: $k(\vec{x_i}, \vec{x_j}) = \tanh(\kappa \vec{x_i} \cdot \vec{x_j} + c)$ for some (not every) $\kappa > 0$ and $c < 0$.

The kernel is related to the transform $\varphi(\vec{x_i})$ by the equation $k(\vec{x_i}, \vec{x_j}) = \varphi(\vec{x_i}) \cdot \varphi(\vec{x_j})$. The value **w** is also in the transformed space, with $\vec{w} = \sum_i \alpha_i y_i \varphi(\vec{x_i})$. Dot products with **w** for classification can again be computed by the kernel trick, i.e. $\vec{w} \cdot \varphi(\vec{x}) = \sum_i \alpha_i y_i k(\vec{x_i}, \vec{x})$.

Computing the SVM Classifier

Computing the (soft-margin) SVM classifier amounts to minimizing an expression of the form

$$\left[\frac{1}{n} \sum_{i=1}^{n} \max\left(0, 1 - y_i(w \cdot x_i - b)\right) \right] + \lambda \| w \|^2 .$$

We focus on the soft-margin classifier since, as noted above, choosing a sufficiently small value for λ yields the hard-margin classifier for linearly classifiable input data. The classical approach, which involves reducing (2) to a quadratic programming problem, is detailed below. Then, more recent approaches such as sub-gradient descent and coordinate descent.

Primal

Minimizing (2) can be rewritten as a constrained optimization problem with a differentiable objective function in the following way.

For each $i \in \{1,...,n\}$ we introduce a variable $\zeta_i = \max\left(0, 1 - y_i(w \cdot x_i - b)\right)$. Note that ζ_i is the smallest nonnegative number satisfying $y_i(w \cdot x_i - b) \geq 1 - \zeta_i$.

Thus we can rewrite the optimization problem as follows:h

$$\text{minimize } \frac{1}{n} \sum_{i=1}^{n} \zeta_i + \lambda \| w \|^2$$

subject to $y_i(w \cdot x_i - b) \geq 1 - \zeta_i$ and $\zeta_i \geq 0$, for all i.

This is called the *primal* problem.

Dual

By solving for the Lagrangian dual of the above problem, one obtains the simplified problem:

$$\text{maximize } f(c_1 \dots c_n) = \sum_{i=1}^{n} c_i - \frac{1}{2} \sum_{i=1}^{n} \sum_{j=1}^{n} y_i c_i (x_i \cdot x_j) y_j c_j,$$

$$\text{subject to } \sum_{i=1}^{n} c_i y_i = 0, \text{and } 0 \leq c_i \leq \frac{1}{2n\lambda} \text{ for all } i.$$

This is called the *dual* problem. Since the dual maximization problem is a quadratic function of the c_i subject to linear constraints, it is efficiently solvable by quadratic programming algorithms.

Here, the variables c_i are defined such that:

$$\vec{w} = \sum_{i=1}^{n} c_i y_i \vec{x}_i.$$

Moreover, $c_i = 0$ exactly when $\vec{x}_i$ lies on the correct side of the margin, and $0 < c_i < (2n\lambda)^{-1}$ when $\vec{x}_i$ lies on the margin's boundary. It follows that $\vec{w}$ can be written as a linear combination of the support vectors.

The offset, b, can be recovered by finding an $\vec{x}_i$ on the margin's boundary and solving:

$$y_i(\vec{w} \cdot \vec{x}_i - b) = 1 \Leftrightarrow b = \vec{w} \cdot \vec{x}_i - y_i.$$

(Note that $y_i^{-1} = y_i$ since $y_i = \pm 1$.)

Kernel Trick

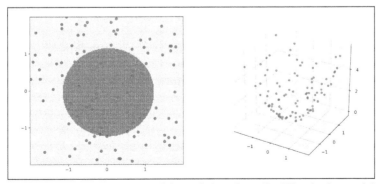

A training example of SVM with kernel given by $\varphi((a, b)) = (a, b, a^2 + b^2)$.

Suppose now that we would like to learn a nonlinear classification rule which corresponds to a linear classification rule for the transformed data points $\varphi(\vec{x}_i)$. Moreover, we are given a kernel function k which satisfies $k(\vec{x}_i, \vec{x}_j) = \varphi(\vec{x}_i) \cdot \varphi(\vec{x}_j)$.

We know the classification vector $\vec{w}$ in the transformed space satisfies:

$$\vec{w} = \sum_{i=1}^{n} c_i y_i \varphi(\vec{x}_i),$$

where, the c_i are obtained by solving the optimization problem:

$$\text{maximize } f(c_1 \ldots c_n) = \sum_{i=1}^{n} c_i - \frac{1}{2} \sum_{i=1}^{n} \sum_{j=1}^{n} y_i c_i (\varphi(\vec{x}_i) \cdot \varphi(\vec{x}_j)) y_j c_j$$

$$= \sum_{i=1}^{n} c_i - \frac{1}{2} \sum_{i=1}^{n} \sum_{j=1}^{n} y_i c_i k(\vec{x}_i, \vec{x}_j) y_j c_j$$

$$\text{subject to } \sum_{i=1}^{n} c_i y_i = 0, \text{and } 0 \le c_i \le \frac{1}{2n\lambda} \text{ for all } i.$$

The coefficients c_i can be solved for using quadratic programming, as before. Again, we can find some index i such that $0 < c_i < (2n\lambda)^{-1}$, so that $\varphi(\vec{x}_i)$ lies on the boundary of the margin in the transformed space, and then solve:

$$b = \vec{w} \cdot \varphi(\vec{x}_i) - y_i = \left[\sum_{j=1}^{n} c_j y_j \varphi(\vec{x}_j) \cdot \varphi(\vec{x}_i) \right] - y_i$$

$$= \left[\sum_{j=1}^{n} c_j y_j k(\vec{x}_j, \vec{x}_i) \right] - y_i.$$

Finally,

$$\vec{z} \mapsto \text{sgn}(\vec{w} \cdot \varphi(\vec{z}) - b) = \text{sgn}\left(\left[\sum_{i=1}^{n} c_i y_i k(\vec{x}_i, \vec{z}) \right] - b \right).$$

Modern Methods

Recent algorithms for finding the SVM classifier include sub-gradient descent and coordinate descent. Both techniques have proven to offer significant advantages over the traditional approach when dealing with large, sparse datasets—sub-gradient methods are especially efficient when there are many training examples, and coordinate descent when the dimension of the feature space is high.

Sub-gradient Descent

Sub-gradient descent algorithms for the SVM work directly with the expression:

$$f(\vec{w}, b) = \left[\frac{1}{n} \sum_{i=1}^{n} \max\left(0, 1 - y_i (\vec{w} \cdot \vec{x}_i - b) \right) \right] + \lambda \| \vec{w} \|^2 .$$

Note that f is a convex function of $\bar{w}$ and b. As such, traditional gradient descent (or SGD) methods can be adapted, where instead of taking a step in the direction of the function's gradient, a step is taken in the direction of a vector selected from the function's sub-gradient. This approach has the advantage that, for certain implementations, the number of iterations does not scale with n, the number of data points.

Coordinate Descent

Coordinate descent algorithms for the SVM work from the dual problem:

$$\text{maximize } f(c_1 \ldots c_n) = \sum_{i=1}^{n} c_i - \frac{1}{2} \sum_{i=1}^{n} \sum_{j=1}^{n} y_i c_i (x_i \cdot x_j) y_j c_j,$$

$$\text{subject to } \sum_{i=1}^{n} c_i y_i = 0, \text{and } 0 \le c_i \le \frac{1}{2n\lambda} \text{ for all } i.$$

For each $i \in \{1,\ldots,n\}$, iteratively, the coefficient c_i is adjusted in the direction of $\partial f / \partial c_i$. Then, the resulting vector of coefficients $(c_1',\ldots,c_n')$ is projected onto the nearest vector of coefficients that satisfies the given constraints. (Typically Euclidean distances are used.) The process is then repeated until a near-optimal vector of coefficients is obtained. The resulting algorithm is extremely fast in practice, although few performance guarantees have been proven.

Empirical Risk Minimization

The soft-margin support vector machine described above is an example of an empirical risk minimization (ERM) algorithm for the *hinge loss*. Seen this way, support vector machines belong to a natural class of algorithms for statistical inference, and many of its unique features are due to the behavior of the hinge loss. This perspective can provide further insight into how and why SVMs work, and allow us to better analyze their statistical properties.

Risk Minimization

In supervised learning, one is given a set of training examples $X_1 \ldots X_n$ with labels $y_1 \ldots y_n$, and wishes to predict y_{n+1} given X_{n+1}. To do so one forms a hypothesis, f, such that $f(X_{n+1})$ is a "good" approximation of y_{n+1}. A "good" approximation is usually defined with the help of a *loss function*, $\ell(y,z)$, which characterizes how bad z is as a prediction of y. We would then like to choose a hypothesis that minimizes the *expected risk*:

$$\varepsilon(f) = \mathbb{E}\left[\ell(y_{n+1}, f(X_{n+1}))\right].$$

In most cases, we don't know the joint distribution of X_{n+1}, y_{n+1} outright. In these cases, a common strategy is to choose the hypothesis that minimizes the *empirical risk*:

$$\hat{\varepsilon}(f) = \frac{1}{n} \sum_{k=1}^{n} \ell(y_k, f(X_k)).$$

Under certain assumptions about the sequence of random variables X_k, y_k (for example, that they are generated by a finite Markov process), if the set of hypotheses being considered is small enough, the minimizer of the empirical risk will closely approximate the minimizer of the expected risk as n grows large. This approach is called empirical risk minimization, or ERM.

Regularization and Stability

In order for the minimization problem to have a well-defined solution, we have to place constraints on the set $\mathcal{H}$ of hypotheses being considered. If $\mathcal{H}$ is a normed space (as is the case for SVM), a particularly effective technique is to consider only those hypotheses f for which $\| f \|_{\mathcal{H}} < k$. This is equivalent to imposing a regularization penalty $\mathcal{R}(f) = \lambda_k \| f \|_{\mathcal{H}}$, and solving the new optimization problem:

$$\hat{f} = \arg\min_{f \in \mathcal{H}} \hat{\varepsilon}(f) + \mathcal{R}(f).$$

This approach is called Tikhonov regularization.

More generally, $\mathcal{R}(f)$ can be some measure of the complexity of the hypothesis f, so that simpler hypotheses are preferred.

SVM and the Hinge Loss

Recall that the (soft-margin) SVM classifier $\hat{w}, b : x \mapsto \mathrm{sgn}(\hat{w} \cdot x - b)$ is chosen to minimize the following expression:

$$\left[\frac{1}{n} \sum_{i=1}^{n} \max\left(0, 1 - y_i(w \cdot x_i - b)\right) \right] + \lambda \| w \|^2.$$

In light of the above discussion, we see that the SVM technique is equivalent to empirical risk minimization with Tikhonov regularization, where in this case the loss function is the hinge loss,

$$\ell(y, z) = \max\left(0, 1 - yz\right).$$

From this perspective, SVM is closely related to other fundamental classification algorithms such as regularized least-squares and logistic regression. The difference between the three lies in the choice of loss function: regularized least-squares amounts to empirical risk minimization with the square-loss, $\ell_{sq}(y, z) = (y - z)^2$; logistic regression employs the log-loss,

$$\ell_{\log}(y, z) = \ln(1 + e^{-yz}).$$

Target Functions

The difference between the hinge loss and these other loss functions is best stated in terms of *target functions* - the function that minimizes expected risk for a given pair of random variables X, y.

In particular, let y_x denote y conditional on the event that $X = x$. In the classification setting, we have:

$$y_x = \begin{cases} 1 & \text{with probability } p_x \\ -1 & \text{with probability } 1 - p_x \end{cases}$$

The optimal classifier is therefore:

$$f^*(x) = \begin{cases} 1 & \text{if } p_x \geq 1/2 \\ -1 & \text{otherwise} \end{cases}$$

For the square-loss, the target function is the conditional expectation function, $f_{sq}(x) = \mathbb{E}[y_x]$; For the logistic loss, it's the logit function, $f_{\log}(x) = \ln(p_x / (1 - p_x))$. While both of these target functions yield the correct classifier, as $\text{sgn}(f_{sq}) = \text{sgn}(f_{\log}) = f^*$, they give us more information than we need. In fact, they give us enough information to completely describe the distribution of y_x.

On the other hand, one can check that the target function for the hinge loss is *exactly* f^*. Thus, in a sufficiently rich hypothesis space—or equivalently, for an appropriately chosen kernel—the SVM classifier will converge to the simplest function (in terms of $\mathcal{R}$) that correctly classifies the data. This extends the geometric interpretation of SVM—for linear classification, the empirical risk is minimized by any function whose margins lie between the support vectors, and the simplest of these is the max-margin classifier.

Properties

SVMs belong to a family of generalized linear classifiers and can be interpreted as an extension of the perceptron. They can also be considered a special case of Tikhonov regularization. A special property is that they simultaneously minimize the empirical *classification error* and maximize the *geometric margin*; hence they are also known as maximum margin classifiers.

A comparison of the SVM to other classifiers has been made by Meyer, Leisch and Hornik.

Parameter Selection

The effectiveness of SVM depends on the selection of kernel, the kernel's parameters, and soft margin parameter C. A common choice is a Gaussian kernel, which has a single parameter γ. The best combination of C and γ is often selected by a grid search with exponentially growing sequences of C and γ, for example, $C \in \{2^{-5}, 2^{-3}, ..., 2^{13}, 2^{15}\}$; $\gamma \in \{2^{-15}, 2^{-13}, ..., 2^{1}, 2^{3}\}$. Typically, each combination of parameter choices is checked using cross validation, and the parameters with best cross-validation accuracy are picked. Alternatively, recent work in Bayesian optimization can be used to select C and γ, often requiring the evaluation of far fewer parameter combinations than grid search. The final model, which is used for testing and for classifying new data, is then trained on the whole training set using the selected parameters.

Issues

Potential drawbacks of the SVM include the following aspects:

- Requires full labeling of input data.

- Uncalibrated class membership probabilities—SVM stems from Vapnik's theory which avoids estimating probabilities on finite data.

- The SVM is only directly applicable for two-class tasks. Therefore, algorithms that reduce the multi-class task to several binary problems have to be applied.

- Parameters of a solved model are difficult to interpret.

LINEAR REGRESSION

Linear Regression is a supervised machine learning algorithm where the predicted output is continuous and has a constant slope. It's used to predict values within a continuous range, (e.g. sales, price) rather than trying to classify them into categories (e.g. cat, dog). There are two main types:

Simple Regression

Simple linear regression uses traditional slope-intercept form, where m and b are the variables our algorithm will try to "learn" to produce the most accurate predictions. x represents our input data and y represents our prediction.

$$y = mx + b$$

Multivariable Regression

A more complex, multi-variable linear equation might look like this, where w represents the co-efficients, or weights, our model will try to learn.

$$f(x,y,z) = w_1 x + w_2 y + w_3 z$$

The variables x, y, z represent the attributes, or distinct pieces of information, we have about each observation. For sales predictions, these attributes might include a company's advertising spend on radio, TV, and newspapers.

$$Sales = w_1 Radio + w_2 TV + w_3 News$$

Simple Regression

Let's say we are given a dataset with the following columns (features): how much a company spends on Radio advertising each year and its annual Sales in terms of units sold. We are trying to develop an equation that will let us to predict units sold based on how much a company spends on radio advertising. The rows (observations) represent companies.

Company	Radio ($)	Sales
Amazon	37.8	22.1
Google	39.3	10.4
Facebook	45.9	18.3
Apple	41.3	18.5

Making Predictions

Our prediction function outputs an estimate of sales given a company's radio advertising spend and our current values for Weight and Bias.

$$Sales = Weight \cdot Radio + Bias$$

Weight

The coefficient for the Radio independent variable. In machine learning we call coefficients weights.

Radio

The independent variable. In machine learning we call these variables features.

Bias

The intercept where our line intercepts the y-axis. In machine learning we can call intercepts *bias*. Bias offsets all predictions that we make.

Our algorithm will try to learn the correct values for Weight and Bias. By the end of our training, our equation will approximate the line of best fit.

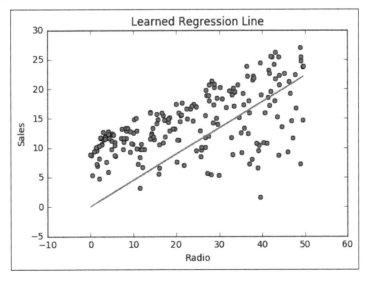

Code

```
def predict_sales(radio, weight, bias):

    return weight*radio + bias
```

Cost Function

The prediction function is nice, but for our purposes we don't really need it. What we need is a cost function so we can start optimizing our weights.

Let's use MSE (L2) as our cost function. MSE measures the average squared difference between an observation's actual and predicted values. The output is a single number representing the cost, or score, associated with our current set of weights. Our goal is to minimize MSE to improve the accuracy of our model.

Math

Given our simple linear equation $y = mx + b$, we can calculate MSE as:

$$MSE = \frac{1}{N} \sum_{i=1}^{n} \left(y_i - \left(mx_i + b \right) \right)^2$$

Code

```
def cost_function(radio, sales, weight, bias):

    companies = len(radio)

    total_error = 0.0

    for i in range(companies):

        total_error += (sales[i] - (weight*radio[i] + bias))**2

    return total_error / companies
```

Gradient Descent

To minimize MSE we use Gradient Descent to calculate the gradient of our cost function.

Math

There are two parameters (coefficients) in our cost function we can control: weight mm and bias bb. Since we need to consider the impact each one has on the final prediction, we use partial derivatives. To find the partial derivatives, we use the Chain rule. We need the chain rule because $\left(y - \left(mx + b \right) \right)^2$ is really 2 nested functions: the inner function $y - \left(mx + b \right)$ and the outer function

Returning to our cost function:

$$f(m,b) = \frac{1}{N} \sum_{i=1}^{n} \left(y_i - (mx_i + b) \right)^2$$

We can calculate the gradient of this cost function as:

$$f'(m,b) = \begin{bmatrix} \dfrac{df}{dm} \\[2mm] \dfrac{df}{db} \end{bmatrix} = \begin{bmatrix} \dfrac{1}{N} \sum -x_i \cdot 2\left(y_i - (mx_i + b)\right) \\[2mm] \dfrac{1}{N} \sum -1 \cdot 2\left(y_i - (mx_i + b)\right) \end{bmatrix}$$

$$= \begin{bmatrix} \dfrac{1}{N} \sum -2x_i \left(y_i - (mx_i + b)\right) \\[2mm] \dfrac{1}{N} \sum -2\left(y_i - (mx_i + b)\right) \end{bmatrix}$$

Code

To solve for the gradient, we iterate through our data points using our new weight and bias values and take the average of the partial derivatives. The resulting gradient tells us the slope of our cost function at our current position (i.e. weight and bias) and the direction we should update to reduce our cost function (we move in the direction opposite the gradient). The size of our update is controlled by the learning rate.

```
def update_weights(radio, sales, weight, bias, learning_rate):
    weight_deriv = 0

    bias_deriv = 0

    companies = len(radio)


    for i in range(companies):
        # Calculate partial derivatives
        # -2x(y - (mx + b))
        weight_deriv += -2*radio[i] * (sales[i] - (weight*radio[i] + bias))


        # -2(y - (mx + b))
        bias_deriv += -2*(sales[i] - (weight*radio[i] + bias))


    # We subtract because the derivatives point in direction of steepest ascent
```

```
    weight -= (weight_deriv / companies) * learning_rate
    bias -= (bias_deriv / companies) * learning_rate


    return weight, bias
```

Training

Training a model is the process of iteratively improving your prediction equation by looping through the dataset multiple times, each time updating the weight and bias values in the direction indicated by the slope of the cost function (gradient). Training is complete when we reach an acceptable error threshold, or when subsequent training iterations fail to reduce our cost.

Before training we need to initialize our weights (set default values), set our hyperparameters (learning rate and number of iterations), and prepare to log our progress over each iteration.

Code

```
def train(radio, sales, weight, bias, learning_rate, iters):
    cost_history = []


    for i in range(iters):
        weight,bias = update_weights(radio, sales, weight, bias, learning_rate)


        #Calculate cost for auditing purposes
        cost = cost_function(radio, sales, weight, bias)
        cost_history.append(cost)


        # Log Progress
        if i % 10 == 0:
            print "iter={:d}    weight={:.2f}    bias={:.4f}    cost={:.2}".
format(i, weight, bias, cost)


    return weight, bias, cost_history
```

Model Evaluation

If our model is working, we should see our cost decrease after every iteration.

Logging

```
iter=1      weight=.03    bias=.0014    cost=197.25

iter=10     weight=.28    bias=.0116    cost=74.65

iter=20     weight=.39    bias=.0177    cost=49.48

iter=30     weight=.44    bias=.0219    cost=44.31

iter=30     weight=.46    bias=.0249    cost=43.28
```

Visualizing

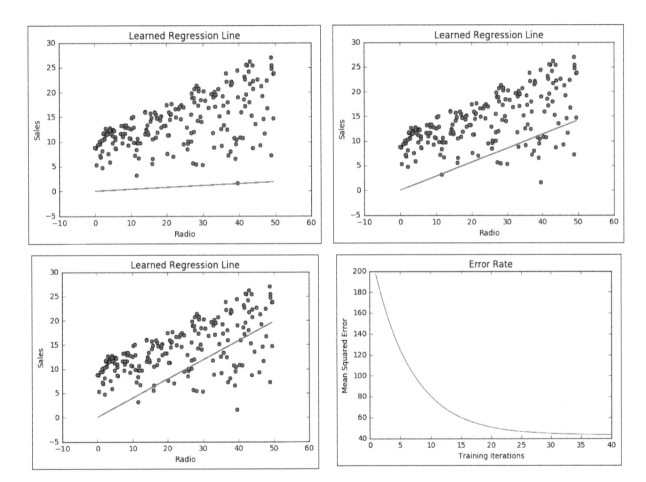

Multivariable Regression

Let's say we are given data on TV, radio, and newspaper advertising spend for a list of companies, and our goal is to predict sales in terms of units sold.

Company	TV	Radio	News	Units
Amazon	230.1	37.8	69.1	22.1

Google	44.5	39.3	23.1	10.4
Facebook	17.2	45.9	34.7	18.3
Apple	151.5	41.3	13.2	18.5

Growing Complexity

As the number of features grows, the complexity of our model increases and it becomes increasingly difficult to visualize, or even comprehend, our data.

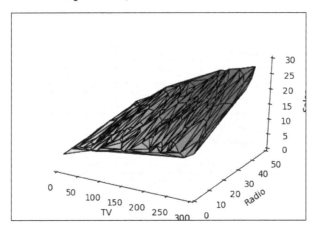

One solution is to break the data apart and compare 1-2 features at a time. In this example we explore how Radio and TV investment impacts Sales.

Normalization

As the number of features grows, calculating gradient takes longer to compute. We can speed this up by "normalizing" our input data to ensure all values are within the same range. This is especially important for datasets with high standard deviations or differences in the ranges of the attributes. Our goal now will be to normalize our features so they are all in the range -1 to 1.

Code

```
For each feature column {

    #1 Subtract the mean of the column (mean normalization)

    #2 Divide by the range of the column (feature scaling)

}
```

Our input is a 200 x 3 matrix containing TV, Radio, and Newspaper data. Our output is a normalized matrix of the same shape with all values between -1 and 1.

```
def normalize(features):

    **
```

```
features      -    (200, 3)

features.T    -    (3, 200)


We transpose the input matrix, swapping

cols and rows to make vector math easier

**


for feature in features.T:

    fmean = np.mean(feature)

    frange = np.amax(feature) - np.amin(feature)


    #Vector Subtraction

    feature -= fmean


    #Vector Division

    feature /= frange


return features
```

Making Predictions

Our predict function outputs an estimate of sales given our current weights (coefficients) and a company's TV, radio, and newspaper spend. Our model will try to identify weight values that most reduce our cost function.

$$Sales = W_1 TV + W_2 Radio + W_3 Newspaper$$

```
def predict(features, weights):

  **

  features - (200, 3)

  weights - (3, 1)

  predictions - (200,1)

  **
```

```
    predictions = np.dot(features, weights)

    return predictions
```

Initialize Weights

```
W1 = 0.0

W2 = 0.0

W3 = 0.0

weights = np.array([

    [W1],

    [W2],

    [W3]

])
```

Cost Function

Now we need a cost function to audit how our model is performing. The math is the same, except we swap the mx+b expression for $W_1x_1 + W_2x_2 + W_3x_3$. We also divide the expression by 2 to make derivative calculations simpler.

$$MSE = \frac{1}{2N}\sum_{i=1}^{n}\left(y_i - \left(W_1x_1 + W_2x_2 + W_3x_3\right)\right)^2$$

```
def cost_function(features, targets, weights):

    **

    features:(200,3)

    targets:  (200,1)

    weights:(3,1)

    returns average squared error among predictions

    **

    N = len(targets)


    predictions = predict(features, weights)
```

```
# Matrix math lets use do this without looping

sq_error = (predictions - targets)**2


# Return average squared error among predictions

return 1.0/(2*N) * sq_error.sum()
```

Gradient Descent

Again using the Chain rule we can compute the gradient–a vector of partial derivatives describing the slope of the cost function for each weight.

$$f'(W_1) = -x_1 \left(y - \left(W_1 x_1 + W_2 x_2 + W_3 x_3 \right) \right)$$
$$f'(W_2) = -x_2 \left(y - \left(W_1 x_1 + W_2 x_2 + W_3 x_3 \right) \right)$$
$$f'(W_3) = -x_3 \left(y - \left(W_1 x_1 + W_2 x_2 + W_3 x_3 \right) \right)$$

```
def update_weights(features, targets, weights, lr):
    '''
    Features:(200, 3)
    Targets: (200, 1)
    Weights:(3, 1)
    '''
    predictions = predict(features, weights)


    #Extract our features
    x1 = features[:,0]
    x2 = features[:,1]
    x3 = features[:,2]


    # Use matrix cross product (*) to simultaneously
    # calculate the derivative for each weight
    d_w1 = -x1*(targets - predictions)
    d_w2 = -x2*(targets - predictions)
    d_w3 = -x3*(targets - predictions)
```

```
    # Multiply the mean derivative by the learning rate

    # and subtract from our weights (remember gradient points in direction of
steepest ASCENT)

    weights[0][0] -= (lr * np.mean(d_w1))

    weights[1][0] -= (lr * np.mean(d_w2))

    weights[2][0] -= (lr * np.mean(d_w3))


    return weights
```

Simplifying with Matrices

The gradient descent code above has a lot of duplication. Can we improve it somehow? One way to refactor would be to loop through our features and weights–allowing our function to handle any number of features. However there is another even better technique: vectorized gradient descent.

Math

We use the same formula as above, but instead of operating on a single feature at a time, we use matrix multiplication to operative on all features and weights simultaneously. We replace the x_i terms with a single feature matrix X.

$$gradient = -X(targets - predictions)$$

Code

```
X = [

    [x1, x2, x3]

    [x1, x2, x3]

    .

    .

    .

    [x1, x2, x3]

]


targets = [
```

```
    [1],

    [2],

    [3]

]


def update_weights_vectorized(X, targets, weights, lr):

    **

    gradient = X.T * (predictions - targets) / N

    X: (200, 3)

    Targets: (200, 1)

    Weights: (3, 1)

    **

    companies = len(X)


    #1 - Get Predictions
    predictions = predict(X, weights)


    #2 - Calculate error/loss
    error = targets - predictions


    #3 Transpose features from (200, 3) to (3, 200)
    # So we can multiply w the (200,1)  error matrix.
    # Returns a (3,1) matrix holding 3 partial derivatives --
    # one for each feature -- representing the aggregate
    # slope of the cost function across all observations
    gradient = np.dot(-X.T,  error)


    #4 Take the average error derivative for each feature
    gradient /= companies


    #5 - Multiply the gradient by our learning rate
    gradient *= lr
```

```
#6 - Subtract from our weights to minimize cost

weights -= gradient


return weights
```

Bias Term

Our train function is the same as for simple linear regression, however we're going to make one final tweak before running: add a bias term to our feature matrix.

In our example, it's very unlikely that sales would be zero if companies stopped advertising. Possible reasons for this might include past advertising, existing customer relationships, retail locations, and salespeople. A bias term will help us capture this base case.

Code

Below we add a constant 1 to our features matrix. By setting this value to 1, it turns our bias term into a constant.

```
bias = np.ones(shape=(len(features),1))

features = np.append(bias, features, axis=1)
```

Model Evaluation

After training our model through 1000 iterations with a learning rate of .0005, we finally arrive at a set of weights we can use to make predictions:

$$Sales = 4.7TV + 3.5Radio + .81Newspaper + 13.9$$

Our MSE cost dropped from 110.86 to 6.25.

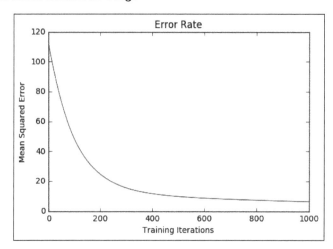

LOGISTIC REGRESSION

Logistic regression is a classification algorithm used to assign observations to a discrete set of classes. Some of the examples of classification problems are Email spam or not spam, Online transactions Fraud or not Fraud, Tumor Malignant or Benign. Logistic regression transforms its output using the logistic sigmoid function to return a probability value.

What are the types of Logistic Regression?

- Binary (eg. Tumor Malignant or Benign).

- Multi-linear functions failsClass (eg. Cats, dogs or Sheep's).

Logistic Regression

Logistic Regression is a Machine Learning algorithm which is used for the classification problems, it is a predictive analysis algorithm and based on the concept of probability.

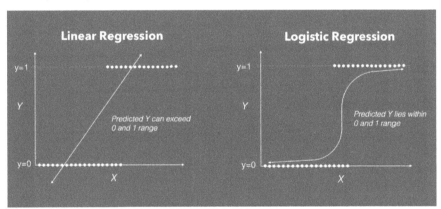

Linear Regression vs Logistic Regression Graph.

We can call a Logistic Regression a Linear Regression model but the Logistic Regression uses a more complex cost function, this cost function can be defined as the 'Sigmoid function' or also known as the 'logistic function' instead of a linear function.

The hypothesis of logistic regression tends it to limit the cost function between 0 and 1. Therefore linear functions fail to represent it as it can have a value greater than 1 or less than 0 which is not possible as per the hypothesis of logistic regression.

$$0 \le h_\theta(x) \le 1$$

Logistic regression hypothesis expectation.

Sigmoid Function

In order to map predicted values to probabilities, we use the Sigmoid function. The function maps any real value into another value between 0 and 1. In machine learning, we use sigmoid to map predictions to probabilities.

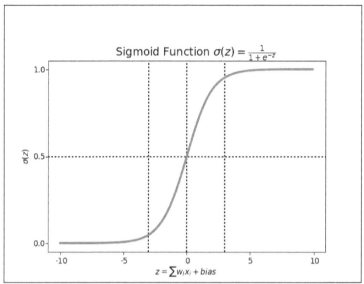

Sigmoid Function Graph.

$$f(x) = \frac{1}{1 + e^{-(x)}}$$

Formula of a sigmoid function.

Hypothesis Representation

When using linear regression we used a formula of the hypothesis i.e.,

$$h\Theta(x) = \beta_0 + \beta_1 X$$

 For logistic regression we are going to modify it a little bit i.e.,

$$\sigma(Z) = \sigma(\beta_0 + \beta_1 X)$$

We have expected that our hypothesis will give values between 0 and 1.

$$Z = \beta_0 + \beta_1 X$$
$$h\Theta(x) = \text{sigmoid}(Z)$$
$$\text{i.e. } h\Theta(x) = 1/(1 + e^{\wedge} - (\beta_0 + \beta_1 X)$$

$$h\theta(X) = \frac{1}{1 + e - (\beta_0 + \beta_1 X)}$$

The Hypothesis of logistic regression.

Decision Boundary

We expect our classifier to give us a set of outputs or classes based on probability when we pass the inputs through a prediction function and returns a probability score between 0 and 1.

For Example, We have 2 classes, let's take them like cats and dogs(1 — dog , 0 — cats). We basically decide with a threshold value above which we classify values into Class 1 and of the value goes below the threshold then we classify it in Class 2.

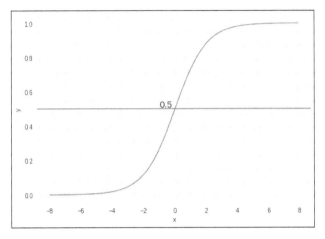

Example:

As shown in the above graph we have chosen the threshold as 0.5, if the prediction function returned a value of 0.7 then we would classify this observation as Class 1(DOG). If our prediction returned a value of 0.2 then we would classify the observation as Class 2(CAT).

Cost Function

We learnt about the cost function $J(\theta)$ in the *Linear regression*, the cost function represents optimization objective i.e. we create a cost function and minimize it so that we can develop an accurate model with minimum error.

$$J(\theta) = \frac{1}{2}\sum_{i=1}^{m}\left(h_\theta\left(x^{(i)}\right) - y^{(x)}\right)^2.$$

The Cost function of Linear regression.

If we try to use the cost function of the linear regression in 'Logistic Regression' then it would be of no use as it would end up being a non-convex function with many local minimums, in which it would be very difficult to minimize the cost value and find the global minimum.

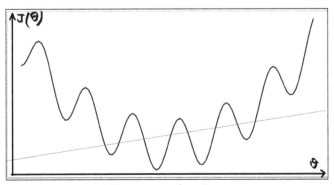

Non-convex function.

For logistic regression, the Cost function is defined as:

$-log(h\theta(x))$ *if* $y = 1$

$-log(1 - h\theta(x))$ *if* $y = 0$

$$\text{Cost}(h_\theta(x), y) = \begin{cases} -log(h_è(x)) & \text{if } y = 1 \\ -log(1 - h_è(x)) & \text{if } y = 0 \end{cases}$$

Cost function of Logistic Regression.

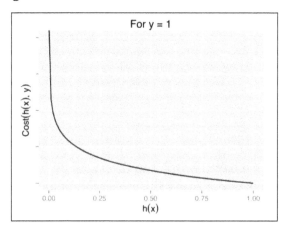

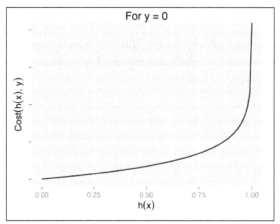

Graph of logistic regression.

The above two functions can be compressed into a single function i.e.,

$$J(\theta) = -\frac{1}{m}\sum\left[y^{(i)}\log\left(h\theta(x(i))\right) + \left(1 - y^{(i)}\right)\log\left(1 - h\theta(x(i))\right)\right]$$

Above functions compressed into one cost function.

Gradient Descent

Now the question arises, how do we reduce the cost value. Well, this can be done by using Gradient Descent. The main goal of Gradient descent is to minimize the cost value. i.e. min $J(\theta)$.

Now to minimize our cost function we need to run the gradient descent function on each parameter i.e.,

$$\theta j := \theta - \alpha \frac{\partial}{\partial \theta j} J(\theta)$$

Objective: To minimize the cost function we have to run the gradient descent function on each parameter:

Want $\min_\theta J(\theta)$:

Repeat

$$\theta_j := \theta_j - \alpha \sum_{i=1}^{m} \left(h_\theta \left(x^{(i)} \right) - y^{(i)} \right) x_j^{(i)}$$

$$\left\{ \qquad \left(\text{simultaneously update all } \theta_j \right) \right.$$

Gradient Descent Simplified

Gradient descent has an analogy in which we have to imagine ourselves at the top of a mountain valley and left stranded and blindfolded, our objective is to reach the bottom of the hill. Feeling the slope of the terrain around you is what everyone would do. Well, this action is analogous to calculating the gradient descent, and taking a step is analogous to one iteration of the update to the parameters.

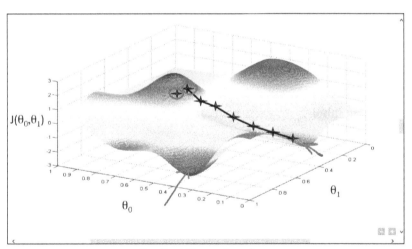

Gradient Descent analogy.

LEARNING VECTOR QUANTIZATION

In computer science, learning vector quantization (LVQ), is a prototype-based supervised classification algorithm. LVQ is the supervised counterpart of vector quantization systems.

LVQ can be understood as a special case of an artificial neural network, more precisely, it applies a winner-take-all Hebbian learning-based approach. It is a precursor to self-organizing maps (SOM) and related to neural gas, and to the k-nearest neighbor algorithm (k-NN). LVQ was invented by Teuvo Kohonen.

An LVQ system is represented by prototypes $W = (w(i),...,w(n))$ which are defined in the feature space of observed data. In winner-take-all training algorithms one determines, for each data point, the prototype which is closest to the input according to a given distance measure. The position of this so-called winner prototype is then adapted, i.e. the winner is moved closer if it correctly classifies the data point or moved away if it classifies the data point incorrectly.

An advantage of LVQ is that it creates prototypes that are easy to interpret for experts in the respective application domain. LVQ systems can be applied to multi-class classification problems in a natural way. It is used in a variety of practical applications.

A key issue in LVQ is the choice of an appropriate measure of distance or similarity for training and classification. Recently, techniques have been developed which adapt a parameterized distance measure in the course of training the system, see e.g. (Schneider, Biehl, and Hammer, 2009) and references therein.

LVQ can be a source of great help in classifying text documents.

Algorithm

Below follows an informal description.

The algorithm consists of 3 basic steps. The algorithm's input is:

- How many neurons the system will have M (in the simplest case it is equal to the number of classes).

- What weight each neuron has $\overrightarrow{w_i}$ for $i = 0,1,...,M-1$.

- The corresponding label c_i to each neuron $\overrightarrow{w_i}$.

- How fast the neurons are learning η.

- And an input list L containing all the vectors of which the labels are known already (training set).

The algorithm's flow is:

- For next input $\vec{x}$ in L find the closest neuron $\overrightarrow{w_m}$, i.e. $d(\vec{x},\overrightarrow{w_m}) = \min_i d(\vec{x},\overrightarrow{w_i})$, where d is the metric used (Euclidean, etc.).

- Update $\overrightarrow{w_m}$. A better explanation is get $\overrightarrow{w_m}$ closer to the input $\vec{x}$, if $\vec{x}$ and $\overrightarrow{w_m}$ belong to the same label and get them further apart if they don't. $\overrightarrow{w_m} \leftarrow \overrightarrow{w_m} + \eta \cdot \left(\vec{x} - \overrightarrow{w_m}\right)$ (closer together) or $\overrightarrow{w_m} \leftarrow \overrightarrow{w_m} - \eta \cdot \left(\vec{x} - \overrightarrow{w_m}\right)$ (further apart).

- While there are vectors left in L go to step 1, else terminate.

$\overrightarrow{w_i}$ and $\vec{x}$ are vectors in feature space.

PERCEPTRON

In machine learning, the perceptron is an algorithm for supervised learning of binary classifiers. A binary classifier is a function which can decide whether or not an input, represented by a vector of numbers, belongs to some specific class. It is a type of linear classifier, i.e. a classification algorithm that makes its predictions based on a linear predictor function combining a set of weights with the feature vector.

In the modern sense, the perceptron is an algorithm for learning a binary classifier called a threshold function: a function that maps its input x (a real-valued vector) to an output value $f(x)$ (a single binary value):

$$f(x) = \begin{cases} 1 & \text{if } w \cdot x + b > 0, \\ 0 & \text{otherwise} \end{cases}$$

where w is a vector of real-valued weights, $w \cdot x$ is the dot product $\sum_{i=1}^{m} w_i x_i$, where m is the number of inputs to the perceptron, and b is the *bias*. The bias shifts the decision boundary away from the origin and does not depend on any input value.

The value of $f(x)$ (0 or 1) is used to classify x as either a positive or a negative instance, in the case of a binary classification problem. If b is negative, then the weighted combination of inputs must produce a positive value greater than $|b|$ in order to push the classifier neuron over the 0 threshold. Spatially, the bias alters the position (though not the orientation) of the decision boundary. The perceptron learning algorithm does not terminate if the learning set is not linearly separable. If the vectors are not linearly separable learning will never reach a point where all vectors are classified properly. The most famous example of the perceptron's inability to solve problems with linearly nonseparable vectors is the Boolean exclusive-or problem. The solution spaces of decision boundaries for all binary functions and learning behaviors are studied in the reference.

In the context of neural networks, a perceptron is an artificial neuron using the Heaviside step function as the activation function. The perceptron algorithm is also termed the single-layer perceptron, to distinguish it from a multilayer perceptron, which is a misnomer for a more complicated neural network. As a linear classifier, the single-layer perceptron is the simplest feedforward neural network.

Learning Algorithm

Below is an example of a learning algorithm for a (single-layer) perceptron. For multilayer perceptrons, where a hidden layer exists, more sophisticated algorithms such as backpropagation must be used. Alternatively, methods such as the delta rule can be used if the function is non-linear and differentiable, although the one below will work as well.

When multiple perceptrons are combined in an artificial neural network, each output neuron operates independently of all the others; thus, learning each output can be considered in isolation.

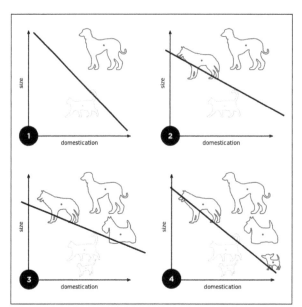

A diagram showing a perceptron updating its linear boundary as more training examples are added.

We first define some variables:

- r is the learning rate of the perceptron. Learning rate is between 0 and 1, larger values make the weight changes more volatile.

- $y = f(z)$ denotes the *output* from the perceptron for an input vector z.

- $D = \{(x_1, d_1), \ldots, (x_s, d_s)\}$ is the *training set* of s samples, where:

  ○ x_j is the n-dimensional input vector.

  ○ d_j is the desired output value of the perceptron for that input.

We show the values of the features as follows:

- $x_{j,i}$ is the value of the ith feature of the jth training *input vector*.

- $x_{j,0} = 1$.

To represent the weights:

- w_i is the ith value in the *weight vector*, to be multiplied by the value of the ith input feature.

- Because $x_{j,0} = 1$, the w_0 is effectively a bias that we use instead of the bias constant b.

To show the time-dependence of w, we use:

- $w_i(t)$ is the weight i at time t.

Unlike other linear classification algorithms such as logistic regression, there is no need for a *learning rate* in the perceptron algorithm. This is because multiplying the update by any constant simply rescales the weights but never changes the sign of the prediction.

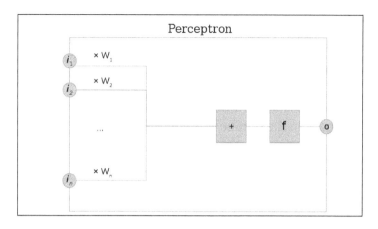

$$o = f\left(\sum_{k=1}^{n} i_k \cdot W_k\right)$$

The appropriate weights are applied to the inputs, and the resulting weighted sum passed to a function that produces the output o.

Steps:

- Initialize the weights and the threshold. Weights may be initialized to 0 or to a small random value. In the example below, we use 0.

- For each example j in our training set D, perform the following steps over the input x_j and desired output d_j :

    ○ Calculate the actual output:

    $$y_j(t) = f[w(t) \cdot x_j]$$
    $$= f[w_0(t)x_{j,0} + w_1(t)x_{j,1} + w_2(t)x_{j,2} + \cdots + w_n(t)x_{j,n}]$$

    ○ Update the weights:

    $$w_i(t+1) = w_i(t) + r \cdot (d_j - y_j(t))x_{j,i},$$ for all features $0 \le i \le n$, r is the learning rate.

- For offline learning, the second step may be repeated until the iteration error $\dfrac{1}{s}\sum_{j=1}^{s}|d_j - y_j(t)|$

    is less than a user-specified error threshold ā, or a predetermined number of iterations have been completed, where s is again the size of the sample set.

The algorithm updates the weights after steps 2a and 2b. These weights are immediately applied to a pair in the training set, and subsequently updated, rather than waiting until all pairs in the training set have undergone these steps.

Convergence

The perceptron is a linear classifier, therefore it will never get to the state with all the input vectors classified correctly if the training set D is not linearly separable, i.e. if the positive examples cannot be separated from the negative examples by a hyperplane. In this case, no "approximate" solution will be gradually approached under the standard learning algorithm, but instead learning will fail completely. Hence, if linear separability of the training set is not known a priori, one of the training variants below should be used.

If the training set *is* linearly separable, then the perceptron is guaranteed to converge. Furthermore, there is an upper bound on the number of times the perceptron will adjust its weights during the training.

Suppose that the input vectors from the two classes can be separated by a hyperplane with a margin ã, i.e. there exists a weight vector $w, \|w\| = 1$, and a bias term b such that $w \cdot x_j > \gamma$ for all $j : d_j = 1$ and $w \cdot x_j < -\gamma$ for all $j : d_j = 0$. Also, let R denote the maximum norm of an input vector. Novikoff proved that in this case the perceptron algorithm converges after making $O(R^2 / \gamma^2)$ updates. The idea of the proof is that the weight vector is always adjusted by a bounded amount in a direction with which it has a negative dot product, and thus can be bounded above by $O(\sqrt{t})$, where t is the number of changes to the weight vector. However, it can also be bounded below by $O(t)$ because if there exists an (unknown) satisfactory weight vector, then every change makes progress in this (unknown) direction by a positive amount that depends only on the input vector.

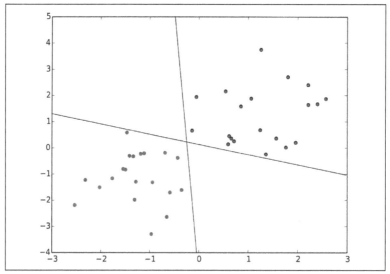

Two classes of points, and two of the infinitely many linear boundaries that separate them. Even though the boundaries are at nearly right angles to one another, the perceptron algorithm has no way of choosing between them.

While the perceptron algorithm is guaranteed to converge on *some* solution in the case of a linearly separable training set, it may still pick *any* solution and problems may admit many solutions of varying quality. The *perceptron of optimal stability*, nowadays better known as the linear support vector machine, was designed to solve this problem.

Variants

The pocket algorithm with ratchet solves the stability problem of perceptron learning by keeping the best solution seen so far "in its pocket". The pocket algorithm then returns the solution in the pocket, rather than the last solution. It can be used also for non-separable data sets, where the aim is to find a perceptron with a small number of misclassifications. However, these solutions appear purely stochastically and hence the pocket algorithm neither approaches them gradually in the course of learning, nor are they guaranteed to show up within a given number of learning steps.

The Maxover algorithm is "robust" in the sense that it will converge regardless of (prior) knowledge of linear separability of the data set. In the linearly separable case, it will solve the training problem – if desired, even with optimal stability (maximum margin between the classes). For non-separable data sets, it will return a solution with a small number of misclassifications. In all cases, the algorithm gradually approaches the solution in the course of learning, without memorizing previous states and without stochastic jumps. Convergence is to global optimality for separable data sets and to local optimality for non-separable data sets.

The Voted Perceptron, is a variant using multiple weighted perceptrons. The algorithm starts a new perceptron every time an example is wrongly classified, initializing the weights vector with the final weights of the last perceptron. Each perceptron will also be given another weight corresponding to how many examples do they correctly classify before wrongly classifying one, and at the end the output will be a weighted vote on all perceptrons.

In separable problems, perceptron training can also aim at finding the largest separating margin between the classes. The so-called perceptron of optimal stability can be determined by means of iterative training and optimization schemes, such as the Min-Over algorithm or the AdaTron. AdaTron uses the fact that the corresponding quadratic optimization problem is convex. The perceptron of optimal stability, together with the kernel trick, are the conceptual foundations of the support vector machine.

The α -perceptron further used a pre-processing layer of fixed random weights, with thresholded output units. This enabled the perceptron to classify analogue patterns, by projecting them into a binary space. In fact, for a projection space of sufficiently high dimension, patterns can become linearly separable.

Another way to solve nonlinear problems without using multiple layers is to use higher order networks (sigma-pi unit). In this type of network, each element in the input vector is extended with each pairwise combination of multiplied inputs (second order). This can be extended to an n-order network.

It should be kept in mind, however, that the best classifier is not necessarily that which classifies all the training data perfectly. Indeed, if we had the prior constraint that the data come from equi-variant Gaussian distributions, the linear separation in the input space is optimal, and the nonlinear solution is overfitted.

Other linear classification algorithms include Winnow, support vector machine and logistic regression.

Multiclass Perceptron

Like most other techniques for training linear classifiers, the perceptron generalizes naturally to multiclass classification. Here, the input x and the output y are drawn from arbitrary sets. A feature representation function $f(x,y)$ maps each possible input/output pair to a finite-dimensional real-valued feature vector. As before, the feature vector is multiplied by a weight vector w, but now the resulting score is used to choose among many possible outputs:

$$\hat{y} = \operatorname{argmax}_y f(x,y) \cdot w.$$

Learning again iterates over the examples, predicting an output for each, leaving the weights unchanged when the predicted output matches the target, and changing them when it does not. The update becomes:

$$w_{t+1} = w_t + f(x,y) - f(x,\hat{y}).$$

This multiclass feedback formulation reduces to the original perceptron when x is a real-valued vector, y is chosen from $\{0,1\}$, and $f(x,y) = yx$.

For certain problems, input/output representations and features can be chosen so that $\operatorname{argmax}_y f(x,y) \cdot w$ can be found efficiently even though y is chosen from a very large or even infinite set.

Since 2002, perceptron training has become popular in the field of natural language processing for such tasks as part-of-speech tagging and syntactic parsing. It has also been applied to large-scale machine learning problems in a distributed computing setting.

LINEAR DISCRIMINANT ANALYSIS

Linear discriminant analysis is an extremely popular dimensionality reduction technique. Dimensionality reduction techniques have become critical in machine learning since many high-dimensional datasets exist these days.

Linear Discriminant Analysis was developed as early as 1936 by Ronald A. Fisher. The original Linear discriminant applied to only a 2-class problem. It was only in 1948 that C.R. Rao generalized it to apply to multi-class problems.

Linear Discriminant Analysis(LDA)

It is used as a dimensionality reduction technique. Also known as a commonly used in the pre-processing step in machine learning and pattern classification projects.

In Python, it helps to reduce high-dimensional data set onto a lower-dimensional space. The goal is to do this while having a decent separation between classes and reducing resources and costs of computing.

Original technique that was developed was known as the Linear Discriminant or Fisher's Discriminant Analysis. This was a two-class technique. The multi-class version, as generalized by C.R. Rao, was called Multiple Discriminant Analysis.

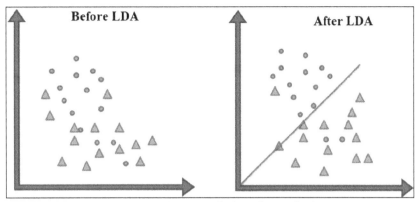

Linear Discriminant Analysis Before and After.

Dimensionality Reduction

To understand in a better, let's begin by understanding what dimensionality reduction is.

Multi-dimensional data is data that has multiple features which have a correlation with one another. Dimensionality reduction simply means plotting multi-dimensional data in just 2 or 3 dimensions.

An alternative to dimensionality reduction is plotting the data using scatter plots, boxplots, histograms, and so on. We can then use these graphs to identify the pattern in the raw data.

However, with charts, it is difficult for a layperson to make sense of the data that has been presented. Moreover, if there are many features in the data, thousands of charts will need to be analyzed to identify patterns.

Dimensionality reduction algorithms solve this problem by plotting the data in 2 or 3 dimensions. This allows us to present the data explicitly, in a way that can be understood by a layperson.

Linear Discriminant Analysis for Dummies

It works on a simple step-by-step basis. Here is an example. These are the three key steps.

(i) Calculate the separability between different classes. This is also known as between-class variance and is defined as the distance between the mean of different classes.

$$S_b = \sum_{i=1}^{g} N_i \left(\overline{x}_i - \overline{x} \right) \left(\overline{x}_i - \overline{x} \right)^T$$

Between Class Variance.

(ii) Calculate the within-class variance. This is the distance between the mean and the sample of every class.

$$S_w = \sum_{i=1}^{g} \left(N_i - 1 \right) S_i = \sum_{i=1}^{g} \sum_{j=1}^{N} \left(\chi_{i,j} - \overline{\chi}_i \right) \left(\chi_{i,j} - \overline{\chi}_i \right)^T$$

Within-Class Variance.

(iii) Construct the lower-dimensional space that maximizes Step1 (between-class variance) and minimizes Step 2(within-class variance). In the equation below P is the lower-dimensional space projection. This is also known as Fisher's criterion.

$$P_{lda} = \arg\max_{P} \frac{\left| P^T S_b P \right|}{\left| P^T S_w P \right|}$$

Fisher's Criterion.

Representation of Linear Discriminant Models

The representation of Linear Discriminant models consists of the statistical properties of the dataset. These are calculated separately for each class. For instance, for a single input variable, it is the mean and variance of the variable for every class.

If there are multiple variables, the same statistical properties are calculated over the multivariate Gaussian. This includes the means and the covariance matrix. All these properties are directly estimated from the data. They directly go into the Linear Discriminant Analysis equation.

The statistical properties are estimated on the basis of certain assumptions. These assumptions help simplify the process of estimation. One such assumption is that each data point has the same variance.

Another assumption is that the data is Gaussian. This means that each variable, when plotted, is shaped like a bell curve. Using these assumptions, the mean and variance of each variable are estimated.

Making Predictions

The linear Discriminant analysis estimates the probability that a new set of inputs belongs to every class. The output class is the one that has the highest probability. That is how the LDA makes its prediction.

LDA uses Bayes' Theorem to estimate the probabilities. If the output class is (k) and the input is (x), here is how Bayes' theorem works to estimate the probability that the data belongs to each class.

$$P\left(Y = x \mid X = x \right) = \left(\text{PIk} * \text{fk}\left(x \right) \right) / \text{sum}\left(\text{PII} * \text{fl}\left(x \right) \right)$$

In the above equation:

Plk: Prior probability. This is the base probability of each class as observed in the training data.

f(x): The estimated probability that x belongs to that particular class. f(x) uses a Gaussian distribution function.

LDA vs. other Dimensionality Reduction Techniques

Two dimensionality-reduction techniques that are commonly used for the same purpose as Linear

Discriminant Analysis are Logistic Regression and PCA (Principal Components Analysis). However, these have certain unique features that make it the technique of choice in many cases. Here are its comparison points against other techniques.

Linear Discriminant Analysis vs. PCA

(i) PCA is an unsupervised algorithm. It ignores class labels altogether and aims to find the principal components that maximize variance in a given set of data. Linear Discriminant Analysis, on the other hand, is a supervised algorithm that finds the linear discriminants that will represent those axes which maximize separation between different classes.

(ii) Linear Discriminant Analysis often outperforms PCA in a multi-class classification task when the class labels are known. In some of these cases, however, PCA performs better. This is usually when the sample size for each class is relatively small. A good example is the comparisons between classification accuracies used in image recognition technology.

(ii) Many times, the two techniques are used together for dimensionality reduction. PCA is used first followed by LDA.

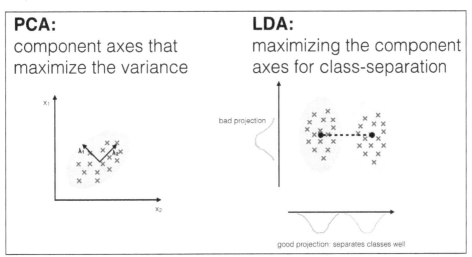

Linear Discriminant Analysis vs PCA.

Linear Discriminant Analysis vs. Logistic Regression

Two-class vs. Multi-class Problems

Logistic regression is both simple and powerful. However, it is traditionally used only in binary classification problems. While it can be extrapolated and used in multi-class classification problems, this is rarely done. When it's a question of multi-class classification problems, linear discriminant analysis is usually the go-to choice. In fact, even with binary classification problems, both logistic regression and linear discriminant analysis are applied at times.

Instability with Well-separated Classes

Logistic regression can become unstable when the classes are well-separated. This is where the Linear Discriminant Analysis comes in.

Instability with few Examples

If there are just a few examples from the parameters need to be estimated, logistic regression tends to become unstable. In this situation too, Linear Discriminant Analysis is the superior option as it tends to stay stable even with fewer examples.

Linear Discriminant Analysis via Scikit Learn

Of course, you can use a step-by-step approach to implement Linear Discriminant Analysis. However, the more convenient and more often-used way to do this is by using the Linear Discriminant Analysis class in the Scikit Learn machine learning library. Here is an example of the code to be used to achieve this.

from sklearn.discriminant_analysis import LinearDiscriminantAnalysis as LDA.

```
# LDA

sklearn_lda = LDA(n_components=2)

X_lda_sklearn = sklearn_lda.fit_transform(X, y)

def plot_scikit_lda(X, title):

    ax = plt.subplot(111)

    for label,marker,color in zip(

        range(1,4),('^', 's', 'o'),('blue', 'red', 'green')):

        plt.scatter(x=X[:,0][y == label],

                    y=X[:,1][y == label] * -1, # flip the figure

                    marker=marker,

                    color=color,

                    alpha=0.5,

                    label=label_dict[label])

    plt.xlabel('LD1')

    plt.ylabel('LD2')

    leg = plt.legend(loc='upper right', fancybox=True)

    leg.get_frame().set_alpha(0.5)

    plt.title(title)

    # hide axis ticks

    plt.tick_params(axis="both", which="both", bottom="off", top="off",

            labelbottom="on", left="off", right="off", labelleft="on")
```

```
# remove axis spines

ax.spines["top"].set_visible(False)

ax.spines["right"].set_visible(False)

ax.spines["bottom"].set_visible(False)

ax.spines["left"].set_visible(False)

plt.grid()

plt.tight_layout

plt.show()
plot_step_lda()

plot_scikit_lda(X_lda_sklearn, title='Default LDA via scikit-learn')
```

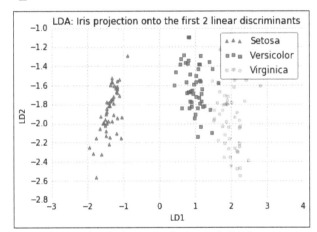

Linear Discriminant Analysis via Scikit Learn.

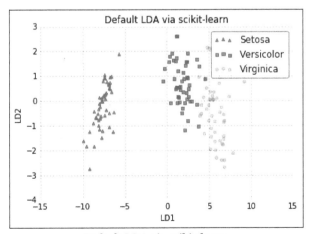

Default LDA via scikit-learn.

Extensions and Variations

Due to its simplicity and ease of use, Linear Discriminant Analysis has seen many extensions and variations. These have all been designed with the objective of improving the efficacy of Linear

Discriminant Analysis examples. Here are some common Linear Discriminant Analysis examples where extensions have been made.

Flexible Discriminant Analysis (FDA)

Regular Linear Discriminant Analysis uses only linear combinations of inputs. The Flexible Discriminant Analysis allows for non-linear combinations of inputs like splines.

Quadratic Discriminant Analysis (QDA)

In Quadratic Discriminant Analysis, each class uses its own estimate of variance when there is a single input variable. In case of multiple input variables, each class uses its own estimate of covariance.

Regularized Discriminant Analysis (RDA)

This method moderates the influence of different variables on the Linear Discriminant Analysis. It does so by regularizing the estimate of variance/covariance.

LDA Python has become very popular because it's simple and easy to understand. While other dimensionality reduction techniques like PCA and logistic regression are also widely used, there are several specific use cases in which LDA is more appropriate. Thorough knowledge of Linear Discriminant Analysis is a must for all data science and machine learning enthusiasts.

RANDOM FORESTS

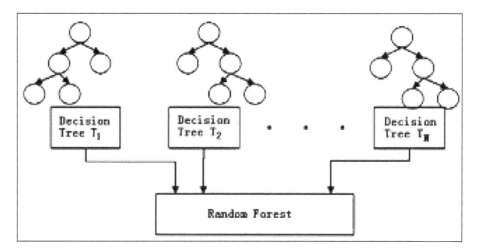

Random forest algorithm is a supervised classification algorithm. As the name suggest, this algorithm creates the forest with a number of trees.

In general, the more trees in the forest the more robust the forest looks like. In the same way in the random forest classifier, the higher the number of trees in the forest gives the high accuracy results.

If you know the decision tree algorithm. You might be thinking are we creating more number of decision trees and how can we create more number of decision trees. As all the calculation of nodes selection will be same for the same dataset.

Yes. You are true. To model more number of decision trees to create the forest you are not going to use the same apache of constructing the decision with information gain or gini index approach.

Basic Decision Tree Concept

Decision tree concept is more to the rule based system. Given the training dataset with targets and features, the decision tree algorithm will come up with some set of rules. The same set rules can be used to perform the prediction on the test dataset.

Suppose you would like to predict that your daughter will like the newly released animation movie or not. To model the decision tree you will use the training dataset like the animated cartoon characters your daughter liked in the past movies.

So once you pass the dataset with the target as your daughter will like the movie or not to the decision tree classifier. The decision tree will start building the rules with the characters your daughter like as nodes and the targets like or not as the leaf nodes. By considering the path from the root node to the leaf node. You can get the rules.

The simple rule could be if some **x** character is playing the leading role then your daughter will like the movie. You can think few more rule based on this example.

Then to predict whether your daughter will like the movie or not. You just need to check the rules which are created by the decision tree to predict whether your daughter will like the newly released movie or not.

In decision tree algorithm calculating these nodes and forming the rules will happen using the information gain and gini index calculations.

In random forest algorithm, Instead of using information gain or gini index for calculating the root node, the process of finding the root node and splitting the feature nodes will happen randomly.

Need of Random Forest Algorithm

- The same random forest algorithm or the random forest classifier can use for both classification and the regression task.

- Random forest classifier will handle the missing values.

- When we have more trees in the forest, random forest classifier won't overfit the model.

- Can model the random forest classifier for categorical values also.

Random Forest Algorithm Real Life Example

Before you drive into the technical details about the random forest algorithm. Let's look into a real life example to understand the layman type of random forest algorithm.

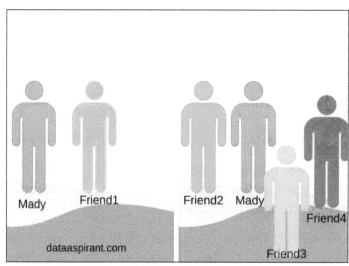
Random Forest Example.

Suppose Mady somehow got 2 weeks leave from his office. He wants to spend his 2 weeks by traveling to the different place. He also wants to go to the place he may like.

So he decided to ask his best friend about the places he may like. Then his friend started asking about his past trips. It's just like his best friend will ask, You have been visited the X place did you like it?

Based on the answers which are given by Mady, his best start recommending the place Mady may like. Here his best formed the decision tree with the answer given by Mady.

As his best friend may recommend his best place to Mady as a friend. The model will be biased with the closeness of their friendship. So he decided to ask few more friends to recommend the best place he may like.

Now his friends asked some random questions and each one recommended one place to Mady. Now Mady considered the place which is high votes from his friends as the final place to visit.

In the above Mady trip planning, two main interesting algorithms decision tree algorithm and random forest algorithm used.

Decision Tree

To recommend the best place to Mady, his best friend asked some questions. Based on the answers given by mady, he recommended a place. This is decision tree algorithm approach. Will explain why it is a decision tree algorithm approach.

Mady friend used the answers given by mady to create rules. Later he used the created rules to recommend the best place which mady will like. These rules could be, mady like a place with lots of tree or waterfalls etc.

In the above approach mady best friend is the decision tree. The vote (recommended place) is the leaf of the decision tree (Target class). The target is finalized by a single person, In a technical way of saying, using an only single decision tree.

Random Forest Algorithm

In the other case when mady asked his friends to recommend the best place to visit. Each friend asked him different questions and come up their recommend a place to visit. Later mady consider all the recommendations and calculated the votes. Votes basically is to pick the popular place from the recommend places from all his friends.

Mady will consider each recommended place and if the same place recommended by some other place he will increase the count. At the end the high count place where mady will go.

In this case, the recommended place (Target Prediction) is considered by many friends. Each friend is the tree and the combined all friends will form the forest. This forest is the random forest. As each friend asked random questions to recommend the best place visit.

Now let's use the above example to understand how the random forest algorithm work.

Working Principle of Random Forests

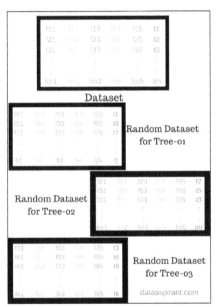

How random forest algorithm works.

Let's look at the pseudocode for random forest algorithm and later we can walk through each step in the random forest algorithm.

The pseudocode for random forest algorithm can split into two stages:

- Random forest creation pseudocode.

- Pseudocode to perform prediction from the created random forest classifier.

First, let's begin with random forest creation pseudocode.

Random Forest pseudocode:

- Randomly select "k" features from total "m" features.

- ◦ Where k << m.

- Among the "k" features, calculate the node "d" using the best split point.

- Split the node into daughter nodes using the best split.

- Repeat 1 to 3 steps until "l" number of nodes has been reached.

- Build forest by repeating steps 1 to 4 for "n" number times to create "n" number of trees.

The beginning of random forest algorithm starts with randomly selecting "k" features out of total "m" features. In the image, you can observe that we are randomly taking features and observations.

In the next stage, we are using the randomly selected "k" features to find the root node by using the best split approach.

The next stage, We will be calculating the daughter nodes using the same best split approach. Will the first 3 stages until we form the tree with a root node and having the target as the leaf node.

Finally, we repeat 1 to 4 stages to create "n" randomly created trees. This randomly created trees forms the random forest.

Random Forest Prediction Pseudocode

To perform prediction using the trained random forest algorithm uses the below pseudocode:

- Takes the test features and use the rules of each randomly created decision tree to predict the oucome and stores the predicted outcome (target).

- Calculate the votes for each predicted target.

- Consider the high voted predicted target as the final prediction from the random forest algorithm.

To perform the prediction using the trained random forest algorithm we need to pass the test features through the rules of each randomly created trees. Suppose let's say we formed 100 random decision trees to from the random forest.

Each random forest will predict different target (outcome) for the same test feature. Then by considering each predicted target votes will be calculated. Suppose the 100 random decision trees are prediction some 3 unique targets x, y, z then the votes of x is nothing but out of 100 random decision tree how many trees prediction is x.

Likewise for other 2 targets (y, z). If x is getting high votes. Let's say out of 100 random decision tree 60 trees are predicting the target will be x. Then the final random forest returns the x as the predicted target.

This concept of voting is known as majority voting.

Now let's look into few applications of random forest algorithm.

Random Forest Algorithm Applications

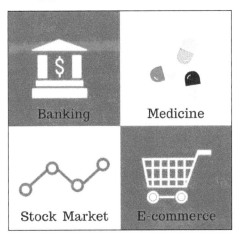

Random Forest Applications.

The random algorithm used in wide varieties applications. In this topic, we are going address few of them.

Below are some the application where random forest algorithm is widely used:

- Banking.

- Medicine.

- Stock Market.

- E-commerce.

Let's begin with the banking sector.

Banking

In the banking sector, random forest algorithm widely used in two main application. These are for finding the loyal customer and finding the fraud customers.

The loyal customer means not the customer who pays well, but also the customer whom can take the huge amount as loan and pays the loan interest properly to the bank. As the growth of the bank purely depends on the loyal customers. The bank customers data highly analyzed to find the pattern for the loyal customer based the customer details.

In the same way, there is need to identify the customer who are not profitable for the bank, like taking the loan and paying the loan interest properly or find the outlier customers. If the bank can identify theses kind of customer before giving the loan the customer. Bank will get a chance to not approve the loan to these kinds of customers. In this case, also random forest algorithm is used to identify the customers who are not profitable for the bank.

Medicine

In medicine field, random forest algorithm is used identify the correct combination of the components to validate the medicine. Random forest algorithm also helpful for identifying the disease by analyzing the patient's medical records.

Stock Market

In the stock market, random forest algorithm used to identify the stock behavior as well as the expected loss or profit by purchasing the particular stock.

E-commerce

In e-commerce, the random forest used only in the small segment of the recommendation engine for identifying the likely hood of customer liking the recommend products base on the similar kinds of customers.

Running random forest algorithm on very large dataset requires high-end GPU systems. If you are not having any GPU system. You can always run the machine learning models in cloud hosted desktop. You can use clouddesktoponline platform to run high-end machine learning models from sitting any corner of the world.

Advantages of Random Forest Algorithm

Below are the advantages of random forest algorithm compared with other classification algorithms:

- The overfitting problem will never come when we use the random forest algorithm in any classification problem.

- The same random forest algorithm can be used for both classification and regression task.

- The random forest algorithm can be used for feature engineering.

  - Which means identifying the most important features out of the available features from the training dataset.

References

- Supervised-learning: searchenterpriseai.techtarget.com, Retrieved 06 June, 2019

- Decision-tree-in-machine-learning: towardsdatascience.com, Retrieved 24 July, 2019

- Linear-regression: ml-cheatsheet.readthedocs.io, Retrieved 10 August, 2019

- Liou, D.-R.; Liou, J.-W.; Liou, C.-Y. (2013). Learning Behaviors of Perceptron. iConcept Press. ISBN 978-1-477554-73-9

- Introduction-to-logistic-regression: towardsdatascience.com, Retrieved 14 April, 2019

- Linear-discriminant-analysis: digitalvidya.com, Retrieved 01 May, 2019

- Random-forest-algorithm-machine-learing: dataaspirant.com, Retrieved 08 February, 2019

- Press, William H.; Teukolsky, Saul A.; Vetterling, William T.; Flannery, Brian P. (2007). "Section 16.5. Support Vector Machines". Numerical Recipes: The Art of Scientific Computing (3rd ed.). New York: Cambridge University Press. ISBN 978-0-521-88068-8. Archived from the original on 2011-08-11

Unsupervised Learning and Algorithms

Unsupervised learning deals with the use of unlabeled data for its working and modeling without supervision. It includes cluster analysis, hidden Markov model, Gaussian mixture model, etc. This chapter closely examines about unsupervised learning and these related algorithms to provide an extensive understanding of the subject.

Unsupervised learning is the training of machine using information that is neither classified nor labeled and allowing the algorithm to act on that information without guidance. Here the task of machine is to group unsorted information according to similarities, patterns and differences without any prior training of data.

Unlike supervised learning, no teacher is provided that means no training will be given to the machine. Therefore machine is restricted to find the hidden structure in unlabeled data by our-self. For instance, suppose it is given an image having both dogs and cats which have not seen ever.

Thus the machine has no idea about the features of dogs and cat so we can't categorize it in dogs and cats. But it can categorize them according to their similarities, patterns, and differences i.e., we can easily categorize the above picture into two parts. First first may contain all pics having dogs in it and second part may contain all pics having cats in it. Here you didn't learn anything before, means no training data or examples.

Unsupervised learning classified into two categories of algorithms:

- Clustering: A clustering problem is where you want to discover the inherent groupings in the data, such as grouping customers by purchasing behavior.

- Association: An association rule learning problem is where you want to discover rules that describe large portions of your data, such as people that buy X also tend to buy Y.

Types of Unsupervised Learning

Unsupervised learning problems further grouped into clustering and association problems.

Clustering

Clustering is an important concept when it comes to unsupervised learning. It mainly deals with finding a structure or pattern in a collection of uncategorized data. Clustering algorithms will process your data and find natural clusters(groups) if they exist in the data. You can also modify how many clusters your algorithms should identify. It allows you to adjust the granularity of these groups.

sample   Cluster/group

There are different types of clustering you can utilize:

Exclusive (Partitioning)

In this clustering method, Data are grouped in such a way that one data can belong to one cluster only.

Example: K-means.

Agglomerative

In this clustering technique, every data is a cluster. The iterative unions between the two nearest clusters reduce the number of clusters.

Example: Hierarchical clustering.

Overlapping

In this technique, fuzzy sets is used to cluster data. Each point may belong to two or more clusters with separate degrees of membership.

Here, data will be associated with an appropriate membership value. Example: Fuzzy C-Means

Probabilistic

This technique uses probability distribution to create the clusters.

Example: Following keywords.
- "Man's shoe".
- "Women's shoe".
- "Women's glove".
- "Man's glove".

can be clustered into two categories "shoe" and "glove" or "man" and "women".

Clustering Types

- Hierarchical clustering.

- K-means clustering.
- K-NN (k nearest neighbors).
- Principal Component Analysis.
- Singular Value Decomposition.
- Independent Component Analysis.

Hierarchical Clustering

Hierarchical clustering is an algorithm which builds a hierarchy of clusters. It begins with all the data which is assigned to a cluster of their own. Here, two close cluster are going to be in the same cluster. This algorithm ends when there is only one cluster left.

K-means Clustering

K means it is an iterative clustering algorithm which helps you to find the highest value for every iteration. Initially, the desired number of clusters are selected. In this clustering method, you need to cluster the data points into k groups. A larger k means smaller groups with more granularity in the same way. A lower k means larger groups with less granularity.

The output of the algorithm is a group of "labels." It assigns data point to one of the k groups. In k-means clustering, each group is defined by creating a centroid for each group. The centroids are like the heart of the cluster, which captures the points closest to them and adds them to the cluster.

K-mean clustering further defines two subgroups:

- Agglomerative clustering.
- Dendrogram.

Agglomerative Clustering

This type of K-means clustering starts with a fixed number of clusters. It allocates all data into the exact number of clusters. This clustering method does not require the number of clusters K as an input. Agglomeration process starts by forming each data as a single cluster.

This method uses some distance measure, reduces the number of clusters (one in each iteration) by merging process. Lastly, we have one big cluster that contains all the objects.

Dendrogram

In the Dendrogram clustering method, each level will represent a possible cluster. The height of dendrogram shows the level of similarity between two join clusters. The closer to the bottom of the process they are more similar cluster which is finding of the group from dendrogram which is not natural and mostly subjective.

K-Nearest Neighbors

K-Nearest neighbour is the simplest of all machine learning classifiers. It differs from other machine learning techniques, in that it doesn't produce a model. It is a simple algorithm which stores all available cases and classifies new instances based on a similarity measure.

It works very well when there is a distance between examples. The learning speed is slow when the training set is large, and the distance calculation is nontrivial.

Principal Components Analysis

In case you want a higher-dimensional space. You need to select a basis for that space and only the 200 most important scores of that basis. This base is known as a principal component. The subset you select constitute is a new space which is small in size compared to original space. It maintains as much of the complexity of data as possible.

Association

Association rules allow you to establish associations amongst data objects inside large databases. This unsupervised technique is about discovering interesting relationships between variables in large databases. For example, people that buy a new home most likely to buy new furniture.

Other Examples:

- A subgroup of cancer patients grouped by their gene expression measurements.

- Groups of shopper based on their browsing and purchasing histories.

- Movie group by the rating given by movies viewers.

Supervised vs. Unsupervised Machine Learning

Parameters	Supervised machine learning technique	Unsupervised machine learning technique
Input Data	Algorithms are trained using labeled data.	Algorithms are used against data which is not labelled
Computational Complexity	Supervised learning is a simpler method.	Unsupervised learning is computationally complex
Accuracy	Highly accurate and trustworthy method.	Less accurate and trustworthy method.

Applications of Unsupervised Machine Learning

Some applications of unsupervised machine learning techniques are:

- Clustering automatically split the dataset into groups base on their similarities.

- Anomaly detection can discover unusual data points in your dataset. It is useful for finding fraudulent transactions.

- Association mining identifies sets of items which often occur together in your dataset.

- Latent variable models are widely used for data preprocessing. Like reducing the number. of features in a dataset or decomposing the dataset into multiple components.

Disadvantages of Unsupervised Learning

- You cannot get precise information regarding data sorting, and the output as data used in unsupervised learning is labeled and not known.

- Less accuracy of the results is because the input data is not known and not labeled by people in advance. This means that the machine requires to do this itself.

- The spectral classes do not always correspond to informational classes.

- The user needs to spend time interpreting and label the classes which follow that classification.

- Spectral properties of classes can also change over time so you can't have the same class information while moving from one image to another.

CLUSTER ANALYSIS

Cluster analysis or clustering is the task of grouping a set of objects in such a way that objects in the same group (called a cluster) are more similar (in some sense) to each other than to those in other groups (clusters). It is a main task of exploratory data mining, and a common technique for statistical data analysis, used in many fields, including machine learning, pattern recognition, image analysis, information retrieval, bioinformatics, data compression, and computer graphics.

Cluster analysis itself is not one specific algorithm, but the general task to be solved. It can be achieved by various algorithms that differ significantly in their understanding of what constitutes a cluster and how to efficiently find them. Popular notions of clusters include groups with small distances between cluster members, dense areas of the data space, intervals or particular statistical distributions. Clustering can therefore be formulated as a multi-objective optimization problem. The appropriate clustering algorithm and parameter settings (including parameters such as the distance function to use, a density threshold or the number of expected clusters) depend on the individual data set and intended use of the results. Cluster analysis as such is not an automatic task, but an iterative process of knowledge discovery or interactive multi-objective optimization that involves trial and failure. It is often necessary to modify data preprocessing and model parameters until the result achieves the desired properties.

Besides the term clustering, there are a number of terms with similar meanings, including automatic classification, numerical taxonomy, botryology, typological analysis, and community detection. The subtle differences are often in the use of the results: while in data mining, the resulting groups are the matter of interest, in automatic classification the resulting discriminative power is of interest.

Cluster analysis was originated in anthropology by Driver and Kroeber in 1932 and introduced to psychology by Joseph Zubin in 1938 and Robert Tryon in 1939 and famously used by Cattell beginning in 1943 for trait theory classification in personality psychology.

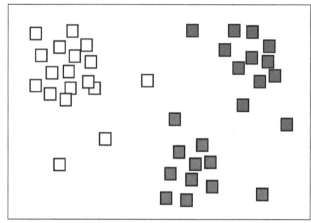

The result of a cluster analysis shown as the
coloring of the squares into three clusters.

The notion of a "cluster" cannot be precisely defined, which is one of the reasons why there are so many clustering algorithms. There is a common denominator: a group of data objects. However, different researchers employ different cluster models, and for each of these cluster models again different algorithms can be given. The notion of a cluster, as found by different algorithms, varies significantly in its properties. Understanding these "cluster models" is key to understanding the differences between the various algorithms. Typical cluster models include:

- Connectivity models: For example, hierarchical clustering builds models based on distance connectivity.

- Centroid models: For example, the k-means algorithm represents each cluster by a single mean vector.

- Distribution models: Clusters are modeled using statistical distributions, such as multivariate normal distributions used by the expectation-maximization algorithm.

- Density models: For example, DBSCAN and OPTICS defines clusters as connected dense regions in the data space.

- Subspace models: In biclustering (also known as co-clustering or two-mode-clustering), clusters are modeled with both cluster members and relevant attributes.

- Group models: Some algorithms do not provide a refined model for their results and just provide the grouping information.

- Graph-based models: A clique, that is, a subset of nodes in a graph such that every two nodes in the subset are connected by an edge can be considered as a prototypical form of cluster. Relaxations of the complete connectivity requirement (a fraction of the edges can be missing) are known as quasi-cliques, as in the HCS clustering algorithm.

- Signed graph models: Every path in a signed graph has a sign from the product of the signs on the edges. Under the assumptions of balance theory, edges may change sign and result in a bifurcated graph. The weaker "clusterability axiom" (no cycle has exactly one negative edge) yields results with more than two clusters, or subgraphs with only positive edges.

- Neural models: The most well known unsupervised neural network is the self-organizing map and these models can usually be characterized as similar to one or more of the above models, and including subspace models when neural networks implement a form of Principal Component Analysis or Independent Component Analysis.

A "clustering" is essentially a set of such clusters, usually containing all objects in the data set. Additionally, it may specify the relationship of the clusters to each other, for example, a hierarchy of clusters embedded in each other. Clusterings can be roughly distinguished as:

- Hard clustering: Each object belongs to a cluster or not.

- Soft clustering: Each object belongs to each cluster to a certain degree (for example, a likelihood of belonging to the cluster).

There are also finer distinctions possible, for example:

- Strict partitioning clustering: Each object belongs to exactly one cluster.

- Strict partitioning clustering with outliers: Objects can also belong to no cluster, and are considered outliers.

- Overlapping clustering (also: alternative clustering, multi-view clustering): Objects may belong to more than one cluster; usually involving hard clusters.

- Hierarchical clustering: Objects that belong to a child cluster also belong to the parent cluster.

- Subspace clustering: While an overlapping clustering, within a uniquely defined subspace, clusters are not expected to overlap.

Algorithms

As listed above, clustering algorithms can be categorized based on their cluster model. The following overview will only list the most prominent examples of clustering algorithms, as there are possibly over 100 published clustering algorithms. Not all provide models for their clusters and can thus not easily be categorized.

There is no objectively "correct" clustering algorithm, but as it was noted, "clustering is in the eye of the beholder." The most appropriate clustering algorithm for a particular problem often needs to be chosen experimentally, unless there is a mathematical reason to prefer one cluster model over another. An algorithm that is designed for one kind of model will generally fail on a data set that contains a radically different kind of model. For example, k-means cannot find non-convex clusters.

Connectivity-based Clustering

Connectivity-based clustering, also known as *hierarchical clustering*, is based on the core idea of objects being more related to nearby objects than to objects farther away. These algorithms connect "objects" to form "clusters" based on their distance. A cluster can be described largely by the maximum distance needed to connect parts of the cluster. At different distances, different clusters will form, which can be represented using a dendrogram, which explains where the common name "hierarchical clustering" comes from: these algorithms do not provide a single partitioning of the data set, but instead provide an extensive hierarchy of clusters that merge with each other at certain distances. In a dendrogram, the y-axis marks the distance at which the clusters merge, while the objects are placed along the x-axis such that the clusters don't mix.

Connectivity-based clustering is a whole family of methods that differ by the way distances are computed. Apart from the usual choice of distance functions, the user also needs to decide on the linkage criterion (since a cluster consists of multiple objects, there are multiple candidates to compute the distance) to use. Popular choices are known as single-linkage clustering (the minimum of object distances), complete linkage clustering (the maximum of object distances), and UPGMA or WPGMA ("Unweighted or Weighted Pair Group Method with Arithmetic Mean", also known as average linkage clustering). Furthermore, hierarchical clustering can be agglomerative (starting with single elements and aggregating them into clusters) or divisive (starting with the complete data set and dividing it into partitions).

These methods will not produce a unique partitioning of the data set, but a hierarchy from which the user still needs to choose appropriate clusters. They are not very robust towards outliers, which will either show up as additional clusters or even cause other clusters to merge (known as "chaining phenomenon", in particular with single-linkage clustering). In the general case, the complexity is $\mathcal{O}(n^3)$ for agglomerative clustering and $\mathcal{O}(2^{n-1})$ for divisive clustering, which makes them too slow for large data sets. For some special cases, optimal efficient methods (of complexity $\mathcal{O}(n^2)$) are known: SLINK for single-linkage and CLINK for complete-linkage clustering. In the data mining community these methods are recognized as a theoretical foundation of cluster analysis, but often considered obsolete. They did however provide inspiration for many later methods such as density based clustering.

Linkage clustering examples:

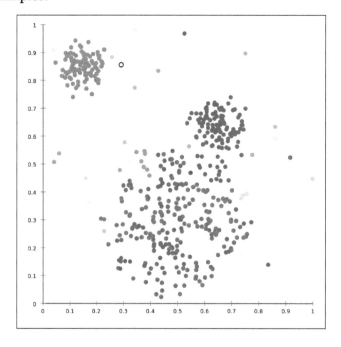

- Single-linkage on Gaussian data. At 35 clusters, the biggest cluster starts fragmenting into smaller parts, while before it was still connected to the second largest due to the single-link effect.

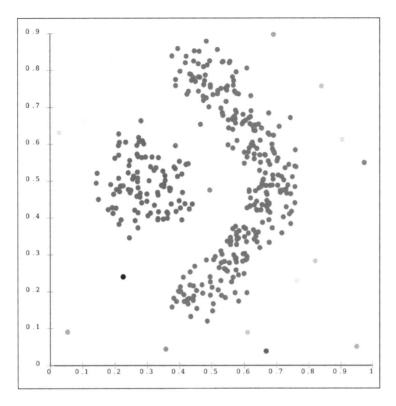

- Single-linkage on density-based clusters. 20 clusters extracted, most of which contain single elements, since linkage clustering does not have a notion of "noise".

Distribution-based Clustering

The clustering model most closely related to statistics is based on distribution models. Clusters can then easily be defined as objects belonging most likely to the same distribution. A convenient property of this approach is that this closely resembles the way artificial data sets are generated: by sampling random objects from a distribution.

While the theoretical foundation of these methods is excellent, they suffer from one key problem known as overfitting, unless constraints are put on the model complexity. A more complex model will usually be able to explain the data better, which makes choosing the appropriate model complexity inherently difficult.

One prominent method is known as Gaussian mixture models (using the expectation-maximization algorithm). Here, the data set is usually modeled with a fixed (to avoid overfitting) number of Gaussian distributions that are initialized randomly and whose parameters are iteratively optimized to better fit the data set. This will converge to a local optimum, so multiple runs may produce different results. In order to obtain a hard clustering, objects are often then assigned to the Gaussian distribution they most likely belong to; for soft clusterings, this is not necessary.

Distribution-based clustering produces complex models for clusters that can capture correlation and dependence between attributes. However, these algorithms put an extra burden on the user: for many real data sets, there may be no concisely defined mathematical model (e.g. assuming Gaussian distributions is a rather strong assumption on the data).

Gaussian mixture model clustering examples:

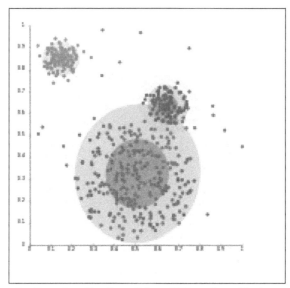

On Gaussian-distributed data, EM works well, since
it uses Gaussians for modelling clusters.

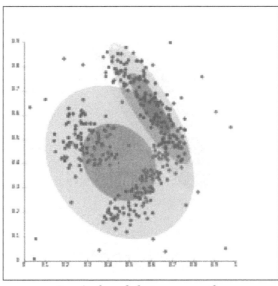

Density-based clusters cannot be
modeled using Gaussian distributions.

Density-based Clustering

In density-based clustering, clusters are defined as areas of higher density than the remainder of the data set. Objects in these sparse areas - that are required to separate clusters - are usually considered to be noise and border points.

The most popular density based clustering method is DBSCAN. In contrast to many newer methods, it features a well-defined cluster model called "density-reachability". Similar to linkage based clustering, it is based on connecting points within certain distance thresholds. However, it only connects points that satisfy a density criterion, in the original variant defined as a minimum number of other objects within this radius. A cluster consists of all density-connected objects (which can form a cluster of an arbitrary shape, in contrast to many other methods) plus all objects that are within these objects' range. Another interesting property of DBSCAN is that its complexity is fairly low – it requires a linear number of range queries on the database – and that it will discover essentially the same results (it is deterministic for core and noise points, but not for border points) in each run, therefore there is no need to run it multiple times. OPTICS is a generalization of DBSCAN that removes the need to choose an appropriate value for the range parameter ε, and produces a hierarchical result related to that of linkage clustering. DeLi-Clu, Density-Link-Clustering combines ideas from single-linkage clustering and OPTICS, eliminating the ε parameter entirely and offering performance improvements over OPTICS by using an R-tree index.

The key drawback of DBSCAN and OPTICS is that they expect some kind of density drop to detect cluster borders. On data sets with, for example, overlapping Gaussian distributions – a common use case in artificial data – the cluster borders produced by these algorithms will often look arbitrary, because the cluster density decreases continuously. On a data set consisting of mixtures of Gaussians, these algorithms are nearly always outperformed by methods such as EM clustering that are able to precisely model this kind of data.

Mean-shift is a clustering approach where each object is moved to the densest area in its vicinity, based on kernel density estimation. Eventually, objects converge to local maxima of density. Similar to k-means clustering, these "density attractors" can serve as representatives for the data set, but mean-shift can detect arbitrary-shaped clusters similar to DBSCAN. Due to the expensive iterative procedure and density estimation, mean-shift is usually slower than DBSCAN or k-Means. Besides that, the applicability of the mean-shift algorithm to multidimensional data is hindered by the unsmooth behaviour of the kernel density estimate, which results in over-fragmentation of cluster tails.

Density-based clustering examples:

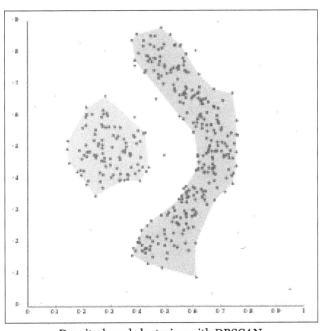

Density-based clustering with DBSCAN.

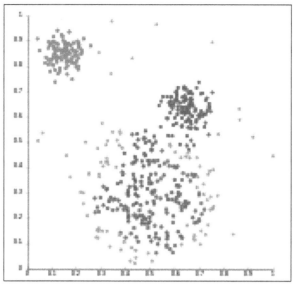

DBSCAN assumes clusters of similar density, and
may have problems separating nearby clusters.

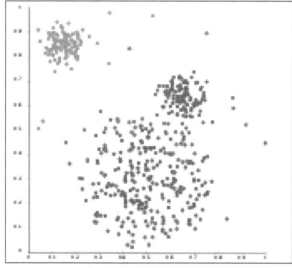

OPTICS is a DBSCAN variant, improving
handling of different densities clusters.

Recent Developments

In recent years, considerable effort has been put into improving the performance of existing algorithms. Among them are *CLARANS* (Ng and Han, 1994), and *BIRCH*. With the recent need to process larger and larger data sets (also known as big data), the willingness to trade semantic meaning
of the generated clusters for performance has been increasing. This led to the development of
pre-clustering methods such as canopy clustering, which can process huge data sets efficiently,
but the resulting "clusters" are merely a rough pre-partitioning of the data set to then analyze the
partitions with existing slower methods such as k-means clustering.

For high-dimensional data, many of the existing methods fail due to the curse of dimensionality,
which renders particular distance functions problematic in high-dimensional spaces. This led to

new clustering algorithms for high-dimensional data that focus on subspace clustering (where only some attributes are used, and cluster models include the relevant attributes for the cluster) and correlation clustering that also looks for arbitrary rotated ("correlated") subspace clusters that can be modeled by giving a correlation of their attributes. Examples for such clustering algorithms are CLIQUE and SUBCLU.

Ideas from density-based clustering methods (in particular the DBSCAN/OPTICS family of algorithms) have been adopted to subspace clustering (HiSC, hierarchical subspace clustering and DiSH) and correlation clustering (HiCO, hierarchical correlation clustering, 4C using "correlation connectivity" and ERiC exploring hierarchical density-based correlation clusters).

Several different clustering systems based on mutual information have been proposed. One is Marina Meilă's *variation of information* metric; another provides hierarchical clustering. Using genetic algorithms, a wide range of different fit-functions can be optimized, including mutual information. Also belief propagation, a recent development in computer science and statistical physics, has led to the creation of new types of clustering algorithms.

Evaluation and Assessment

Evaluation (or "validation") of clustering results is as difficult as the clustering itself. Popular approaches involve "internal" evaluation, where the clustering is summarized to a single quality score, "external" evaluation, where the clustering is compared to an existing "ground truth" classification, "manual" evaluation by a human expert, and "indirect" evaluation by evaluating the utility of the clustering in its intended application.

Internal evaluation measures suffer from the problem that they represent functions that themselves can be seen as a clustering objective. For example, one could cluster the data set by the Silhouette coefficient; except that there is no known efficient algorithm for this. By using such an internal measure for evaluation, one rather compares the similarity of the optimization problems, and not necessarily how useful the clustering is.

External evaluation has similar problems: if we have such "ground truth" labels, then we would not need to cluster; and in practical applications we usually do not have such labels. On the other hand, the labels only reflect one possible partitioning of the data set, which does not imply that there does not exist a different, and maybe even better, clustering.

Neither of these approaches can therefore ultimately judge the actual quality of a clustering, but this needs human evaluation, which is highly subjective. Nevertheless, such statistics can be quite informative in identifying bad clusterings, but one should not dismiss subjective human evaluation.

Internal Evaluation

When a clustering result is evaluated based on the data that was clustered itself, this is called internal evaluation. These methods usually assign the best score to the algorithm that produces clusters with high similarity within a cluster and low similarity between clusters. One drawback of using internal criteria in cluster evaluation is that high scores on an internal measure do not necessarily result in effective information retrieval applications. Additionally, this evaluation is biased towards algorithms that use the same cluster model. For example, k-means clustering naturally optimizes object distances, and a distance-based internal criterion will likely overrate the resulting clustering.

Therefore, the internal evaluation measures are best suited to get some insight into situations where one algorithm performs better than another, but this shall not imply that one algorithm produces more valid results than another. Validity as measured by such an index depends on the claim that this kind of structure exists in the data set. An algorithm designed for some kind of models has no chance if the data set contains a radically different set of models, or if the evaluation measures a radically different criterion. For example, k-means clustering can only find convex clusters, and many evaluation indexes assume convex clusters. On a data set with non-convex clusters neither the use of k-means, nor of an evaluation criterion that assumes convexity, is sound.

More than a dozen of internal evaluation measures exist, usually based on the intuition that items in the same cluster should be more similar than items in different clusters. For example, the following methods can be used to assess the quality of clustering algorithms based on internal criterion:

- Davies–Bouldin index:

  The Davies–Bouldin index can be calculated by the following formula:

  $$DB = \frac{1}{n}\sum_{i=1}^{n}\max_{j\neq i}\left(\frac{\sigma_i + \sigma_j}{d(c_i, c_j)}\right)$$

  where n is the number of clusters, c_x is the centroid of cluster x, σ_x is the average distance of all elements in cluster x to centroid c_x, and $d(c_i, c_j)$ is the distance between centroids c_i and c_j. Since algorithms that produce clusters with low intra-cluster distances (high intra-cluster similarity) and high inter-cluster distances (low inter-cluster similarity) will have a low Davies–Bouldin index, the clustering algorithm that produces a collection of clusters with the smallest Davies–Bouldin index is considered the best algorithm based on this criterion.

- Dunn index:

  The Dunn index aims to identify dense and well-separated clusters. It is defined as the ratio between the minimal inter-cluster distance to maximal intra-cluster distance. For each cluster partition, the Dunn index can be calculated by the following formula:

  $$D = \frac{\min_{1 \le i < j \le n} d(i, j)}{\max_{1 \le k \le n} d'(k)},$$

  where $d(i,j)$ represents the distance between clusters i and j, and $d'(k)$ measures the intra-cluster distance of cluster k. The inter-cluster distance $d(i,j)$ between two clusters may be any number of distance measures, such as the distance between the centroids of the clusters. Similarly, the intra-cluster distance $d'(k)$ may be measured in a variety ways, such as the maximal distance between any pair of elements in cluster k. Since internal criterion seek clusters with high intra-cluster similarity and low inter-cluster similarity, algorithms that produce clusters with high Dunn index are more desirable.

- Silhouette coefficient:

  The silhouette coefficient contrasts the average distance to elements in the same cluster with the average distance to elements in other clusters. Objects with a high silhouette value are considered well clustered, objects with a low value may be outliers. This index works well with k-means clustering, and is also used to determine the optimal number of clusters.

External Evaluation

In external evaluation, clustering results are evaluated based on data that was not used for clustering, such as known class labels and external benchmarks. Such benchmarks consist of a set of pre-classified items, and these sets are often created by (expert) humans. Thus, the benchmark sets can be thought of as a gold standard for evaluation. These types of evaluation methods measure how close the clustering is to the predetermined benchmark classes. However, it has recently been discussed whether this is adequate for real data, or only on synthetic data sets with a factual ground truth, since classes can contain internal structure, the attributes present may not allow separation of clusters or the classes may contain anomalies. Additionally, from a knowledge discovery point of view, the reproduction of known knowledge may not necessarily be the intended result. In the special scenario of constrained clustering, where meta information (such as class labels) is used already in the clustering process, the hold-out of information for evaluation purposes is non-trivial.

A number of measures are adapted from variants used to evaluate classification tasks. In place of counting the number of times a class was correctly assigned to a single data point (known as true positives), such *pair counting* metrics assess whether each pair of data points that is truly in the same cluster is predicted to be in the same cluster.

As with internal evaluation, several external evaluation measures exist, for example:

- Purity: Purity is a measure of the extent to which clusters contain a single class. Its calculation can be thought of as follows: For each cluster, count the number of data points from the most common class in said cluster. Now take the sum over all clusters and divide by the total number of data points. Formally, given some set of clusters M and some set of classes D, both partitioning N data points, purity can be defined as:

$$\frac{1}{N} \sum_{m \in M} \max_{d \in D} |m \cap d|$$

  This measure doesn't penalize having many clusters. So for example, a purity score of 1 is possible by putting each data point in its own cluster. Also purity doesn't work well for imbalanced data: if a size 1000 dataset consists of two classes, one class contains 999 points and the other has only 1 point. No matter how bad a clustering algorithm performs, it will always give a very high purity value.

- Rand index:

The Rand index computes how similar the clusters (returned by the clustering algorithm) are to the benchmark classifications. One can also view the Rand index as a measure of the percentage of correct decisions made by the algorithm. It can be computed using the following formula:

$$RI = \frac{TP + TN}{TP + FP + FN + TN}$$

where TP is the number of true positives, TN is the number of true negatives, FP is the number of false positives, and FN is the number of false negatives. One issue with the Rand index is that false positives and false negatives are equally weighted. This may be an undesirable characteristic for some clustering applications. The F-measure addresses this concern, as does the chance-corrected adjusted Rand index.

- F-measure:

The F-measure can be used to balance the contribution of false negatives by weighting recall through a parameter $\beta \geq 0$. Let precision and recall (both external evaluation measures in themselves) be defined as follows:

$$P = \frac{TP}{TP + FP}$$

$$R = \frac{TP}{TP + FN}$$

where P is the precision rate and R is the recall rate. We can calculate the F-measure by using the following formula:

$$F_\beta = \frac{(\beta^2 + 1) \cdot P \cdot R}{\beta^2 \cdot P + R}$$

When $\beta = 0, F_0 = P$. In other words, recall has no impact on the F-measure when $\beta = 0$, and increasing β allocates an increasing amount of weight to recall in the final F-measure.

Also TN is not taken into account and can vary from 0 upward without bound.

- Jaccard index:

The Jaccard index is used to quantify the similarity between two datasets. The Jaccard index takes on a value between 0 and 1. An index of 1 means that the two dataset are identical, and an index of 0 indicates that the datasets have no common elements. The Jaccard index is defined by the following formula:

$$J(A, B) = \frac{|A \cap B|}{|A \cup B|} = \frac{TP}{TP + FP + FN}$$

This is simply the number of unique elements common to both sets divided by the total number of unique elements in both sets.

Also TN is not taken into account and can vary from 0 upward without bound.

- Dice index:

The Dice symmetric measure doubles the weight on TP while still ignoring TN :

$$DSC = \frac{2TP}{2TP + FP + FN}$$

- Fowlkes–Mallows index:

The Fowlkes–Mallows index computes the similarity between the clusters returned by the clustering algorithm and the benchmark classifications. The higher the value of the Fowlkes–Mallows index the more similar the clusters and the benchmark classifications are. It can be computed using the following formula:

$$FM = \sqrt{\frac{TP}{TP + FP} \cdot \frac{TP}{TP + FN}}$$

where TP is the number of true positives, FP is the number of false positives, and FN is the number of false negatives. The FM index is the geometric mean of the precision and recall P and R, and is thus also known as the G-measure, while the F-measure is their harmonic mean. Moreover, precision and recall are also known as Wallace's indices B^I and B^{II}. Chance normalized versions of recall, precision and G-measure correspond to Informedness, Markedness and Matthews Correlation and relate strongly to Kappa.

- The mutual information is an information theoretic measure of how much information is shared between a clustering and a ground-truth classification that can detect a non-linear similarity between two clusterings. Normalized mutual information is a family of corrected-for-chance variants of this that has a reduced bias for varying cluster numbers.

- Confusion matrix:

A confusion matrix can be used to quickly visualize the results of a classification (or clustering) algorithm. It shows how different a cluster is from the gold standard cluster.

Cluster Tendency

To measure cluster tendency is to measure to what degree clusters exist in the data to be clustered, and may be performed as an initial test, before attempting clustering. One way to do this is to compare the data against random data. On average, random data should not have clusters.

- Hopkins Statistic.

There are multiple formulations of the Hopkins statistic. A typical one is as follows. Let X be the set of n data points in d dimensional space. Consider a random sample (without replacement) of $m \ll n$ data points with members x_i. Also generate a set Y of m uniformly randomly distributed data points. Now define two distance measures, u_i to be the distance of $y_i \in Y$ from its nearest neighbor in X and w_i to be the distance of $x_i \in X$ from its nearest neighbor in X. We then define the Hopkins statistic as:

$$H = \frac{\sum_{i=1}^{m} u_i^d}{\sum_{i=1}^{m} u_i^d + \sum_{i=1}^{m} w_i^d},$$

With this definition, uniform random data should tend to have values near to 0.5, and clustered data should tend to have values nearer to 1.

However, data containing just a single Gaussian will also score close to 1, as this statistic measures deviation from a *uniform* distribution, not multimodality, making this statistic largely useless in application (as real data never is remotely uniform).

k-means Clustering

k-means clustering is a method of vector quantization, originally from signal processing, that is popular for cluster analysis in data mining. *k*-means clustering aims to partition n observations into k clusters in which each observation belongs to the cluster with the nearest mean, serving as a prototype of the cluster. This results in a partitioning of the data space into Voronoi cells. *k*-Means minimizes within-cluster variances (squared Euclidean distances), but not regular Euclidean distances, which would be the more difficult Weber problem: the mean optimizes squared errors, whereas only the geometric median minimizes Euclidean distances. Better Euclidean solutions can for example be found using k-medians and k-medoids.

The problem is computationally difficult (NP-hard); however, efficient heuristic algorithms converge quickly to a local optimum. These are usually similar to the expectation-maximization algorithm for mixtures of Gaussian distributions via an iterative refinement approach employed by both k-means and Gaussian mixture modeling. They both use cluster centers to model the data; however, k-means clustering tends to find clusters of comparable spatial extent, while the expectation-maximization mechanism allows clusters to have different shapes.

The algorithm has a loose relationship to the *k*-nearest neighbor classifier, a popular machine learning technique for classification that is often confused with *k*-means due to the name. Applying the 1-nearest neighbor classifier to the cluster centers obtained by *k*-means classifies new data into the existing clusters. This is known as nearest centroid classifier or Rocchio algorithm.

Given a set of observations $(x_1, x_2, ..., x_n)$, where each observation is a d-dimensional real vector, *k*-means clustering aims to partition the n observations into k ($\leq n$) sets S = $\{S_1, S_2, ..., S_k\}$ so as to minimize the within-cluster sum of squares (WCSS) (i.e. variance). Formally, the objective is to find:

$$\arg \min_{S} \sum_{i=1}^{k} \sum_{x \in S_i} \|x - \mu_i\|^2 = \arg \min_{S} \sum_{i=1}^{k} |S_i| \operatorname{Var} S_i$$

where μ_i is the mean of points in S_i. This is equivalent to minimizing the pairwise squared deviations of points in the same cluster:

$$\arg\min_{S} \sum_{i=1}^{k} \frac{1}{2|S_i|} \sum_{x,y \in S_i} \|x - y\|^2$$

The equivalence can be deduced from identity:

$$\sum_{x \in S_i} \|x - \mu_i\|^2 = \sum_{x \neq y \in S_i} (x - \mu_i)(\mu_i - y).$$

Because the total variance is constant, this is equivalent to maximizing the sum of squared deviations between points in *different* clusters (between-cluster sum of squares, BCSS), which follows from the law of total variance.

The term "*k*-means" was first used by James MacQueen in 1967, though the idea goes back to Hugo Steinhaus in 1956. The standard algorithm was first proposed by Stuart Lloyd of Bell Labs in 1957 as a technique for pulse-code modulation, though it wasn't published as a journal article until 1982. In 1965, Edward W. Forgy published essentially the same method, which is why it is sometimes referred to as Lloyd-Forgy.

Algorithms

Standard Algorithm (Naive k-means)

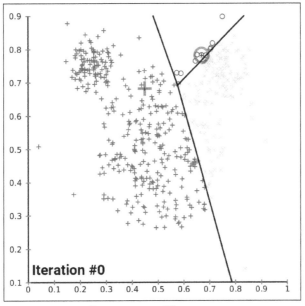

Convergence of *k*-means.

The most common algorithm uses an iterative refinement technique. Due to its ubiquity, it is often called "the *k*-means algorithm"; it is also referred to as Lloyd's algorithm, particularly in the computer science community. It is sometimes also referred to as "naive *k*-means", because there exist much faster alternatives.

Given an initial set of k means $m_1^{(1)},...,m_k^{(1)}$, the algorithm proceeds by alternating between two steps:

Assignment step: Assign each observation to the cluster whose mean has the least squared Euclidean distance, this is intuitively the "nearest" mean. (Mathematically, this means partitioning the observations according to the Voronoi diagram generated by the means).

$$S_i^{(t)} = \left\{ x_p : \left\| x_p - m_i^{(t)} \right\|^2 \leq \left\| x_p - m_j^{(t)} \right\|^2 \; \forall j, 1 \leq j \leq k \right\},$$

where each x_p is assigned to exactly one $S^{(t)}$, even if it could be assigned to two or more of them.

Update step: Calculate the new means (centroids) of the observations in the new clusters.

$$m_i^{(t+1)} = \frac{1}{\left| S_i^{(t)} \right|} \sum_{x_j \in S_i^{(t)}} x_j$$

The algorithm has converged when the assignments no longer change. The algorithm does not guarantee to find the optimum.

The algorithm is often presented as assigning objects to the nearest cluster by distance. Using a different distance function other than (squared) Euclidean distance may stop the algorithm from converging. Various modifications of k-means such as spherical k-means and k-medoids have been proposed to allow using other distance measures.

Initialization Methods

Commonly used initialization methods are Forgy and Random Partition. The Forgy method randomly chooses k observations from the dataset and uses these as the initial means. The Random Partition method first randomly assigns a cluster to each observation and then proceeds to the update step, thus computing the initial mean to be the centroid of the cluster's randomly assigned points. The Forgy method tends to spread the initial means out, while Random Partition places all of them close to the center of the data set. According to Hamerly et al., the Random Partition method is generally preferable for algorithms such as the k-harmonic means and fuzzy k-means. For expectation maximization and standard k-means algorithms, the Forgy method of initialization is preferable. A comprehensive study by Celebi et al., however, found that popular initialization methods such as Forgy, Random Partition, and Maximin often perform poorly, whereas Bradley and Fayyad's approach performs "consistently" in "the best group" and k-means++ performs "generally well".

Demonstration of the Standard Algorithm

The algorithm does not guarantee convergence to the global optimum. The result may depend on the initial clusters. As the algorithm is usually fast, it is common to run it multiple times with different starting conditions. However, worst-case performance can be slow: in particular certain point sets, even in two dimensions, converge in exponential time, that is $2^{\Omega(n)}$. These point sets do not seem to arise in practice: this is corroborated by the fact that the smoothed running time of k-means is polynomial.

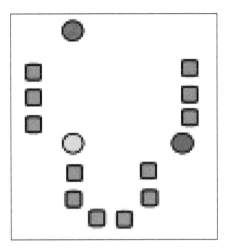

1. k initial "means" (in this case $k=3$) are randomly generated within the data domain (shown in color).

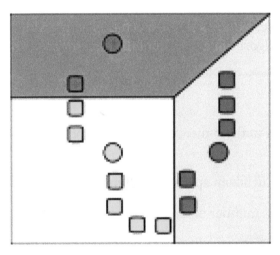

2. k clusters are created by associating every observation with the nearest mean. The partitions here represent the Voronoi diagram generated by the means.

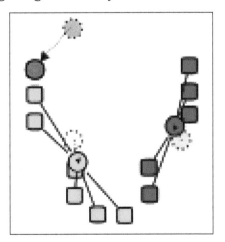

3. The centroid of each of the k clusters becomes the new mean.

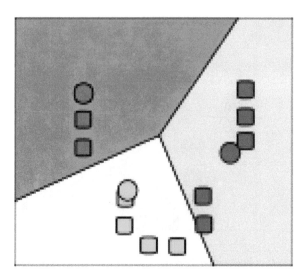

4. Steps 2 and 3 are repeated until convergence has been reached.

The "assignment" step is referred to as the "expectation step", while the "update step" is a maximization step, making this algorithm a variant of the *generalized* expectation-maximization algorithm.

Complexity

Finding the optimal solution to the k-means clustering problem for observations in d dimensions is:

- NP-hard in general Euclidean space (of d dimensions) even for two clusters.

- NP-hard for a general number of clusters k even in the plane.

- If k and d (the dimension) are fixed, the problem can be exactly solved in time $O(n^{dk+1})$, where n is the number of entities to be clustered.

Thus, a variety of heuristic algorithms such as Lloyd's algorithm given above are generally used.

The running time of Lloyd's algorithm (and most variants) is $O(nkdi)$, where:

- n is the number of d-dimensional vectors (to be clustered).

- k the number of clusters.

- i the number of iterations needed until convergence.

On data that does have a clustering structure, the number of iterations until convergence is often small, and results only improve slightly after the first dozen iterations. Lloyd's algorithm is therefore often considered to be of "linear" complexity in practice, although it is in the worst case superpolynomial when performed until convergence.

- In the worst-case, Lloyd's algorithm needs $i = 2^{\Omega(\sqrt{n})}$ iterations, so that the worst-case complexity of Lloyd's algorithm is superpolynomial.

Lloyd's k-means algorithm has polynomial smoothed running time. It is shown that for arbitrary set of n points in $[0,1]^d$, if each point is independently perturbed by a normal distribution with mean o and variance σ^2, then the expected running time of k-means algorithm is bounded by $O(n^{34}k^{34}d^8 \log^4(n)/\sigma^6)$, which is a polynomial in n, k, d and $1/\sigma$.

Better bounds are proven for simple cases. For example, in it is shown that the running time of k-means algorithm is bounded by $O(dn^4 M^2)$ for n points in an integer lattice $\{1,...,M\}^d$.

Lloyd's algorithm is the standard approach for this problem. However, it spends a lot of processing time computing the distances between each of the k cluster centers and the n data points. Since points usually stay in the same clusters after a few iterations, much of this work is unnecessary, making the naive implementation very inefficient. Some implementations use caching and the triangle inequality in order to create bounds and accelerate Lloyd's algorithm.

Variations

- Jenks natural breaks optimization: *k*-means applied to univariate data.

- *k*-medians clustering uses the median in each dimension instead of the mean, and this way minimizes L_1 norm (Taxicab geometry).

- *k*-medoids (also: Partitioning Around Medoids, PAM) uses the medoid instead of the mean, and this way minimizes the sum of distances for *arbitrary* distance functions.

- Fuzzy C-Means Clustering is a soft version of *k*-means, where each data point has a fuzzy degree of belonging to each cluster.

- Gaussian mixture models trained with expectation-maximization algorithm (EM algorithm) maintains probabilistic assignments to clusters, instead of deterministic assignments, and multivariate Gaussian distributions instead of means.

- *k*-means++ chooses initial centers in a way that gives a provable upper bound on the WCSS objective.

- The filtering algorithm uses kd-trees to speed up each *k*-means step.

- Some methods attempt to speed up each *k*-means step using the triangle inequality.

- Escape local optima by swapping points between clusters.

- The Spherical *k*-means clustering algorithm is suitable for textual data.

- Hierarchical variants such as Bisecting *k*-means, X-means clustering and G-means clustering repeatedly split clusters to build a hierarchy, and can also try to automatically determine the optimal number of clusters in a dataset.

- Internal cluster evaluation measures such as cluster silhouette can be helpful at determining the number of clusters.

- Minkowski weighted *k*-means automatically calculates cluster specific feature weights, supporting the intuitive idea that a feature may have different degrees of relevance at different features. These weights can also be used to re-scale a given data set, increasing the likelihood of a cluster validity index to be optimized at the expected number of clusters.

- Mini-batch k-means: k-means variation using "mini batch" samples for data sets that do not fit into memory.

Hartigan–Wong Method

Hartigan–Wong's method provides a more sophisticated though more computationally expensive way to perform k-means. It is still a heuristic method.

$\varphi(S_j)$ is the individual cost of S_j defined by $\sum_{x \in S_j}(x - \mu_j)^2$, with μ_j the center of the cluster.

Assignment step: Hartigan and Wong's method starts by partitioning the points into random clusters $\{S_j\}_{j \in \{1, \cdots k\}}$.

Update step: Next it determines the $n, m \in \{1, \ldots, k\}$ and $x \in S_n$ for which the following function reaches a minimum.

$$\Delta(m, n, x) = \varphi(S_n) + \varphi(S_m) - \varphi(S_n \setminus \{x\}) - \varphi(S_m \cup \{x\}).$$

For the x, n, m that reach this minimum, x moves from the cluster S_n to the cluster S_m.

Termination: The algorithm terminates once $\Delta(m, n, x)$ is larger than zero for all x, n, m.

The algorithm can be sped up by immediately moving x from the cluster S_n to the cluster S_m as soon as an x, n, m have been found for which $\Delta(m, n, x) < 0$. This speed up can make the cost of the final result higher.

The function Δ can be relatively efficiently evaluated by making use of the equality.

$$\Delta(x, n, m) = \frac{\check{Z}S_n\check{Z}}{\check{Z}S_n\check{Z}-1} \cdot \| \mu_n - x \|^2 - \frac{\check{Z}S_m\check{Z}}{\check{Z}S_m\check{Z}+1} \cdot \| \mu_m - x \|^2 \ .$$

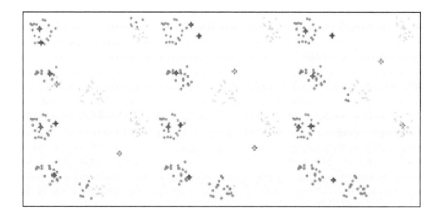

A typical example of the k-means convergence to a local minimum. In this example, the result of k-means clustering (the right figure) contradicts the obvious cluster structure of the data set. The small circles are the data points, the four ray stars are the centroids (means). The initial configuration is on the left figure. The algorithm converges after five iterations presented on the figures, from the left to the right. The illustration was prepared with the Mirkes Java applet.

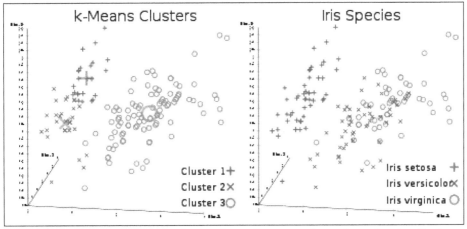

k-means clustering result for the Iris flower data set and actual species visualized using ELKI. Cluster means are marked using larger, semi-transparent symbols.

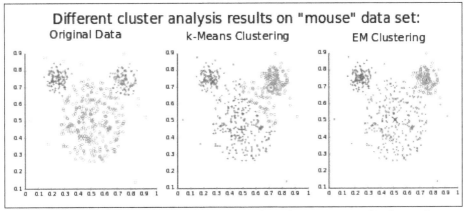

k-means clustering vs. EM clustering on an artificial dataset ("mouse"). The tendency of *k*-means to produce equal-sized clusters leads to bad results here, while EM benefits from the Gaussian distributions with different radius present in the data set.

Three key features of *k*-means that make it efficient are often regarded as its biggest drawbacks:

- Euclidean distance is used as a metric and variance is used as a measure of cluster scatter.

- The number of clusters *k* is an input parameter: an inappropriate choice of *k* may yield poor results. That is why, when performing *k*-means, it is important to run diagnostic checks for determining the number of clusters in the data set.

- Convergence to a local minimum may produce counterintuitive ("wrong") results.

A key limitation of *k*-means is its cluster model. The concept is based on spherical clusters that are separable so that the mean converges towards the cluster center. The clusters are expected to be of similar size, so that the assignment to the nearest cluster center is the correct assignment. When for example applying *k*-means with a value of $k = 3$ onto the well-known Iris flower data set, the result often fails to separate the three Iris species contained in the data set. With $k = 2$, the two visible clusters (one containing two species) will be discovered, whereas with $k = 3$ one of the two clusters will be split into two even parts. In fact, $k = 2$ is more appropriate for this data set, despite the data set's containing 3 *classes*. As with any other clustering algorithm, the k-means result makes assumptions that the data satisfy certain criteria. It works well on some data sets, and fails on others.

The result of k-means can be seen as the Voronoi cells of the cluster means. Since data is split halfway between cluster means, this can lead to suboptimal splits as can be seen in the "mouse" example. The Gaussian models used by the expectation-maximization algorithm (arguably a generalization of k-means) are more flexible by having both variances and covariances. The EM result is thus able to accommodate clusters of variable size much better than k-means as well as correlated clusters (not in this example). K-means is closely related to nonparametric Bayesian modeling.

Applications

k-means clustering is rather easy to apply to even large data sets, particularly when using heuristics such as Lloyd's algorithm. It has been successfully used in market segmentation, computer vision, and astronomy among many other domains. It often is used as a preprocessing step for other algorithms, for example to find a starting configuration.

Vector Quantization

Two-channel (for illustration purposes -- red and green only) color image.

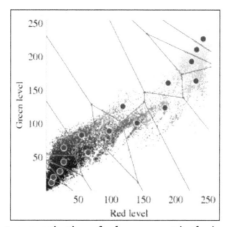

Vector quantization of colors present in the image
above into Voronoi cells using k-means.

k-means originates from signal processing, and still finds use in this domain. For example, in computer graphics, color quantization is the task of reducing the color palette of an image to a fixed number of colors k. The k-means algorithm can easily be used for this task and produces competitive results. A use case for this approach is image segmentation. Other uses of vector quantization include non-random sampling, as k-means can easily be used to choose k different but prototypical objects from a large data set for further analysis.

Cluster Analysis

In cluster analysis, the k-means algorithm can be used to partition the input data set into k partitions (clusters).

However, the pure k-means algorithm is not very flexible, and as such is of limited use (except for when vector quantization as above is actually the desired use case). In particular, the parameter k is known to be hard to choose (as discussed above) when not given by external constraints. Another limitation is that it cannot be used with arbitrary distance functions or on non-numerical data. For these use cases, many other algorithms are superior.

Feature Learning

k-means clustering has been used as a feature learning (or dictionary learning) step, in either (semi-)supervised learning or unsupervised learning. The basic approach is first to train a k-means clustering representation, using the input training data (which need not be labelled). Then, to project any input datum into the new feature space, an "encoding" function, such as the thresholded matrix-product of the datum with the centroid locations, computes the distance from the datum to each centroid, or simply an indicator function for the nearest centroid, or some smooth transformation of the distance. Alternatively, transforming the sample-cluster distance through a Gaussian RBF, obtains the hidden layer of a radial basis function network.

This use of k-means has been successfully combined with simple, linear classifiers for semi-supervised learning in NLP (specifically for named entity recognition) and in computer vision. On an object recognition task, it was found to exhibit comparable performance with more sophisticated feature learning approaches such as autoencoders and restricted Boltzmann machines. However, it generally requires more data, for equivalent performance, because each data point only contributes to one "feature".

Relation to other Algorithms

Gaussian Mixture Model

The slow "standard algorithm" for k-means clustering, and its associated expectation-maximization algorithm, is a special case of a Gaussian mixture model, specifically, the limiting case when fixing all covariances to be diagonal, equal and have infinitesimal small variance. Instead of small variances, a hard cluster assignment can also be used to show another equivalence of k-means clustering to a special case of "hard" Gaussian mixture modelling. This does not mean that it is efficient to use Gaussian mixture modelling to compute k-means, but just that there is a theoretical relationship, and that Gaussian mixture modelling can be interpreted as a generalization of k-means; on the contrary, it has been suggested to use k-means clustering to find starting points for Gaussian mixture modelling on difficult data.

K-SVD

Another generalization of the k-means algorithm is the K-SVD algorithm, which estimates data points as a sparse linear combination of "codebook vectors". k-means corresponds to the special case of using a single codebook vector, with a weight of 1.

Principal Component Analysis

The relaxed solution of k-means clustering, specified by the cluster indicators, is given by principal component analysis (PCA). The PCA subspace spanned by the principal directions is identical to the cluster centroid subspace. The intuition is that k-means describe spherically shaped (ball-like) clusters. If the data has 2 clusters, the line connecting the two centroids is the best 1-dimensional projection direction, which is also the first PCA direction. Cutting the line at the center of mass separates the clusters (this is the continuous relaxation of the discrete cluster indicator). If the data have three clusters, the 2-dimensional plane spanned by three cluster centroids is the best 2-D projection. This plane is also defined by the first two PCA dimensions. Well-separated clusters are effectively modelled by ball-shaped clusters and thus discovered by k-means. Non-ball-shaped clusters are hard to separate when they are close. For example, two half-moon shaped clusters intertwined in space do not separate well when projected onto PCA subspace. k-means should not be expected to do well on this data. It is straightforward to produce counterexamples to the statement that the cluster centroid subspace is spanned by the principal directions.

Mean Shift Clustering

Basic mean shift clustering algorithms maintain a set of data points the same size as the input data set. Initially, this set is copied from the input set. Then this set is iteratively replaced by the mean of those points in the set that are within a given distance of that point. By contrast, k-means restricts this updated set to k points usually much less than the number of points in the input data set, and replaces each point in this set by the mean of all points in the *input set* that are closer to that point than any other (e.g. within the Voronoi partition of each updating point). A mean shift algorithm that is similar then to k-means, called *likelihood mean shift*, replaces the set of points undergoing replacement by the mean of all points in the input set that are within a given distance of the changing set. One of the advantages of mean shift over k-means is that the number of clusters is not pre-specified, because mean shift is likely to find only a few clusters if only a small number exist. However, mean shift can be much slower than k-means, and still requires selection of a bandwidth parameter. Mean shift has soft variants.

Independent Component Analysis

Under sparsity assumptions and when input data is pre-processed with the whitening transformation, k-means produces the solution to the linear independent component analysis (ICA) task. This aids in explaining the successful application of k-means to feature learning.

Bilateral Filtering

k-means implicitly assumes that the ordering of the input data set does not matter. The bilateral filter is similar to k-means and mean shift in that it maintains a set of data points that are iteratively replaced by means. However, the bilateral filter restricts the calculation of the (kernel weighted) mean to include only points that are close in the ordering of the input data. This makes it applicable to problems such as image denoising, where the spatial arrangement of pixels in an image is of critical importance.

HIDDEN MARKOV MODEL

Hidden Markov Model (HMM) is a statistical Markov model in which the system being modeled is assumed to be a Markov process with unobservable (i.e. *hidden*) states.

The hidden Markov model can be represented as the simplest dynamic Bayesian network. The mathematics behind the HMM were developed by L. E. Baum and coworkers. HMM is closely related to earlier work on the optimal nonlinear filtering problem by Ruslan L. Stratonovich, who was the first to describe the forward-backward procedure.

In simpler Markov models (like a Markov chain), the state is directly visible to the observer, and therefore the state transition probabilities are the only parameters, while in the hidden Markov model, the state is not directly visible, but the output (in the form of data or "token" in the following), dependent on the state, is visible. Each state has a probability distribution over the possible output tokens. Therefore, the sequence of tokens generated by an HMM gives some information about the sequence of states; this is also known as pattern theory, a topic of grammar induction.

The adjective *hidden* refers to the state sequence through which the model passes, not to the parameters of the model; the model is still referred to as a hidden Markov model even if these parameters are known exactly.

Hidden Markov models are especially known for their application in reinforcement learning and temporal pattern recognition such as speech, handwriting, gesture recognition, part-of-speech tagging, musical score following, partial discharges and bioinformatics.

A hidden Markov model can be considered a generalization of a mixture model where the hidden variables (or latent variables), which control the mixture component to be selected for each observation, are related through a Markov process rather than independent of each other. Recently, hidden Markov models have been generalized to pairwise Markov models and triplet Markov models which allow consideration of more complex data structures and the modeling of nonstationary data.

Let X_n and Y_n be discrete-time stochastic processes and $n \geq 1$. The pair (X_n, Y_n) is a *hidden markov model* if:

- X_n is a Markov process and is not directly observable ("hidden").

- $P\left(Y_n \in A \mid X_1 = x_1, \ldots, X_n = x_n\right) = P\left(Y_n \in A \mid X_n = x_n\right).$

  for every $n \geq 1, x_1, \ldots, x_n$, and an arbitrary measurable set A.

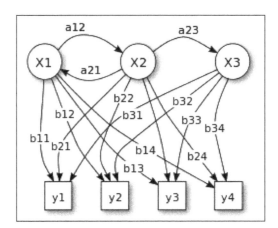

Probabilistic parameters of a hidden Markov model (example):

- X — States.

- y — Possible observations.

- a — State transition probabilities.

- b — Output probabilities.

In its discrete form, a hidden Markov process can be visualized as a generalization of the urn problem with replacement (where each item from the urn is returned to the original urn before the next step). Consider this example: in a room that is not visible to an observer there is a genie. The room contains urns X1, X2, X3, ... each of which contains a known mix of balls, each ball labeled y1, y2, y3, ... The genie chooses an urn in that room and randomly draws a ball from that urn. They then put the ball onto a conveyor belt, where the observer can observe the sequence of the balls but not the sequence of urns from which they were drawn. The genie has some procedure to choose urns; the choice of the urn for the n-th ball depends only upon a random number and the choice of the urn for the $(n - 1)$-th ball. The choice of urn does not directly depend on the urns chosen before this single previous urn; therefore, this is called a Markov process. It can be described by the upper part of figure.

The Markov process itself cannot be observed, only the sequence of labeled balls, thus this arrangement is called a "hidden Markov process". This is illustrated by the lower part of the diagram shown in figure, where one can see that balls y1, y2, y3, y4 can be drawn at each state. Even if the observer knows the composition of the urns and has just observed a sequence of three balls, *e.g.* y1, y2 and y3 on the conveyor belt, the observer still cannot be *sure* which urn (*i.e.*, at which state) the genie has drawn the third ball from. However, the observer can work out other information, such as the likelihood that the third ball came from each of the urns.

Structural Architecture

The diagram below shows the general architecture of an instantiated HMM. Each oval shape represents a random variable that can adopt any of a number of values. The random variable $x(t)$ is the hidden state at time t (with the model from the above diagram, $x(t) \in \{ x_1, x_2, x_3 \}$). The random variable $y(t)$ is the observation at time t (with $y(t) \in \{ y_1, y_2, y_3, y_4 \}$). The arrows in the diagram (often called a trellis diagram) denote conditional dependencies.

From the diagram, it is clear that the conditional probability distribution of the hidden variable $x(t)$ at time t, given the values of the hidden variable x at all times, depends *only* on the value of the hidden variable $x(t-1)$; the values at time $t-2$ and before have no influence. This is called the Markov property. Similarly, the value of the observed variable $y(t)$ only depends on the value of the hidden variable $x(t)$ (both at time t).

In the standard type of hidden Markov model considered here, the state space of the hidden variables is discrete, while the observations themselves can either be discrete (typically generated from a categorical distribution) or continuous (typically from a Gaussian distribution). The parameters of a hidden Markov model are of two types, *transition probabilities* and *emission probabilities* (also known as *output probabilities*). The transition probabilities control the way the hidden state at time t is chosen given the hidden state at time $t-1$.

The hidden state space is assumed to consist of one of N possible values, modelled as a categorical distribution. This means that for each of the N possible states that a hidden variable at time t can be in, there is a transition probability from this state to each of the N possible states of the hidden variable at time $t+1$, for a total of N^2 transition probabilities. Note that the set of transition probabilities for transitions from any given state must sum to 1. Thus, the $N \times N$ matrix of transition probabilities is a Markov matrix. Because any one transition probability can be determined once the others are known, there are a total of $N(N-1)$ transition parameters.

In addition, for each of the N possible states, there is a set of emission probabilities governing the distribution of the observed variable at a particular time given the state of the hidden variable at that time. The size of this set depends on the nature of the observed variable. For example, if the observed variable is discrete with M possible values, governed by a categorical distribution, there will be $M-1$ separate parameters, for a total of $N(M-1)$ emission parameters over all hidden states. On the other hand, if the observed variable is an M-dimensional vector distributed according to an arbitrary multivariate Gaussian distribution, there will be M parameters controlling the means and $\dfrac{M(M+1)}{2}$ parameters controlling the covariance matrix, for a total of $N\left(M + \dfrac{M(M+1)}{2}\right) = \dfrac{NM(M+3)}{2} = O(NM^2)$ emission parameters. (In such a case, unless the value of M is small, it may be more practical to restrict the nature of the covariances between individual elements of the observation vector, e.g. by assuming that the elements are independent of each other, or less restrictively, are independent of all but a fixed number of adjacent elements.)

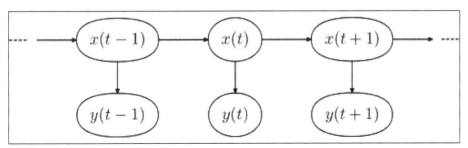

Inference

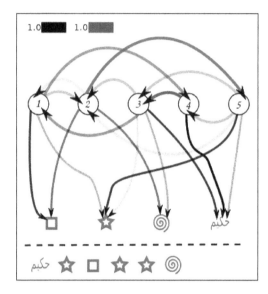

The state transition and output probabilities of an HMM are indicated by the line opacity in the upper part of the diagram. Given that we have observed the output sequence in the lower part of the diagram, we may be interested in the most likely sequence of states that could have produced it. Based on the arrows that are present in the diagram, the following state sequences are candidates:

5 3 2 5 3 2

4 3 2 5 3 2

3 1 2 5 3 2

We can find the most likely sequence by evaluating the joint probability of both the state sequence and the observations for each case (simply by multiplying the probability values, which here correspond to the opacities of the arrows involved). In general, this type of problem (i.e. finding the most likely explanation for an observation sequence) can be solved efficiently using the Viterbi algorithm.

Several inference problems are associated with hidden Markov models, as outlined below.

Probability of an Observed Sequence

The task is to compute in a best way, given the parameters of the model, the probability of a particular output sequence. This requires summation over all possible state sequences:

The probability of observing a sequence,

$$Y = y(0), y(1), \ldots, y(L-1)$$

of length L is given by,

$$P(Y) = \sum_X P(Y \mid X) P(X),$$

where the sum runs over all possible hidden-node sequences,

$$X = x(0), x(1), \ldots, x(L-1).$$

Applying the principle of dynamic programming, this problem, too, can be handled efficiently using the forward algorithm.

Probability of the Latent Variables

A number of related tasks ask about the probability of one or more of the latent variables, given the model's parameters and a sequence of observations $y(1), \ldots, y(t)$.

Filtering

The task is to compute, given the model's parameters and a sequence of observations, the distribution over hidden states of the last latent variable at the end of the sequence, i.e. to compute $P(x(t) \mid y(1), \ldots, y(t))$. This task is normally used when the sequence of latent variables is thought of as the underlying states that a process moves through at a sequence of points of time, with corresponding observations at each point in time. Then, it is natural to ask about the state of the process at the end.

This problem can be handled efficiently using the forward algorithm.

Smoothing

This is similar to filtering but asks about the distribution of a latent variable somewhere in the middle of a sequence, i.e. to compute $P(x(k) \mid y(1), \ldots, y(t))$ for some $k < t$. From the perspective described above, this can be thought of as the probability distribution over hidden states for a point in time k in the past, relative to time t.

The forward-backward algorithm is an goo method for computing the smoothed values for all hidden state variables.

The task, unlike the previous two, asks about the joint probability of the *entire* sequence of hidden states that generated a particular sequence of observations. This task is generally applicable when HMM's are applied to different sorts of problems from those for which the tasks of filtering and smoothing are applicable. An example is part-of-speech tagging, where the hidden states represent the underlying parts of speech corresponding to an observed sequence of words. In this case, what is of interest is the entire sequence of parts of speech, rather than simply the part of speech for a single word, as filtering or smoothing would compute.

This task requires finding a maximum over all possible state sequences, and can be solved efficiently by the Viterbi algorithm.

Statistical Significance

For some of the above problems, it may also be interesting to ask about statistical significance. What is the probability that a sequence drawn from some null distribution will have an HMM probability (in the case of the forward algorithm) or a maximum state sequence probability (in the case of the

Viterbi algorithm) at least as large as that of a particular output sequence? When an HMM is used to evaluate the relevance of a hypothesis for a particular output sequence, the statistical significance indicates the false positive rate associated with failing to reject the hypothesis for the output sequence.

A Concrete Example

Consider two friends, Alice and Bob, who live far apart from each other and who talk together daily over the telephone about what they did that day. Bob is only interested in three activities: walking in the park, shopping, and cleaning his apartment. The choice of what to do is determined exclusively by the weather on a given day. Alice has no definite information about the weather, but she knows general trends. Based on what Bob tells her he did each day, Alice tries to guess what the weather must have been like.

Alice believes that the weather operates as a discrete Markov chain. There are two states, "Rainy" and "Sunny", but she cannot observe them directly, that is, they are *hidden* from her. On each day, there is a certain chance that Bob will perform one of the following activities, depending on the weather: "walk", "shop", or "clean". Since Bob tells Alice about his activities, those are the *observations*. The entire system is that of a hidden Markov model (HMM).

Alice knows the general weather trends in the area, and what Bob likes to do on average. In other words, the parameters of the HMM are known. They can be represented as follows in Python:

```python
states = ('Rainy', 'Sunny')


observations = ('walk', 'shop', 'clean')


start_probability = {'Rainy': 0.6, 'Sunny': 0.4}


transition_probability = {
  'Rainy' : {'Rainy': 0.7, 'Sunny': 0.3},
  'Sunny' : {'Rainy': 0.4, 'Sunny': 0.6},
  }


emission_probability = {
  'Rainy' : {'walk': 0.1, 'shop': 0.4, 'clean': 0.5},
  'Sunny' : {'walk': 0.6, 'shop': 0.3, 'clean': 0.1},
  }
```

In this piece of code, `start_probability` represents Alice's belief about which state the HMM is in when Bob first calls her (all she knows is that it tends to be rainy on average). The particular probability distribution used here is not the equilibrium one, which is (given the transition probabilities) approximately `{'Rainy': 0.57, 'Sunny': 0.43}`. The `transition_probability` represents the change of the weather in the underlying Markov chain. In this example, there is only a 30% chance that tomorrow will be sunny if today is rainy. The `emission_probability` represents how likely Bob is to perform a certain activity on each day. If it is rainy, there is a 50% chance that he is cleaning his apartment; if it is sunny, there is a 60% chance that he is outside for a walk.

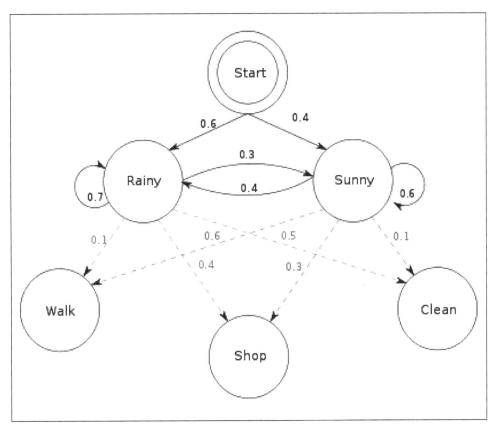

Learning

The parameter learning task in HMMs is to find, given an output sequence or a set of such sequences, the best set of state transition and emission probabilities. The task is usually to derive the maximum likelihood estimate of the parameters of the HMM given the set of output sequences. No tractable algorithm is known for solving this problem exactly, but a local maximum likelihood can be derived efficiently using the Baum–Welch algorithm or the Baldi–Chauvin algorithm. The Baum–Welch algorithm is a special case of the expectation-maximization algorithm. If the HMMs are used for time series prediction, more sophisticated Bayesian inference methods, like Markov chain Monte Carlo (MCMC) sampling are proven to be favorable over finding a single maximum likelihood model both in terms of accuracy and stability.

Since MCMC imposes significant computational burden, in cases where computational scalability is also of interest, one may alternatively resort to variational approximations to Bayesian inference, e.g. Indeed, approximate variational inference offers computational efficiency comparable to expectation-maximization, while yielding an accuracy profile only slightly inferior to exact MCMC-type Bayesian inference.

Mathematical Description

A basic hidden Markov model can be described as follows:

N	=	number of states
T	=	number of observations
$\theta_{i=1\ldots N}$	=	emission parameter for an observation associated with state i
$\varphi_{i=1\ldots N,j=1\ldots N}$	=	probability of transition from state i to state j
		N-dimensional vector, composed of $\varphi_{i,j=1\ldots N}$;
$\varphi_{i=1\ldots N}$	=	the i-th row of the matrix $\varphi_{i=1\ldots N,j=1\ldots N}$ (sum of it is 1)
$x_{t=1\ldots T}$	=	(hidden) state at time t
$y_{t=1\ldots T}$	=	observation at time t
$F(y|\theta)$	~	probability distribution of an observation, parametrized on θ
$x_{t=2\ldots T}$	~	Categorical($\varphi_{x_{t-1}}$)
$y_{t=1\ldots T}$	~	$F(\theta_{x_t})$

Note that, in the above model (and also the one below), the prior distribution of the initial state x_1 is not specified. Typical learning models correspond to assuming a discrete uniform distribution over possible states (i.e. no particular prior distribution is assumed).

In a Bayesian setting, all parameters are associated with random variables, as follows:

N,T	=	as above
$\theta_{i=1\ldots N}, \varphi_{i=1\ldots N,j=1\ldots N}, \ddot{o}_{i=1\ldots N}$	=	as above
$x_{t=1\ldots T}, y_{t=1\ldots T}, F(y\,|\,\theta)$	=	as above
α	=	shared hyperparameter for emission parameters
β	=	shared hyperparameter for transition parameters
$H(\theta\,|\,\alpha)$	=	prior probability distribution of emission parameters, parametrized on α
$\theta_{i=1\ldots N}$	~	$H(\alpha)$
$\varphi_{i=1\ldots N}$	~	Symmetric-Dirichlet$_N(\beta)$
$x_{t=2\ldots T}$	~	Categorical($\varphi_{x_{t-1}}$)
$y_{t=1\ldots T}$	~	$F(\theta_{x_t})$

These characterizations use F and H to describe arbitrary distributions over observations and parameters, respectively. Typically H will be the conjugate prior of F. The two most common choices of F are Gaussian and categorical.

Compared with a Simple Mixture Model

As mentioned above, the distribution of each observation in a hidden Markov model is a mixture density, with the states of the corresponding to mixture components. It is useful to compare the above characterizations for an HMM with the corresponding characterizations, of a mixture model, using the same notation.

A non-Bayesian mixture model:

N	=	Number of mixture components.
T	=	Number of observations.
$\theta_{i=1...N}$	=	Parameter of distribution of observation associated with component i.
$\varphi_{i=1...N}$	=	Mixture weight, i.e. prior probability of component i.
φ	=	N-dimensional vector, composed of $\varphi_{1...N}$; must sum to 1.
$x_{t=1...T}$	=	Component of observation t.
$y_{t=1...T}$	=	Observation t.
$F(y\|\theta)$	=	Probability distribution of an observation, parametrized on θ.
$x_{t=1...T}$	~	Categorical(φ).
$y_{t=1...T}$	~	$F(\theta_{x_t})$.

A Bayesian mixture model:

N,T	=	As above.
$\theta_{i=1...N},\varphi_{i=1...N},\varphi$	=	As above.
$x_{t=1...T},y_{t=1...T},F(y\|\theta)$	=	As above.
α	=	Shared hyperparameter for component parameters.
β	=	Shared hyperparameter for mixture weights.
$H(\theta\|\alpha)$	=	Prior probability distribution of component parameters, parametrized on α.
$\theta_{i=1...N}$	~	$H(\alpha)$.
φ	~	Symmetric-Dirichlet$_N(\beta)$.
$x_{t=1...T}$	~	Categorical(φ).
$y_{t=1...T}$	~	$F(\theta_{x_t})$.

Examples:

The following mathematical descriptions are fully written out and explained, for ease of implementation.

A typical non-Bayesian HMM with Gaussian observations looks like this:

N	$=$	Number of states.
T	$=$	Number of observations.
$\varphi_{i=1\ldots N,\,j=1\ldots N}$	$=$	Probability of transition from state i to state j.
$\varphi_{i=1\ldots N}$	$=$	N-dimensional vector, composed of $\varphi_{i,1\ldots N}$; must sum to 1.
$\mu_{i=1\ldots N}$	$=$	Mean of observations associated with state i.
$\sigma^2_{i=1\ldots N}$	$=$	Variance of observations associated with state i.
$x_{t=1\ldots T}$	$=$	State of observation at time t.
$y_{t=1\ldots T}$	$=$	Observation at time t.
$x_{t=2\ldots T}$	$\sim$	Categorical($\varphi_{x_{t-1}}$).
$y_{t=1\ldots T}$	$\sim$	$\mathcal{N}(\mu_{x_t}, \sigma^2_{x_t})$.

A typical Bayesian HMM with Gaussian observations looks like this:

N	$=$	Number of states.
T	$=$	Number of observations.
$\varphi_{i=1\ldots N,\,j=1\ldots N}$	$=$	Probability of transition from state i to state j.
$\varphi_{i=1\ldots N}$	$=$	N-dimensional vector, composed of $\varphi_{i,1\ldots N}$; must sum to 1.
$\mu_{i=1\ldots N}$	$=$	Mean of observations associated with state i.
$\sigma^2_{i=1\ldots N}$	$=$	Variance of observations associated with state i.
$t=\ldots T$	$=$	State of observation at time t.
$y_{t=1\ldots T}$	$=$	Observation at time t.
β	$=$	Concentration hyperparameter controlling the density of the transition matrix.
μ_0, λ	$=$	Shared hyperparameters of the means for each state.
ν, σ^2_0	$=$	Shared hyperparameters of the variances for each state.
$\varphi_{i=1\ldots N}$	$\sim$	Symmetric-Dirichlet$_N(\beta)$.
$x_{t=2\ldots T}$	$\sim$	Categorical($\varphi_{x_{t-1}}$).
$\mu_{i=1\ldots N}$	$\sim$	$\mathcal{N}(\mu_0, \lambda\sigma^2_i)$.
$\sigma^2_{i=1\ldots N}$	$\sim$	Inverse-Gamma(ν, σ^2_0).
$y_{t=1\ldots T}$	$\sim$	$\mathcal{N}(\mu_{x_t}, \sigma^2_{x_t})$.

A typical non-Bayesian HMM with categorical observations looks like this:

N	=	Number of states.
T	=	Number of observations
$\varphi_{i=1\ldots N, j=1\ldots N}$	=	Probability of transition from state t to state j.
$\theta_{i=1\ldots N}$	=	N - dimensional vector, composed of $\varphi_{i,1\ldots N}$; must sum to 1.
V	=	Dimension of categorical observations, e.g. size of word vocabulary.
$\theta_{i=1\ldots N, j=1\ldots V}$	=	Probability for state i of observing the j th item.
$\theta_{i=1\ldots N}$	=	V- dimensional vector, composed of $\theta_{i,1\ldots V}$; must sum to 1.
$x_{t=1\ldots T}$	=	State of observation at time t.
$y_{t=1\ldots T}$	=	Observation at time t.
$x_{t=2\ldots T}$	~	Categorical($\varphi_{x_{t-1}}$).
$y_{t=1\ldots T}$	~	Categorical(θ_{x_t}) ·

A typical Bayesian HMM with categorical observations looks like this:

N	=	Number of states.
T	=	Number of observations.
$\varphi_{i=1\ldots N, j=1\ldots N}$	=	Probability of transition from state i to state j.
$\varphi_{i=1\ldots N}$	=	N-dimensional vector, composed of $\varphi_{i,1\ldots N}$; must sum to 1.
V	=	dimension of categorical observations, e.g. size of word vocabulary.
$\theta_{i=1\ldots N, j=1\ldots V}$	=	Probability for state i of observing the j th item.
$\theta_{i=1\ldots N}$	=	V-dimensional vector, composed $\theta_{i,1\ldots V}$; must sum to 1.
$x_{t=1\ldots T}$	=	State of observation at time t.
$y_{t=1\ldots T}$	=	Observation at time t.
α	=	Shared concentration hyperparameter of θ for each state.
β	~	Concentration hyperparameter controlling the density of the transition matrix.
$\varphi_{i=1\ldots N}$	~	Symmetric-Dirichlet$_N(\beta)$.
$\theta_{1\ldots V}$	~	Symmetric-Dirichlet$_V(\alpha)$.
$x_{t=2\ldots T}$	~	Categorical($ö_{x_{t-1}}$).
$y_{t=1\ldots T}$	~	Categorical($è_{x_t}$).

Note that in the above Bayesian characterizations, β (a concentration parameter) controls the density of the transition matrix. That is, with a high value of β (significantly above 1), the probabilities controlling the transition out of a particular state will all be similar, meaning there will be a significant probability of transitioning to any of the other states. In other words, the path followed by the Markov chain of hidden states will be highly random. With a low value of β (significantly below 1), only a small number of the possible transitions out of a given state will have significant probability, meaning that the path followed by the hidden states will be somewhat predictable.

A Two-level Bayesian HMM

An alternative for the above two Bayesian examples would be to add another level of prior parameters for the transition matrix. That is, replace the lines:

β	=	concentration hyperparameter controlling the density of the transition matrix
$\varphi_{i=1...N}$	~	Symmetric-Dirichlet$_N(\beta)$

with the following:

γ	=	concentration hyperparameter controlling how many states are intrinsically likely
β	=	concentration hyperparameter controlling the density of the transition matrix
η	=	N-dimensional vector of probabilities, specifying the intrinsic probability of a given state
η	~	Symmetric-Dirichlet$_N(\gamma)$
$\varphi_{i=1...N}$	~	Dirichlet$_N(\beta N \varsigma)$

What this means is the following:

- η is a probability distribution over states, specifying which states are inherently likely. The greater the probability of a given state in this vector, the more likely is a transition to that state (regardless of the starting state).

- γ controls the density of β. Values significantly above 1 cause a dense vector where all states will have similar prior probabilities. Values significantly below 1 cause a sparse vector where only a few states are inherently likely (have prior probabilities significantly above 0).

- β controls the density of the transition matrix, or more specifically, the density of the N different probability vectors $\varphi_{i=1...N}$ specifying the probability of transitions out of state i to any other state.

Imagine that the value of β is significantly above 1. Then the different φ vectors will be dense, i.e. the probability mass will be spread out fairly evenly over all states. However, to the extent that this mass is unevenly spread, η controls which states are likely to get more mass than others.

Now, imagine instead that φ is significantly below 1. This will make the φ vectors sparse, i.e. almost all the probability mass is distributed over a small number of states, and for the rest, a transition to that state will be very unlikely. Notice that there are different φ vectors for each starting state, and so even if all the vectors are sparse, different vectors may distribute the mass to different ending states. However, for all of the vectors, η controls which ending states are likely to get mass assigned to them. For example, if β is 0.1, then each φ will be sparse and, for any given starting state i, the set of states J_i to which transitions are likely to occur will be very small, typically having only one or two members. Now, if the probabilities in η are all the same (or equivalently, one of the above models without η is used), then for different i, there will be different states in the corresponding J_i, so that all states are equally likely to occur in any given J_i. On the other hand, if the values in η are unbalanced, so that one state has a much higher probability than others, almost all J_i will contain this state; hence, regardless of the starting state, transitions will nearly always occur to this given state.

Hence, a two-level model such as just described allows independent control over (1) the overall density of the transition matrix, and (2) the density of states to which transitions are likely (i.e. the density of the prior distribution of states in any particular hidden variable (x_i)In both cases this is done while still assuming ignorance over which particular states are more likely than others. If it is desired to inject this information into the model, the probability vector η can be directly specified; or, if there is less certainty about these relative probabilities, a non-symmetric Dirichlet distribution can be used as the prior distribution over η. That is, instead of using a symmetric Dirichlet distribution with the single parameter γ (or equivalently, a general Dirichlet with a vector all of whose values are equal to γ), use a general Dirichlet with values that are variously greater or less than γ, according to which state is more or less preferred.

Poisson Hidden Markov Model

Poisson hidden Markov models (PHMM) are special cases of hidden Markov models where a Poisson process has a rate which varies in association with changes between the different states of a Markov model. PHMMs are not necessarily Markovian processes themselves because the underlying Markov chain or Markov process cannot be observed and only the Poisson signal is observed.

Applications

HMMs can be applied in many fields where the goal is to recover a data sequence that is not immediately observable (but other data that depend on the sequence are). Applications include:

- Computational finance.

- Single-molecule kinetic analysis.

- Cryptanalysis.

- Speech recognition, including Siri.

- Speech synthesis.

- Part-of-speech tagging.

- Document separation in scanning solutions.

- Machine translation.

- Partial discharge.

- Gene prediction.

- Handwriting recognition.

- Alignment of bio-sequences.

- Time series analysis.

- Activity recognition.

- Protein folding.

- Sequence classification.

- Metamorphic virus detection.

- DNA motif discovery.

- Chromatin state discovery.

- Transportation forecasting.

- Solar irradiance variability.

Types

Hidden Markov models can model complex Markov processes where the states emit the observations according to some probability distribution. One such example is the Gaussian distribution; in such a Hidden Markov Model the states output are represented by a Gaussian distribution.

Moreover, it could represent even more complex behavior when the output of the states is represented as mixture of two or more Gaussians, in which case the probability of generating an observation is the product of the probability of first selecting one of the Gaussians and the probability of generating that observation from that Gaussian. In cases of modeled data exhibiting artifacts such as outliers and skewness, one may resort to finite mixtures of heavier-tailed elliptical distributions, such as the multivariate Student's-t distribution, or appropriate non-elliptical distributions, such as the multivariate Normal Inverse-Gaussian.

Extensions

In the hidden Markov models considered above, the state space of the hidden variables is discrete, while the observations themselves can either be discrete (typically generated from a categorical distribution) or continuous (typically from a Gaussian distribution). Hidden Markov models can also be generalized to allow continuous state spaces. Examples of such models are those where the Markov process over hidden variables is a linear dynamical system, with a linear relationship among related variables and where all hidden and observed variables follow a Gaussian distribution. In simple cases, such as the linear dynamical system just mentioned, exact inference is tractable (in this case, using the Kalman filter); however, in general, exact inference in HMMs with continuous latent variables is infeasible, and approximate methods must be used, such as the extended Kalman filter or the particle filter.

Hidden Markov models are generative models, in which the joint distribution of observations and hidden states, or equivalently both the prior distribution of hidden states (the transition probabilities) and conditional distribution of observations given states (the emission probabilities), is modeled. The above algorithms implicitly assume a uniform prior distribution over the transition probabilities. However, it is also possible to create hidden Markov models with other types of prior distributions. An obvious candidate, given the categorical distribution of the transition probabilities, is the Dirichlet distribution, which is the conjugate prior distribution of the categorical distribution. Typically, a symmetric Dirichlet distribution is chosen, reflecting ignorance about which states are inherently more likely than others. The single parameter of this distribution (termed the concentration parameter) controls the relative density or sparseness of the resulting transition matrix. A choice of 1 yields a uniform distribution. Values greater than 1 produce a dense matrix, in which the transition probabilities between pairs of states are likely to be nearly equal. Values less than 1 result in a sparse matrix in which, for each given source state, only a small number of destination states have non-negligible transition probabilities. It is also possible to use a two-level prior Dirichlet distribution, in which one Dirichlet distribution (the upper distribution) governs the parameters of another Dirichlet distribution (the lower distribution), which in turn governs the transition probabilities. The upper distribution governs the overall distribution of states, determining how likely each state is to occur; its concentration parameter determines the density or sparseness of states. Such a two-level prior distribution, where both concentration parameters are set to produce sparse distributions, might be useful for example in unsupervised part-of-speech tagging, where some parts of speech occur much more commonly than others; learning algorithms that assume a uniform prior distribution generally perform poorly on this task. The parameters of models of this sort, with non-uniform prior distributions, can be learned using Gibbs sampling or extended versions of the expectation-maximization algorithm.

An extension of the previously described hidden Markov models with Dirichlet priors uses a Dirichlet process in place of a Dirichlet distribution. This type of model allows for an unknown and potentially infinite number of states. It is common to use a two-level Dirichlet process, similar to the previously described model with two levels of Dirichlet distributions. Such a model is called a hierarchical Dirichlet process hidden Markov model, or HDP-HMM for short. It was originally described under the name "Infinite Hidden Markov Model" and was further formalized in.

A different type of extension uses a discriminative model in place of the generative model of standard HMMs. This type of model directly models the conditional distribution of the hidden states given the observations, rather than modeling the joint distribution. An example of this model is the so-called maximum entropy Markov model (MEMM), which models the conditional distribution of the states using logistic regression (also known as a "maximum entropy model"). The advantage of this type of model is that arbitrary features (i.e. functions) of the observations can be modeled, allowing domain-specific knowledge of the problem at hand to be injected into the model. Models of this sort are not limited to modeling direct dependencies between a hidden state and its associated observation; rather, features of nearby observations, of combinations of the associated observation and nearby observations, or in fact of arbitrary observations at any distance from a given hidden state can be included in the process used to determine the value of a hidden state. Furthermore, there is no need for these features to be statistically independent of each other, as would be the case if such features were used in a generative model. Finally, arbitrary features over pairs of adjacent hidden states can be used rather than simple transition probabilities. The disadvantages of such models are: (1) The types of prior distributions that can be placed on hidden states are severely limited; (2) It is not possible to predict the probability of seeing an arbitrary observation. This second limitation is often not an issue in practice, since many common usages of HMM's do not require such predictive probabilities.

A variant of the previously described discriminative model is the linear-chain conditional random field. This uses an undirected graphical model (aka Markov random field) rather than the directed graphical models of MEMM's and similar models. The advantage of this type of model is that it does not suffer from the so-called *label bias* problem of MEMM's, and thus may make more accurate predictions. The disadvantage is that training can be slower than for MEMM's.

Yet another variant is the *factorial hidden Markov model*, which allows for a single observation to be conditioned on the corresponding hidden variables of a set of K independent Markov chains, rather than a single Markov chain. It is equivalent to a single HMM, with N^K states (assuming there are N states for each chain), and therefore, learning in such a model is difficult: for a sequence of length T, a straightforward Viterbi algorithm has complexity $O(N^{2K}T)$. To find an exact solution, a junction tree algorithm could be used, but it results in an $O(N^{K+1}KT)$ complexity. In practice, approximate techniques, such as variational approaches, could be used.

All of the above models can be extended to allow for more distant dependencies among hidden states, e.g. allowing for a given state to be dependent on the previous two or three states rather than a single previous state; i.e. the transition probabilities are extended to encompass sets of three or four adjacent states (or in general K adjacent states). The disadvantage of such models is that dynamic-programming algorithms for training them have an $O(N^K T)$ running time, for K adjacent states and T total observations (i.e. a length-T Markov chain).

Another recent extension is the *triplet Markov model*, in which an auxiliary underlying process is added to model some data specificities. Many variants of this model have been proposed. One should also mention the interesting link that has been established between the *theory of evidence* and the *triplet Markov models* and which allows to fuse data in Markovian context and to model nonstationary data.

Finally, a different rationale towards addressing the problem of modeling nonstationary data by means of hidden Markov models was suggested in 2012. It consists in employing a small recurrent neural network (RNN), specifically a reservoir network, to capture the evolution of the temporal dynamics in the observed data. This information, encoded in the form of a high-dimensional vector, is used as a conditioning variable of the HMM state transition probabilities. Under such a setup, we eventually obtain a nonstationary HMM the transition probabilities of which evolve over time in a manner that is inferred from the data itself, as opposed to some unrealistic ad-hoc model of temporal evolution.

The model suitable in the context of longitudinal data is named latent Markov model. The basic version of this model has been extended to include individual covariates, random effects and to model more complex data structures such as multilevel data.

GAUSSIAN MIXTURE MODEL

A *Gaussian Mixture* is a function that is comprised of several Gaussians, each identified by $k \in \{1,\ldots, K\}$, where K is the number of clusters of our dataset. Each Gaussian k in the mixture is comprised of the following parameters:

- A mean μ that defines its centre.

- A covariance Σ that defines its width. This would be equivalent to the dimensions of an ellipsoid in a multivariate scenario.

- A mixing probability π that defines how big or small the Gaussian function will be.

Let us now illustrate these parameters graphically:

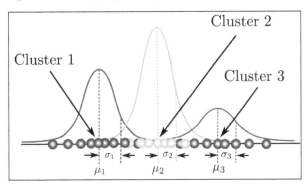

Here, we can see that there are three Gaussian functions, hence $K = 3$. Each Gaussian explains the data contained in each of the three clusters available. The mixing coefficients are themselves probabilities and must meet this condition:

$$\sum_{k=1}^{K} \pi_k = 1$$

Now how do we determine the optimal values for these parameters? To achieve this we must ensure that each Gaussian fits the data points belonging to each cluster. This is exactly what maximum likelihood does.

In general, the Gaussian density function is given by:

$$\mathcal{N}\left(x|\mu,\sum \right) = \frac{1}{\left(2\pi\right)^{D/2}\left|\sum\right|^{1/2}}\exp\left(-\frac{1}{2}(x-\mu)^T\sum\nolimits^{-1}(x-\mu)\right)$$

Where x represents our data points, D is the number of dimensions of each data point. μ and Σ are the mean and covariance, respectively. If we have a dataset comprised of $N = 1000$ three-dimensional points ($D = 3$), then x will be a 1000×3 matrix. μ will be a 1×3 vector, and Σ will be a 3×3 matrix. For later purposes, we will also find it useful to take the log of this equation, which is given by:

$$\ln \mathcal{N}\left(x|\mu,\sum \right) = -\frac{D}{2}\ln 2\pi - \frac{1}{2}\ln\sum - \frac{1}{2}(x-\mu)^T\sum\nolimits^{-1}(x-\mu)$$

If we differentiate this equation with respect to the mean and covariance and then equate it to zero, then we will be able to find the optimal values for these parameters, and the solutions will correspond to the Maximum Likelihood Estimates (MLE) for this setting. However, because we are dealing with not just one, but many Gaussians, things will get a bit complicated when time comes for us to find the parameters for the whole mixture.

Initial Derivations

We are now going to introduce some additional notation. Just a word of warning. Math is coming on! Don't worry. I'll try to keep the notation as clean as possible for better understanding of the derivations. First, let's suppose we want to know what is the probability that a data point xn comes from Gaussian k. We can express this as:

$$p\left(z_{nk} = 1 \middle| \mathbf{x}_n\right)$$

Which reads "*given a data point x, what is the probability it came from Gaussian k?*" In this case, z is a *latent variable* that takes only two possible values. It is one when x came from Gaussian k, and zero otherwise. Actually, we don't get to see this z variable in reality, but knowing its probability of occurrence will be useful in helping us determine the Gaussian mixture parameters.

Likewise, we can state the following:

$$\pi_k = p\left(z_k = 1\right)$$

Which means that the overall probability of observing a point that comes from Gaussian k is actually equivalent to the mixing coefficient for that Gaussian. This makes sense, because the bigger the Gaussian is, the higher we would expect this probability to be. Now let z be the set of all possible latent variables z, hence:

$$z = \left\{z_1, \ldots, z_K\right\}$$

We know beforehand that each z occurs independently of others and that they can only take the value of one when k is equal to the cluster the point comes from. Therefore:

$$p(z) = p\left(z_1 = 1\right)^{z_1} p\left(z_2 = 1\right)^{z_2} \ldots p\left(z_K = 1\right)^{z_K} = \prod_{k=1}^{K} \pi_k^{z_k}$$

Now, what about finding the probability of observing our data given that it came from Gaussian k? Turns out to be that it is actually the Gaussian function itself! Following the same logic we used to define $p(z)$, we can state:

$$p\left(\mathbf{x}_n \middle| z\right) = \prod_{k=1}^{K} \mathcal{N}\left(\mathbf{x}_n \middle| \mu_k, \textstyle\sum_k\right)^{z_k}$$

Ok, now you may be asking, why are we doing all this? Remember our initial aim was to determine what the probability of z given our observation x? Well, it turns out to be that the equations we have just derived, along with the Bayes rule, will help us determine this probability. From the product rule of probabilities, we know that:

$$p(x_n, z) = p(x_n | z) p(z)$$

Hmm, it seems to be that now we are getting somewhere. The operands on the right are what we have just found. Perhaps some of you may be anticipating that we are going to use the Bayes rule to get the probability we eventually need. However, first we will need p(xn), not p(xn, z). So how do we get rid of z here? Yes, you guessed it right. Marginalization! We just need to sum up the terms on z, hence:

$$p(x_n) = \sum_{k=1}^{K} p(x_n | z) p(z) = \sum_{k=1}^{K} \pi_k \mathcal{N}(x_n | \mu_k, \Sigma_k)$$

This is the equation that defines a Gaussian Mixture, and you can clearly see that it depends on all parameters that we mentioned previously! To determine the optimal values for these we need to determine the maximum likelihood of the model. We can find the likelihood as the joint probability of all observations xn, defined by:

$$p(X) = \prod_{n=1}^{N} p(x_n) = \prod_{n=1}^{N} \sum_{k=1}^{K} \pi_k \mathcal{N}(x_n | \mu_k, \Sigma_k)$$

Like we did for the original Gaussian density function, let's apply the log to each side of the equation:

$$\ln p(X) = \sum_{n=1}^{N} \ln \sum_{k=1}^{K} \pi_k \mathcal{N}(x_n | \mu_k, \Sigma_k)$$

Great! Now in order to find the optimal parameters for the Gaussian mixture, all we have to do is to differentiate this equation with respect to the parameters and we are done, right? Wait! Not so fast. We have an issue here. We can see that there is a logarithm that is affecting the second summation. Calculating the derivative of this expression and then solving for the parameters is going to be very hard.

What can we do? Well, we need to use an iterative method to estimate the parameters. But first, remember we were supposed to find the probability of z given x? Well, let's do that since at this point we already have everything in place to define what this probability will look like.

From Bayes rule, we know that:

$$p(z_k = 1 | x_n) = \frac{p(x_n | z_k = 1) p(z_k = 1)}{\sum_{j=1}^{K} p(x_n | z_j = 1) p(z_j = 1)}$$

From our earlier derivations we learned that:

$$p(z_k = 1) = \pi_k, \quad p(x_n | z_k = 1) = \mathcal{N}(x_n | \mu_k, \Sigma_k)$$

So let's now replace these in the previous equation:

$$p\left(z_k = 1 \middle| x_n\right) = \frac{\pi_k \mathcal{N}\left(x_n \middle| \mu_k, \sum_k\right)}{\sum_{j=1}^{K} \pi_j \mathcal{N}\left(x_n \middle| \mu_j, \sum_j\right)} = \gamma\left(z_{nk}\right)$$

Moving forward we are going to see this expression a lot. Next we will continue our discussion with a method that will help us easily determine the parameters for the Gaussian mixture.

Expectation — Maximization Algorithm

Well, at this point we have derived some expressions for the probabilities that we will find useful in determining the parameters of our model. However, previously we could see that simply evaluating to find such parameters would prove to be very hard. Fortunately, there is an iterative method we can use to achieve this purpose. It is called the Expectation — Maximization, or simply EM algorithm. It is widely used for optimization problems where the objective function has complexities such as the one we've just encountered for the GMM case.

Let the parameters of our model be:

$$\theta = \left\{\pi, \mu, \sum\right\}$$

Let us now define the steps that the general EM algorithm will follow.

Step 1: Initialise θ accordingly. For instance, we can use the results obtained by a previous K-Means run as a good starting point for our algorithm.

Step 2 (Expectation step): Evaluate.

$$p\left(Z \middle| X, \theta\right)$$

Actually, we have already found an expression for this. If the take the expectation of $z\{nk\}$, then we get:

$$p\left(z_{nk} \middle| X, \theta\right) = \mathbb{E}\left[z_{nk}\right] = \sum_{j=1}^{K} z_{nj} \gamma\left(z_{nj}\right) = \gamma\left(z_{nk}\right)$$

Do you now see why it was important for us to find this probability? Yeah, because it is evaluated as part of the EM algorithm.

Step 3 (Maximization step): Find the revised parameters θ^* using:

$$\theta^* = \arg\max_\theta \mathcal{Q}\left(\theta^*, \theta\right)$$

Where,

$$\mathcal{Q}\left(\theta^*, \theta\right) = \mathbb{E}\left[\ln p\left(X, Z \middle| \theta^*\right)\right] = \sum_z p\left(Z \middle| X, \theta\right) \ln p\left(X, Z \middle| \theta^*\right)$$

Okay, we already found $p(Z|X,\theta)$ in step 2, but we are missing $p(X,Z|\theta*)$. How can we find it? Well, actually it's not that difficult. It is just the complete likelihood of the model, including both X and Z, and we can find it by using the following expression:

$$p\left(X,Z|\theta*\right) = \prod_{n=1}^{N}\prod_{k=1}^{K}\pi^{z_{nk}}\mathcal{N}\left(x_n|\mu_k,\sum_k\right)^{z_{nk}}$$

which is the result of calculating the joint probability of all observations and latent variables and is an extension of our initial derivations for p(x). The log of this expression is given by,

$$\ln p\left(X,Z|\theta*\right) = \sum_{n=1}^{N}\sum_{k=1}^{K}z_{nk}\left[\ln\pi_k + \ln\mathcal{N}\left(x_n|\mu_k,\sum_k\right)\right]$$

And we have finally gotten rid of this troublesome logarithm that affected the summation in (3). With all of this in place, it will be much easier for us to estimate the parameters by just maximizing Q with respect to the parameters. Besides, remember that the latent variable z will only be 1 once everytime the summation is evaluated. With that knowledge, we can easily get rid of it as needed for our derivations.

Let us now determine the optimal parameters. Replacing equations (5) and (7) in (6) and applying a suitable Lagrange multiplier for the mixing coefficients π, we get:

$$Q(\theta*,\theta) = \sum_{n=1}^{N}\sum_{k=1}^{K}\gamma\left(z_{nk}\right)\left[\ln\pi_k + \ln\mathcal{N}\left(x_n|\mu k,\sum_k\right)\right] - \lambda\left(\sum_{k=1}^{K}\pi_k - 1\right)$$

And now we can easily determine the parameters by using maximum likelihood. Let's now take the derivative of Q with respect to π and set it equal to zero:

$$\frac{\partial Q(\theta*,\theta)}{\partial\pi_k} = \sum_{n=1}^{N}\frac{\gamma\left(z_{nk}\right)}{\pi_k} - \lambda = 0$$

Then, by rearranging the terms and applying a summation over k to both sides of the equation, we obtain:

$$\sum_{n=1}^{N}\gamma\left(z_{nk}\right)\pi_k\lambda \Rightarrow \sum_{k=1}^{K}\sum_{n=1}^{N}\gamma\left(z_{nk}\right) = \sum_{k=1}^{K}\pi_k\lambda$$

From (1), we know that the summation of all mixing coefficients π equals one. In addition, we know that summing up the probabilities γ over k will also give us 1. Thus we get $\lambda = N$. Using this result, we can solve for π:

$$\pi_k = \frac{\sum_{n=1}^{N}\gamma\left(z_{nk}\right)}{N}$$

Similarly, if we differentiate Q with respect to μ and Σ, equate the derivative to zero and then solve for the parameters by making use of the log-likelihood equation (2) we defined, we obtain:

$$\mu_k^* = \frac{\sum_{n=1}^{N} \gamma(z_{nk}) x_n}{\sum_{n=1}^{N} \gamma(z_{nk})},$$

$$\Sigma_k^* = \frac{\sum_{n=1}^{N} \gamma(z_{nk})(x_n - \mu_k)(x_n - \mu_k)^T}{\sum_{n=1}^{N} \gamma(z_{nk})}$$

Then we will use these revised values to determine γ in the next EM iteration and so on and so forth until we see some convergence in the likelihood value. We can use equation (3) to monitor the log-likelihood in each step and we are always guaranteed to reach a local maximum.

Implementation in Python

From our previous derivations, we stated that the EM algorithm follows an iterative approach to find the parameters of a Gaussian Mixture Model. Our first step was to initialise our parameters. In this case, we can use the values of K-means to suit this purpose. The Python code for this would look like:

```
def initialize_clusters(X, n_clusters):

    clusters = []

    idx = np.arange(X.shape)


    kmeans = KMeans().fit(X)

    mu_k = kmeans.cluster_centers_


    for i in range(n_clusters):

        clusters.append({

            'pi_k': 1.0 / n_clusters,

            'mu_k': mu_k[i],

            'cov_k': np.identity(X.shape, dtype=np.float64)

        })


    return clusters
```

Next, we execute the expectation step. Here we calculate:

$$\gamma(z_{nk}) = \frac{\pi_k \mathcal{N}\left(x_n \middle| \mu_k, \Sigma_k\right)}{\sum_{j=1}^{K} \pi_j \mathcal{N}\left(x_n \middle| \mu_j, \Sigma_j\right)}$$

And the corresponding Python code would look like:

```
def expectation_step(X, clusters):
    totals = np.zeros((X.shape, 1), dtype=np.float64)


    for cluster in clusters:
    pi_k = cluster['pi_k']
    mu_k = cluster['mu_k']
    cov_k = cluster['cov_k']


    gamma_nk = (pi_k * gaussian(X, mu_k, cov_k)).astype(np.float64)


    for i in range(X.shape):
        totals[i] += gamma_nk[i]


    cluster['gamma_nk'] = gamma_nk
    cluster['totals'] = totals


 for cluster in clusters:
     cluster['gamma_nk'] /= cluster['totals']
```

Note that in order to calculate the summation we just make use of the terms in the numerator and divide accordingly.

We then have the maximization step, where we calculate:

$$\pi_k^* = \frac{\sum_{n=1}^{N} \gamma(z_{nk})}{N}$$

$$\mu_k^* = \frac{\sum_{n=1}^{N} \gamma(z_{nk}) \mathbf{x}_n}{\sum_{n=1}^{N} \gamma(z_{nk})}, \quad \Sigma_k^* = \frac{\sum_{n=1}^{N} \gamma(z_{nk})(\mathbf{x}_n - \mu_k)(\mathbf{x}_n - \mu_k)^T}{\sum_{n=1}^{N} \gamma(z_{nk})}$$

The corresponding Python code for this would be the following:

```
def maximization_step(X, clusters):
    N = float(X.shape)


    for cluster in clusters:
```

```
gamma_nk = cluster['gamma_nk']
cov_k = np.zeros((X.shape, X.shape))


N_k = np.sum(gamma_nk, axis=0)


pi_k = N_k / N
mu_k = np.sum(gamma_nk * X, axis=0) / N_k


for j in range(X.shape):
    diff = (X[j] - mu_k).reshape(-1, 1)
    cov_k += gamma_nk[j] * np.dot(diff, diff.T)


cov_k /= N_k


cluster['pi_k'] = pi_k
cluster['mu_k'] = mu_k
cluster['cov_k'] = cov_k
```

Note that in order to simplify the calculations a bit, we have made use of:

$$N_k = \times \sum_{n=1}^{N} \gamma\left(z_{nk}\right)$$

Finally, we also have the log-likelihood calculation, which is given by,

$$\ln p(X) = \sum_{n=1}^{N} \ln \sum_{k=1}^{K} \pi_k \mathcal{N}\left(x_n | \mu_k, \Sigma_k\right)$$

The Python code for this would be,

```
def get_likelihood(X, clusters):

    likelihood = []

    sample_likelihoods = np.log(np.array([cluster['totals'] for cluster in clus-
ters]))

    return np.sum(sample_likelihoods), sample_likelihoods
```

We have pre-computed the value of the second summation in the expectation step, so we just make use of that here. In addition, it is always useful to create graphs to see how the likelihood is making progress.

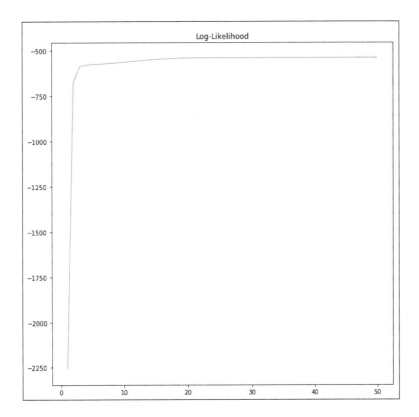

We can clearly see that the algorithm converges after about 20 epochs. EM guarantees that a local maximum will be reached after a given number of iterations of the procedure.

Finally, as part of the implementation we also generate an animation that shows us how the cluster settings improve after each iteration.

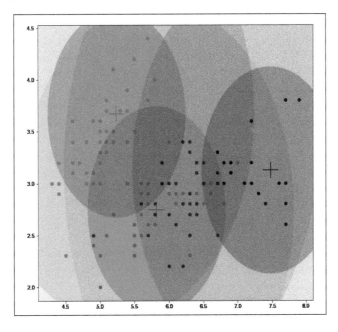

Note how the GMM improves the centroids estimated by K-means. As we converge, the values for the parameters for each cluster do not change any further.

References

- Supervised-unsupervised-learning: geeksforgeeks.org, Retrieved 14 January, 2019

- Unsupervised-machine-learning: guru99.com, Retrieved 24 March, 2019

- Phillips, Steven J. (2002-01-04). "Acceleration of K-Means and Related Clustering Algorithms". In Mount, David M.; Stein, Clifford (eds.). Acceleration of k-Means and Related Clustering Algorithms. Lecture Notes in Computer Science. 2409. Springer Berlin Heidelberg. pp. 166–177. doi:10.1007/3-540-45643-0_13. ISBN 978-3-540-43977-6

- Pieczynski, Wojciech (2007). "Multisensor triplet Markov chains and theory of evidence". International Journal of Approximate Reasoning. 45: 1–16. doi:10.1016/j.ijar.2006.05.001

- Gaussian-mixture-models-explained: towardsdatascience.com, Retrieved 24 August, 2019

- Everitt, Brian (2011). Cluster analysis. Chichester, West Sussex, U.K: Wiley. ISBN 9780470749913

Reinforcement Learning and Algorithms

Reinforcement learning is one of the basic machine paradigms of machine learning which uses dynamic programming techniques for maximizing notions of cumulative reward in an environment. It involves value function, Monte Carlo method, brute-force search, etc. This chapter has been carefully written to provide an easy understanding of reinforcement learning and its algorithms.

Reinforcement Learning (RL) is a type of machine learning technique that enables an agent to learn in an interactive environment by trial and error using feedback from its own actions and experiences.

Though both supervised and reinforcement learning use mapping between input and output, unlike supervised learning where feedback provided to the agent is correct set of actions for performing a task, reinforcement learning uses rewards and punishment as signals for positive and negative behavior.

As compared to unsupervised learning, reinforcement learning is different in terms of goals. While the goal in unsupervised learning is to find similarities and differences between data points, in reinforcement learning the goal is to find a suitable action model that would maximize the total cumulative reward of the agent. The figure below represents the basic idea and elements involved in a reinforcement learning model.

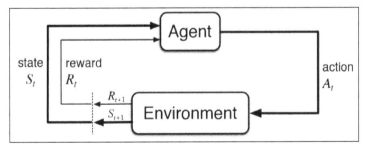

Formulating Basic Reinforcement Learning Problem

Some key terms that describe the elements of a RL problem are:

- Environment: Physical world in which the agent operates.
- State: Current situation of the agent.
- Reward: Feedback from the environment.
- Policy: Method to map agent's state to actions.
- Value: Future reward that an agent would receive by taking an action in a particular state.

A Reinforcement Learning problem can be best explained through games. Let's take the game of PacMan where the goal of the agent (PacMan) is to eat the food in the grid while avoiding the ghosts on its way. The grid world is the interactive environment for the agent. PacMan receives a reward for eating food and punishment if it gets killed by the ghost (loses the game). The states are the location of PacMan in the grid world and the total cumulative reward is PacMan winning the game.

In order to build an optimal policy, the agent faces the dilemma of exploring new states while maximizing its reward at the same time. This is called Exploration vs Exploitation trade-off.

Markov Decision Processes (MDPs) are mathematical frameworks to describe an environment in reinforcement learning and almost all RL problems can be formalized using MDPs. An MDP consists of a set of finite environment states S, a set of possible actions A(s) in each state, a real valued reward function R(s) and a transition model P(s', s | a). However, real world environments are more likely to lack any prior knowledge of environment dynamics. Model-free RL methods come handy in such cases.

Q-learning is a commonly used model free approach which can be used for building a self-playing PacMan agent. It revolves around the notion of updating Q values which denotes value of doing action a in state s. The value update rule is the core of the Q-learning algorithm.

$$Q(s_t, a_t) \leftarrow \underbrace{(1-\alpha) \cdot Q(s_t, a_t)}_{\text{old value}} + \underbrace{\alpha}_{\text{learning rate}} \cdot \overbrace{\left(\underbrace{r_t}_{\text{reward}} + \underbrace{\gamma}_{\text{discount factor}} \cdot \underbrace{\max_a Q(s_{t+1}, a)}_{\text{estimate of optimal future value}} \right)}^{\text{learned value}}$$

Most used Reinforcement Learning Algorithms

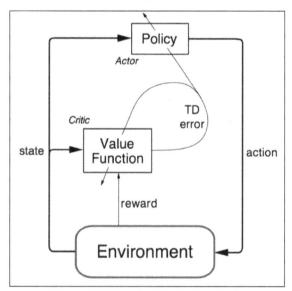

Actor-critic architecture for Reinforcement Learning.

Q-learning and SARSA (State-Action-Reward-State-Action) are two commonly used model-free RL algorithms. They differ in terms of their exploration strategies while their exploitation strategies are similar. While Q-learning is an off-policy method in which the agent learns the value based on action a* derived from the another policy, SARSA is an on-policy method where it learns the value based on its current action a derived from its current policy. These two methods are simple to implement but lack generality as they do not have the ability to estimate values for unseen states.

This can be overcome by more advanced algorithms such as Deep Q-Networks which use Neural Networks to estimate Q-values. But DQNs can only handle discrete, low-dimensional action spaces. DDPG(Deep Deterministic Policy Gradient)is a model-free, off-policy, actor-critic algorithm that tackles this problem by learning policies in high dimensional, continuous action spaces.

Practical Applications of Reinforcement Learning

Since, RL requires a lot of data, therefore it is most applicable in domains where simulated data is readily available like gameplay, robotics.

- RL is quite widely used in building AI for playing computer games. AlphaGo Zero is the first computer program to defeat a world champion in the ancient Chinese game of Go. Others include ATARI games, Backgammon, etc.

- In robotics and industrial automation, RL is used to enable the robot to create an efficient adaptive control system for itself which learns from its own experience and behavior. DeepMind's work on Deep Reinforcement Learning for Robotic Manipulation with Asynchronous Policy updates is a good example of the same.

- Other applications of RL include text summarization engines, dialog agents (text, speech) which can learn from user interactions and improve with time, learning optimal treatment policies in healthcare and RL based agents for online stock trading.

BRUTE-FORCE SEARCH

In computer science, brute-force search or exhaustive search, also known as generate and test, is a very general problem-solving technique and algorithmic paradigm that consists of systematically enumerating all possible candidates for the solution and checking whether each candidate satisfies the problem's statement.

A brute-force algorithm to find the divisors of a natural number n would enumerate all integers from 1 to n, and check whether each of them divides n without remainder. A brute-force approach for the eight queens puzzle would examine all possible arrangements of 8 pieces on the 64-square chessboard, and, for each arrangement, check whether each (queen) piece can attack any other.

While a brute-force search is simple to implement, and will always find a solution if it exists, its cost is proportional to the number of candidate solutions – which in many practical problems tends to grow very quickly as the size of the problem increases (combinatorial explosion). Therefore, brute-force search is typically used when the problem size is limited, or when there are problem-specific heuristics that can be used to reduce the set of candidate solutions to a manageable size. The method is also used when the simplicity of implementation is more important than speed.

This is the case, for example, in critical applications where any errors in the algorithm would have very serious consequences; or when using a computer to prove a mathematical theorem. Brute-force search is also useful as a baseline method when benchmarking other algorithms or meta-heuristics. Indeed, brute-force search can be viewed as the simplest metaheuristic. Brute force search should not be confused with backtracking, where large sets of solutions can be discarded without being explicitly enumerated (as in the textbook computer solution to the eight queens problem above). The brute-force method for finding an item in a table – namely, check all entries of the latter, sequentially – is called linear search.

Implementing the Brute-force Search

Basic Algorithm

In order to apply brute-force search to a specific class of problems, one must implement four procedures, *first, next, valid,* and *output.* These procedures should take as a parameter the data P for the particular instance of the problem that is to be solved, and should do the following:

- First (P): Generate a first candidate solution for P.

- Next (P, c): Generate the next candidate for P after the current one c.

- Valid (P, c): Check whether candidate c is a solution for P.

- Output (P, c): Use the solution c of P as appropriate to the application.

The *next* procedure must also tell when there are no more candidates for the instance P, after the current one c. A convenient way to do that is to return a "null candidate", some conventional data value Λ that is distinct from any real candidate. Likewise the *first* procedure should return Λ if there are no candidates at all for the instance P. The brute-force method is then expressed by the algorithm:

```
c ← first(P)
while c ≠ Λ do
 if valid(P,c) then output(P, c)
 c ← next(P,c)
end while
```

For example, when looking for the divisors of an integer n, the instance data P is the number n. The call *first*(n) should return the integer 1 if $n \geq 1$, or Λ otherwise; the call *next*(n,c) should return $c + 1$ if $c < n$, and Λ otherwise; and *valid*(n,c) should return true if and only if c is a divisor of n. (In fact, if we choose Λ to be $n + 1$, the tests $n \geq 1$ and $c < n$ are unnecessary.)The brute-force search algorithm above will call *output* for every candidate that is a solution to the given instance P. The algorithm is easily modified to stop after finding the first solution, or a specified number of solutions; or after testing a specified number of candidates, or after spending a given amount of CPU time.

Combinatorial Explosion

The main disadvantage of the brute-force method is that, for many real-world problems, the number of natural candidates is prohibitively large. For instance, if we look for the divisors of a number as described above, the number of candidates tested will be the given number n. So if n has sixteen decimal digits, say, the search will require executing at least 10^{15} computer instructions, which will take several days on a typical PC. If n is a random 64-bit natural number, which has about 19 decimal digits on the average, the search will take about 10 years. This steep growth in the number of candidates, as the size of the data increases, occurs in all sorts of problems. For instance, if we are seeking a particular rearrangement of 10 letters, then we have 10! = 3,628,800 candidates to consider, which a typical PC can generate and test in less than one second. However, adding one more letter – which is only a 10% increase in the data size – will multiply the number of candidates by 11, a 1000% increase. For 20 letters, the number of candidates is 20!, which is about 2.4×10^{18} or 2.4 quintillion; and the search will take about 10 years. This unwelcome phenomenon is commonly called the combinatorial explosion, or the curse of dimensionality.

One example of a case where combinatorial complexity leads to solvability limit is in solving chess. Chess is not a solved game. In 2005 all chess game endings with six pieces or less were solved, showing the result of each position if played perfectly. It took ten more years to complete the tablebase with one more chess piece added, thus completing a 7-piece tablebase. Adding one more piece to a chess ending (thus making an 8-piece tablebase) is considered intractable due to the added combinatorial complexity.

Speeding up Brute-force Searches

One way to speed up a brute-force algorithm is to reduce the search space, that is, the set of candidate solutions, by using heuristics specific to the problem class. For example, in the eight queens problem the challenge is to place eight queens on a standard chessboard so that no queen attacks any other. Since each queen can be placed in any of the 64 squares, in principle there are 64^8 = 281,474,976,710,656 possibilities to consider. However, because the queens are all alike, and that no two queens can be placed on the same square, the candidates are all possible ways of choosing of a set of 8 squares from the set all 64 squares; which means 64 choose 8 = 64!/(56!*8!) = 4,426,165,368 candidate solutions – about 1/60,000 of the previous estimate. Further, no arrangement with two queens on the same row or the same column can be a solution. Therefore, we can further restrict the set of candidates to those arrangements.

As this example shows, a little bit of analysis will often lead to dramatic reductions in the number of candidate solutions, and may turn an intractable problem into a trivial one.

In some cases, the analysis may reduce the candidates to the set of all valid solutions; that is, it may yield an algorithm that directly enumerates all the desired solutions (or finds one solution, as appropriate), without wasting time with tests and the generation of invalid candidates. For example, for the problem "find all integers between 1 and 1,000,000 that are evenly divisible by 417" a naive brute-force solution would generate all integers in the range, testing each of them for divisibility. However, that problem can be solved much more efficiently by starting with 417 and repeatedly adding 417 until the number exceeds 1,000,000 – which takes only 2398 (= 1,000,000 ÷ 417) steps, and no tests.

Reordering the Search Space

In applications that require only one solution, rather than all solutions, the expected running time of a brute force search will often depend on the order in which the candidates are tested. As a general rule, one should test the most promising candidates first. For example, when searching for a proper divisor of a random number n, it is better to enumerate the candidate divisors in increasing order, from 2 to $n - 1$, than the other way around – because the probability that n is divisible by c is $1/c$. Moreover, the probability of a candidate being valid is often affected by the previous failed trials. For example, consider the problem of finding a 1 bit in a given 1000-bit string P. In this case, the candidate solutions are the indices 1 to 1000, and a candidate c is valid if $P[c] = 1$. Now, suppose that the first bit of P is equally likely to be 0 or 1, but each bit thereafter is equal to the previous one with 90% probability. If the candidates are enumerated in increasing order, 1 to 1000, the number t of candidates examined before success will be about 6, on the average. On the other hand, if the candidates are enumerated in the order 1,11,21,31...991,2,12,22,32 etc., the expected value of t will be only a little more than 2.More generally, the search space should be enumerated in such a way that the next candidate is most likely to be valid, *given that the previous trials were not*. So if the valid solutions are likely to be "clustered" in some sense, then each new candidate should be as far as possible from the previous ones, in that same sense. The converse holds, of course, if the solutions are likely to be spread out more uniformly than expected by chance.

Alternatives to Brute-force Search

There are many other search methods, or metaheuristics, which are designed to take advantage of various kinds of partial knowledge one may have about the solution. Heuristics can also be used to make an early cutoff of parts of the search. One example of this is the minimax principle for searching game trees, that eliminates many subtrees at an early stage in the search. In certain fields, such as language parsing, techniques such as chart parsing can exploit constraints in the problem to reduce an exponential complexity problem into a polynomial complexity problem. In many cases, such as in Constraint Satisfaction Problems, one can dramatically reduce the search space by means of Constraint propagation, that is efficiently implemented in Constraint programming languages. The search space for problems can also be reduced by replacing the full problem with a simplified version. For example, in computer chess, rather than computing the full minimax tree of all possible moves for the remainder of the game, a more limited tree of minimax possibilities is computed, with the tree being pruned at a certain number of moves, and the remainder of the tree being approximated by a static evaluation function.

In Cryptography

In cryptography, a *brute-force attack* involves systematically checking all possible keys until the correct key is found. This strategy can in theory be used against any encrypted data (except a one-time pad) by an attacker who is unable to take advantage of any weakness in an encryption system that would otherwise make his or her task easier.

The key length used in the encryption determines the practical feasibility of performing a brute force attack, with longer keys exponentially more difficult to crack than shorter ones. Brute force attacks can be made less effective by obfuscating the data to be encoded, something that makes it more difficult for an attacker to recognise when he has cracked the code. One of the measures of the strength of an encryption system is how long it would theoretically take an attacker to mount a successful brute force attack against it.

VALUE FUNCTION

The value function of an optimization problem gives the value attained by the objective function at a solution, while only depending on the parameters of the problem. In a controlled dynamical system, the value function represents the optimal payoff of the system over the interval *[t, T]* when started at the time-*t* state variable *x(t)=x*. If the objective function represents some cost that is to be minimized, the value function can be interpreted as the cost to finish the optimal program, and is thus referred to as "cost-to-go function." In an economic context, where the objective function usually represents utility, the value function is conceptually equivalent to the indirect utility function.

In a problem of optimal control, the value function is defined as the supremum of the objective function taken over the set of admissible controls. Given $(t_0, x_0) \in [0, t_1] \times \mathbb{R}^d$, a typical optimal control problem is:

$$\text{maximize} \quad J(t_0, x_0; u) = \int_{t_0}^{t_1} I(t, x(t), u(t)) dt + \phi(x(t_1))$$

subject to,

$$\frac{dx(t)}{dt} = f(t, x(t), u(t))$$

with initial state variable $x(t_0) = x_0$. The objective function $J(t_0, x_0; u)$ is to be maximized over all admissible controls $u \in U[t_0, t_1]$, where u is a Lebesgue measurable function from $[t_0, t_1]$ to some prescribed arbitrary set in $\mathbb{R}^m$. The value function is then defined as

$$V(t_0, x_0) = \sup_{u \in U} J(t_0, x_0; u)$$

If the optimal pair of control and state trajectories is (x^*, u^*), then $V(t_0, x_0) = J(t_0, x_0; u^*)$. In economics, the function $u^* = h(x)$ is called a policy function.

Bellman's principle of optimality roughly states that any optimal policy at time t, $t_0 \le t \le t_1$ taking the current state $x(t)$ as "new" initial condition must be optimal for the remaining problem. If the value function happens to be continuously differentiable, this gives rise to an important functional recurrence equation known as Hamilton–Jacobi–Bellman equation,

$$-\frac{\partial V(t, x)}{\partial t} = \max_u H\left(t, x, u, \frac{\partial V(t, x)}{\partial x}\right)$$

where the maximand on the right-hand side is the Hamiltonian, with $\partial V(t, x) / \partial x$ playing the role of the costate variables. The value function is a viscosity solution to the Hamilton–Jacobi–Bellman equation.

In an online closed-loop approximate optimal control, the value function is also a Lyapunov function that establishes global asymptotic stability of the closed-loop system.

MONTE CARLO METHOD

Monte Carlo methods, or Monte Carlo experiments, are a broad class of computational algorithms that rely on repeated random sampling to obtain numerical results. The underlying concept is to use randomness to solve problems that might be deterministic in principle. They are often used in physical and mathematical problems and are most useful when it is difficult or impossible to use other approaches. Monte Carlo methods are mainly used in three problem classes: optimization, numerical integration, and generating draws from a probability distribution.

In physics-related problems, Monte Carlo methods are useful for simulating systems with many coupled degrees of freedom, such as fluids, disordered materials, strongly coupled solids, and cellular structures. Other examples include modeling phenomena with significant uncertainty in inputs such as the calculation of risk in business and, in mathematics, evaluation of multidimensional definite integrals with complicated boundary conditions. In application to systems engineering problems (space, oil exploration, aircraft design, etc.), Monte Carlo–based predictions of failure, cost overruns and schedule overruns are routinely better than human intuition or alternative "soft" methods.

In principle, Monte Carlo methods can be used to solve any problem having a probabilistic interpretation. By the law of large numbers, integrals described by the expected value of some random variable can be approximated by taking the empirical mean (a.k.a. the sample mean) of independent samples of the variable. When the probability distribution of the variable is parametrized, mathematicians often use a Markov chain Monte Carlo (MCMC) sampler. The central idea is to design a judicious Markov chain model with a prescribed stationary probability distribution. That is, in the limit, the samples being generated by the MCMC method will be samples from the desired (target) distribution. By the ergodic theorem, the stationary distribution is approximated by the empirical measures of the random states of the MCMC sampler.

In other problems, the objective is generating draws from a sequence of probability distributions satisfying a nonlinear evolution equation. These flows of probability distributions can always be interpreted as the distributions of the random states of a Markov process whose transition probabilities depend on the distributions of the current random states. In other instances we are given a flow of probability distributions with an increasing level of sampling complexity (path spaces models with an increasing time horizon, Boltzmann–Gibbs measures associated with decreasing temperature parameters, and many others). These models can also be seen as the evolution of the law of the random states of a nonlinear Markov chain. A natural way to simulate these sophisticated nonlinear Markov processes is to sample multiple copies of the process, replacing in the evolution equation the unknown distributions of the random states by the sampled empirical measures. In contrast with traditional Monte Carlo and MCMC methodologies these mean field particle techniques rely on sequential interacting samples. The terminology *mean field* reflects the fact that each of the *samples* (a.k.a. particles, individuals, walkers, agents, creatures, or phenotypes) interacts with the empirical measures of the process. When the size of the system tends to infinity, these random empirical measures converge to the deterministic distribution of the random states of the nonlinear Markov chain, so that the statistical interaction between particles vanishes.

Monte Carlo method applied to approximating the value of π.

Monte Carlo methods vary, but tend to follow a particular pattern:

- Define a domain of possible inputs.

- Generate inputs randomly from a probability distribution over the domain.

- Perform a deterministic computation on the inputs.

- Aggregate the results.

For example, consider a quadrant (circular sector) inscribed in a unit square. Given that the ratio of their areas is $\pi/4$, the value of π can be approximated using a Monte Carlo method:

- Draw a square, then inscribe a quadrant within it.

- Uniformly scatter a given number of points over the square.

- Count the number of points inside the quadrant, i.e. having a distance from the origin of less than 1.

- The ratio of the inside-count and the total-sample-count is an estimate of the ratio of the two areas, $\pi/4$. Multiply the result by 4 to estimate π.

In this procedure the domain of inputs is the square that circumscribes the quadrant. We generate random inputs by scattering grains over the square then perform a computation on each input (test whether it falls within the quadrant). Aggregating the results yields our final result, the approximation of π.

There are two important considerations:

- If the points are not uniformly distributed, then the approximation will be poor.

- There are many points. The approximation is generally poor if only a few points are randomly placed in the whole square. On average, the approximation improves as more points are placed.

Uses of Monte Carlo methods require large amounts of random numbers, and it was their use that spurred the development of pseudorandom number generators, which were far quicker to use than the tables of random numbers that had been previously used for statistical sampling.

There is no consensus on how *Monte Carlo* should be defined. For example, Ripley defines most probabilistic modeling as *stochastic simulation*, with *Monte Carlo* being reserved for Monte Carlo integration and Monte Carlo statistical tests. Sawilowsky distinguishes between a simulation, a Monte Carlo method, and a Monte Carlo simulation: a simulation is a fictitious representation of reality, a Monte Carlo method is a technique that can be used to solve a mathematical or statistical problem, and a Monte Carlo simulation uses repeated sampling to obtain the statistical properties of some phenomenon (or behavior). Examples:

- Simulation: Drawing one pseudo-random uniform variable from the interval [0,1] can be used to simulate the tossing of a coin: If the value is less than or equal to 0.50 designate the outcome as heads, but if the value is greater than 0.50 designate the outcome as tails. This is a simulation, but not a Monte Carlo simulation.

- Monte Carlo method: Pouring out a box of coins on a table, and then computing the ratio of coins that land heads versus tails is a Monte Carlo method of determining the behavior of repeated coin tosses, but it is not a simulation.

- Monte Carlo simulation: Drawing a large number of pseudo-random uniform variables from the interval [0,1] at one time, or once at many different times, and assigning values less than or equal to 0.50 as heads and greater than 0.50 as tails, is a *Monte Carlo simulation* of the behavior of repeatedly tossing a coin.

Kalos and Whitlock point out that such distinctions are not always easy to maintain. For example, the emission of radiation from atoms is a natural stochastic process. It can be simulated directly, or its average behavior can be described by stochastic equations that can themselves be solved using Monte Carlo methods. "Indeed, the same computer code can be viewed simultaneously as a 'natural simulation' or as a solution of the equations by natural sampling."

Monte Carlo and Random Numbers

The main idea behind this method is that the results are computed based on repeated random sampling and statistical analysis. The Monte Carlo simulation is, in fact, random experimentations, in the case that, the results of these experiments are not well known. Monte Carlo simulations are typically characterized by many unknown parameters, many of which are difficult to obtain experimentally. Monte Carlo simulation methods do not always require truly random numbers to be useful (although, for some applications such as primality testing, unpredictability is vital). Many of the most useful techniques use deterministic, pseudorandom sequences, making it easy to test and re-run simulations. The only quality usually necessary to make good simulations is for the pseudo-random sequence to appear "random enough" in a certain sense.

What this means depends on the application, but typically they should pass a series of statistical tests. Testing that the numbers are uniformly distributed or follow another desired distribution when a large enough number of elements of the sequence are considered is one of the simplest and most common ones. Weak correlations between successive samples are also often desirable/ necessary.

Sawilowsky lists the characteristics of a high-quality Monte Carlo simulation:

- The (pseudo-random) number generator has certain characteristics (e.g. a long "period" before the sequence repeats).
- The (pseudo-random) number generator produces values that pass tests for randomness.
- There are enough samples to ensure accurate results.
- The proper sampling technique is used.
- The algorithm used is valid for what is being modeled.
- It simulates the phenomenon in question.

Pseudo-random number sampling algorithms are used to transform uniformly distributed pseudo-random numbers into numbers that are distributed according to a given probability distribution.

Low-discrepancy sequences are often used instead of random sampling from a space as they ensure even coverage and normally have a faster order of convergence than Monte Carlo simulations using random or pseudorandom sequences. Methods based on their use are called quasi-Monte Carlo methods.

In an effort to assess the impact of random number quality on Monte Carlo simulation outcomes, astrophysical researchers tested cryptographically-secure pseudorandom numbers generated via Intel's RDRAND instruction set, as compared to those derived from algorithms, like the Mersenne Twister, in Monte Carlo simulations of radio flares from brown dwarfs. RDRAND is the closest pseudorandom number generator to a true random number generator. No statistically significant difference was found between models generated with typical pseudorandom number generators and RDRAND for trials consisting of the generation of 10^7 random numbers.

Monte Carlo Simulation versus "what if" Scenarios

There are ways of using probabilities that are definitely not Monte Carlo simulations – for example, deterministic modeling using single-point estimates. Each uncertain variable within a model is assigned a "best guess" estimate. Scenarios (such as best, worst, or most likely case) for each input variable are chosen and the results recorded.

By contrast, Monte Carlo simulations sample from a probability distribution for each variable to produce hundreds or thousands of possible outcomes. The results are analyzed to get probabilities of different outcomes occurring. For example, a comparison of a spreadsheet cost construction model run using traditional "what if" scenarios, and then running the comparison again with Monte Carlo simulation and triangular probability distributions shows that the Monte Carlo analysis has a narrower range than the "what if" analysis. This is because the "what if" analysis gives equal weight to all scenarios, while the Monte Carlo method hardly samples in the very low probability regions. The samples in such regions are called "rare events".

Applications

Monte Carlo methods are especially useful for simulating phenomena with significant uncertainty in inputs and systems with many coupled degrees of freedom. Areas of application include:

Physical Sciences

Monte Carlo methods are very important in computational physics, physical chemistry, and related applied fields, and have diverse applications from complicated quantum chromodynamics calculations to designing heat shields and aerodynamic forms as well as in modeling radiation transport for radiation dosimetry calculations. In statistical physics Monte Carlo molecular modeling is an alternative to computational molecular dynamics, and Monte Carlo methods are used to compute statistical field theories of simple particle and polymer systems. Quantum Monte Carlo methods solve the many-body problem for quantum systems. In radiation materials science, the binary collision approximation for simulating ion implantation is usually based on a Monte Carlo approach to select the next colliding atom.

In experimental particle physics, Monte Carlo methods are used for designing detectors, understanding their behavior and comparing experimental data to theory. In astrophysics, they are used in such diverse manners as to model both galaxy evolution and microwave radiation transmission through a rough planetary surface. Monte Carlo methods are also used in the ensemble models that form the basis of modern weather forecasting.

Engineering

Monte Carlo methods are widely used in engineering for sensitivity analysis and quantitative probabilistic analysis in process design. The need arises from the interactive, co-linear and non-linear behavior of typical process simulations. For example,

- In microelectronics engineering, Monte Carlo methods are applied to analyze correlated and uncorrelated variations in analog and digital integrated circuits.

- In geostatistics and geometallurgy, Monte Carlo methods underpin the design of mineral processing flowsheets and contribute to quantitative risk analysis.

- In wind energy yield analysis, the predicted energy output of a wind farm during its lifetime is calculated giving different levels of uncertainty (P90, P50, etc.)

- impacts of pollution are simulated and diesel compared with petrol.

- In fluid dynamics, in particular rarefied gas dynamics, where the Boltzmann equation is solved for finite Knudsen number fluid flows using the direct simulation Monte Carlo method in combination with highly efficient computational algorithms.

- In autonomous robotics, Monte Carlo localization can determine the position of a robot. It is often applied to stochastic filters such as the Kalman filter or particle filter that forms the heart of the SLAM (simultaneous localization and mapping) algorithm.

- In telecommunications, when planning a wireless network, design must be proved to work for a wide variety of scenarios that depend mainly on the number of users, their locations and the services they want to use. Monte Carlo methods are typically used to generate these users and their states. The network performance is then evaluated and, if results are not satisfactory, the network design goes through an optimization process.

- In reliability engineering, Monte Carlo simulation is used to compute system-level response given the component-level response. For example, for a transportation network subject to an earthquake event, Monte Carlo simulation can be used to assess the k-terminal reliability of the network given the failure probability of its components, e.g. bridges, roadways, etc.

- In signal processing and Bayesian inference, particle filters and sequential Monte Carlo techniques are a class of mean field particle methods for sampling and computing the posterior distribution of a signal process given some noisy and partial observations using interacting empirical measures.

Climate Change and Radiative Forcing

The Intergovernmental Panel on Climate Change relies on Monte Carlo methods in probability density function analysis of radiative forcing.

Probability density function (PDF) of ERF due to total GHG, aerosol forcing and total anthropogenic forcing. The GHG consists of WMGHG, ozone and stratospheric water vapour. The combination of the individual RF agents to derive total forcing over the Industrial Era are done by Monte Carlo simulations and based on the method in Boucher and Haywood. PDF of the ERF from surface albedo changes and combined contrails and contrail-induced cirrus are included in the total anthropogenic forcing, but not shown as a separate PDF. We currently do not have ERF estimates for some forcing mechanisms: ozone, land use, solar, etc.

Computational Biology

Monte Carlo methods are used in various fields of computational biology, for example for Bayesian inference in phylogeny, or for studying biological systems such as genomes, proteins, or membranes. The systems can be studied in the coarse-grained or *ab initio* frameworks depending on the desired accuracy. Computer simulations allow us to monitor the local environment of a particular molecule to see if some chemical reaction is happening for instance.

In cases where it is not feasible to conduct a physical experiment, thought experiments can be conducted (for instance: breaking bonds, introducing impurities at specific sites, changing the local/global structure, or introducing external fields).

Computer Graphics

Path tracing, occasionally referred to as Monte Carlo ray tracing, renders a 3D scene by randomly tracing samples of possible light paths. Repeated sampling of any given pixel will eventually cause the average of the samples to converge on the correct solution of the rendering equation, making it one of the most physically accurate 3D graphics rendering methods in existence.

Applied Statistics

The standards for Monte Carlo experiments in statistics were set by Sawilowsky. In applied statistics, Monte Carlo methods may be used for at least four purposes:

- To compare competing statistics for small samples under realistic data conditions. Although type I error and power properties of statistics can be calculated for data drawn from classical theoretical distributions (*e.g.*, normal curve, Cauchy distribution) for asymptotic conditions (*i. e*, infinite sample size and infinitesimally small treatment effect), real data often do not have such distributions.

- To provide implementations of hypothesis tests that are more efficient than exact tests such as permutation tests (which are often impossible to compute) while being more accurate than critical values for asymptotic distributions.

- To provide a random sample from the posterior distribution in Bayesian inference. This sample then approximates and summarizes all the essential features of the posterior.

- To provide efficient random estimates of the Hessian matrix of the negative log-likelihood function that may be averaged to form an estimate of the Fisher information matrix.

Monte Carlo methods are also a compromise between approximate randomization and permutation tests. An approximate randomization test is based on a specified subset of all permutations (which entails potentially enormous housekeeping of which permutations have been considered). The Monte Carlo approach is based on a specified number of randomly drawn permutations (exchanging a minor loss in precision if a permutation is drawn twice—or more frequently—for the efficiency of not having to track which permutations have already been selected).

Artificial Intelligence for Games

Monte Carlo methods have been developed into a technique called Monte-Carlo tree search that is useful for searching for the best move in a game. Possible moves are organized in a search tree and many random simulations are used to estimate the long-term potential of each move. A black box simulator represents the opponent's moves.

The Monte Carlo tree search (MCTS) method has four steps:

- Starting at root node of the tree, select optimal child nodes until a leaf node is reached.

- Expand the leaf node and choose one of its children.

- Play a simulated game starting with that node.

- Use the results of that simulated game to update the node and its ancestors.

The net effect, over the course of many simulated games, is that the value of a node representing a move will go up or down, hopefully corresponding to whether or not that node represents a good move.

Monte Carlo Tree Search has been used successfully to play games such as Go, Tantrix, Battleship, Havannah, and Arimaa.

Design and Visuals

Monte Carlo methods are also efficient in solving coupled integral differential equations of radiation fields and energy transport, and thus these methods have been used in global illumination computations that produce photo-realistic images of virtual 3D models, with applications in video games, architecture, design, computer generated films, and cinematic special effects.

Search and Rescue

The US Coast Guard utilizes Monte Carlo methods within its computer modeling software SAROPS in order to calculate the probable locations of vessels during search and rescue operations. Each simulation can generate as many as ten thousand data points that are randomly distributed based upon provided variables. Search patterns are then generated based upon extrapolations of these data in order to optimize the probability of containment (POC) and the probability of detection (POD), which together will equal an overall probability of success (POS). Ultimately this serves as a practical application of probability distribution in order to provide the swiftest and most expedient method of rescue, saving both lives and resources.

Finance and Business

Monte Carlo simulation is commonly used to evaluate the risk and uncertainty that would affect the outcome of different decision options. Monte Carlo simulation allows the business risk analyst to incorporate the total effects of uncertainty in variables like sales volume, commodity and labour prices, interest and exchange rates, as well as the effect of distinct risk events like the cancellation of a contract or the change of a tax law.

Monte Carlo methods in finance are often used to evaluate investments in projects at a business unit or corporate level, or to evaluate financial derivatives. They can be used to model project schedules, where simulations aggregate estimates for worst-case, best-case, and most likely durations for each task to determine outcomes for the overall project. Monte Carlo methods are also used in option pricing, default risk analysis. Additionally, they can be used to estimate the financial impact of medical interventions.

Law

A Monte Carlo approach was used for evaluating the potential value of a proposed program to help female petitioners in Wisconsin be successful in their applications for harassment and domestic abuse restraining orders. It was proposed to help women succeed in their petitions by providing them with greater advocacy thereby potentially reducing the risk of rape and physical assault. However, there were many variables in play that could not be estimated perfectly, including the effectiveness of restraining orders, the success rate of petitioners both with and without advocacy, and many others. The study ran trials that varied these variables to come up with an overall estimate of the success level of the proposed program as a whole.

Use in Mathematics

In general, the Monte Carlo methods are used in mathematics to solve various problems by generating suitable random numbers and observing that fraction of the numbers that obeys some property or properties. The method is useful for obtaining numerical solutions to problems too complicated to solve analytically. The most common application of the Monte Carlo method is Monte Carlo integration.

Integration

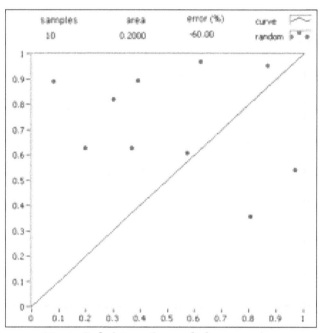

Monte-Carlo integration works by comparing random points with the value of the function.

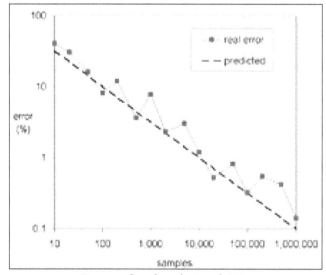

Errors reduce by a factor of $1/\sqrt{N}$.

Deterministic numerical integration algorithms work well in a small number of dimensions, but encounter two problems when the functions have many variables. First, the number of function evaluations needed increases rapidly with the number of dimensions. For example, if 10 evaluations provide adequate accuracy in one dimension, then 10^{100} points are needed for 100 dimensions—far too many to be computed. This is called the curse of dimensionality. Second, the boundary of a multidimensional region may be very complicated, so it may not be feasible to reduce the problem to an iterated integral. 100 dimensions is by no means unusual, since in many physical problems, a "dimension" is equivalent to a degree of freedom.

Monte Carlo methods provide a way out of this exponential increase in computation time. As long as the function in question is reasonably well-behaved, it can be estimated by randomly selecting points in 100-dimensional space, and taking some kind of average of the functions values at these points. By the central limit theorem, this method displays convergence—i.e., quadrupling the number of sampled points halves the error, regardless of the number of dimensions

A refinement of this method, known as importance sampling in statistics, involves sampling the points randomly, but more frequently where the integrand is large. To do this precisely one would have to already know the integral, but one can approximate the integral by an integral of a similar function or use adaptive routines such as stratified sampling, recursive stratified sampling, adaptive umbrella sampling or the VEGAS algorithm.

A similar approach, the quasi-Monte Carlo method, uses low-discrepancy sequences. These sequences "fill" the area better and sample the most important points more frequently, so quasi-Monte Carlo methods can often converge on the integral more quickly.

Another class of methods for sampling points in a volume is to simulate random walks over it (Markov chain Monte Carlo). Such methods include the Metropolis–Hastings algorithm, Gibbs sampling, Wang and Landau algorithm, and interacting type MCMC methodologies such as the sequential Monte Carlo samplers.

Simulation and Optimization

Another powerful and very popular application for random numbers in numerical simulation is in numerical optimization. The problem is to minimize (or maximize) functions of some vector that often has many dimensions. Many problems can be phrased in this way: for example, a computer chess program could be seen as trying to find the set of, say, 10 moves that produces the best evaluation function at the end. In the traveling salesman problem the goal is to minimize distance traveled. There are also applications to engineering design, such as multidisciplinary design optimization. It has been applied with quasi-one-dimensional models to solve particle dynamics problems by efficiently exploring large configuration space. Reference is a comprehensive review of many issues related to simulation and optimization.

The traveling salesman problem is what is called a conventional optimization problem. That is, all the facts (distances between each destination point) needed to determine the optimal path to follow are known with certainty and the goal is to run through the possible travel choices to come up with the one with the lowest total distance. However, let's assume that instead of wanting to minimize the total distance traveled to visit each desired destination, we wanted to minimize the total time needed to reach each destination. This goes beyond conventional optimization since travel time is inherently uncertain (traffic jams, time of day, etc.). As a result, to determine our optimal path we would want to use simulation - optimization to first understand the range of potential times it could take to go from one point to another (represented by a probability distribution in this case rather than a specific distance) and then optimize our travel decisions to identify the best path to follow taking that uncertainty into account.

Inverse Problems

Probabilistic formulation of inverse problems leads to the definition of a probability distribution in the model space. This probability distribution combines prior information with new information obtained by measuring some observable parameters (data). As, in the general case, the theory linking data with model parameters is nonlinear, the posterior probability in the model space may not be easy to describe (it may be multimodal, some moments may not be defined, etc.).

When analyzing an inverse problem, obtaining a maximum likelihood model is usually not sufficient, as we normally also wish to have information on the resolution power of the data. In the general case we may have many model parameters, and an inspection of the marginal probability densities of interest may be impractical, or even useless. But it is possible to pseudorandomly generate a large collection of models according to the posterior probability distribution and to analyze and display the models in such a way that information on the relative likelihoods of model properties is conveyed to the spectator. This can be accomplished by means of an efficient Monte Carlo method, even in cases where no explicit formula for the *a priori* distribution is available.

The best-known importance sampling method, the Metropolis algorithm, can be generalized, and this gives a method that allows analysis of (possibly highly nonlinear) inverse problems with complex *a priori* information and data with an arbitrary noise distribution.

TEMPORAL DIFFERENCE LEARNING

Temporal difference (TD) learning is an approach to learning how to predict a quantity that depends on future values of a given signal. The name TD derives from its use of changes, or differences, in predictions over successive time steps to drive the learning process. The prediction at any given time step is updated to bring it closer to the prediction of the same quantity at the next time step. It is a supervised learning process in which the training signal for a prediction is a future prediction. TD algorithms are often used in reinforcement learning to predict a measure of the total amount of reward expected over the future, but they can be used to predict other quantities as well. Continuous-time TD algorithms have also been developed.

Suppose a system receives as input a time sequence of vectors (x_t, y_t), $t = 0, 1, 2, \ldots$, where each x_t is an arbitrary signal and y_t is a real number. TD learning applies to the problem of producing at each discrete time step t, an estimate, or prediction, p_t, of the following quantity:

$$Y_t = y_{t+1} + \gamma y_{t+2} + \gamma^2 y_{t+3} + \cdots = \sum_{i=1}^{\infty} \gamma^{i-1} y_{t+i},$$

where $\bar{a}$ is a discount factor, with $0 \leq \gamma < 1$. Each estimate is a prediction because it involves future values of y. The signal x_t is the information available to the system at time t to enable it to make the prediction p_t. In other words, p_t is a function of x_t, and we can write $p_t = P(x_t)$, where P is a prediction function. The discount factor determines how strongly future values of y influence current predictions. When $\gamma = 0, p_t$ predicts just the next value of y, that is, y_{t+1}. As $\bar{a}$ increases toward one, values of y in the more distant future become more significant. The problem, then, is to select a function p so that $p_t = P(x_t) \approx Y_t$ as closely as possible for $t = 0,1,2,\ldots$. This is the infinite-horizon discounted prediction problem. TD algorithms apply to other prediction.

It is not always possible to find a prediction function that does a good job of solving this problem. If there are no regularities in the relationship between signals x_t and future values of y, then the best predictions will be no better than random guessing. However, if there are regularities in this relationship, then predictions may be possible that are more accurate than chance. The usual way to model possible regularities is to assume that the signals x_t are derived from the states of a Markov chain, on which the numbers y also functionally depend. Depending on how the x_t represent the Markov chain's states (e.g., do these signals unambiguously identify states, or are some states unobservable), a prediction function may exist that accurately gives the expected value of the quantity Y_t for each t.

The Simplest TD Algorithm

A good way to explain TD learning is to start with a simple case and then extend it to the full algorithm. Consider first the problem of making a one-step-ahead prediction, i.e., the above problem with $\gamma = 0$, meaning that one wants $P_t = y_{t+1}$ for each t. Incremental error-correction supervised learning can be used to update the prediction function as inputs arrive. Letting P_t denote the prediction function at step t, the algorithm updates P_t to a new prediction function P_{t+1} at each step. To do this, it uses the error between the current prediction, p_t, and the prediction target (the quantity being predicted), y_{t+1}. This error can be obtained by computing p_t by applying the current prediction function, P_t, to x_t, waiting one time step while remembering p_t, then observing y_{t+1} to obtain the information required to compute the error $y_{t+1} - p_t = y_{t+1} - P_t(x_t)$.

The simplest example of a prediction function is one implemented as a lookup table. Suppose x_t can take only a finite number of values and that there is an entry in a lookup table to store a prediction for each of these values. At step t, the table entry for input x_t is $p_t = P_t(x_t)$. When y_{t+1} is observed, the table entry for x_t is changed from its current value of p_t to $p_t + \alpha(y_{t+1} - p_t) = (1-\alpha)p_t + \alpha y_{t+1}$, where α is a positive fraction that controls how quickly new data is incorporated into the table and old data forgotten. Only the table entry corresponding to x_t is changed from step t to step $t+1$, to produce the a table, P_{t+1}. The fraction α is called the learning rate or step-size parameter. Note that if $\alpha = 1$, the table entry is simply set to y_{t+1}, which is appropriate if the predictive relationship is deterministic. Using $\alpha < 1$, on the other hand, causes the table entries to approach the expected prediction targets when the predictive relationship is not deterministic.

To extend this approach to the full prediction problem with $\tilde{a} \neq 0$, the prediction target would be $Y_t = y_{t+1} + \gamma y_{t+2} + \gamma^2 y_{t+3} + \cdots$ instead of just y_{t+1}. The algorithm above would have to update the table entry for x_t by changing its value from p_t to $p_t + \alpha(Y_t - p_t) = (1-\alpha)p_t + \alpha T_t$. But to do this would require waiting for the arrival of all the future values of y instead of waiting for just the next value. This would prevent the approach from forming a useful learning rule. TD algorithms use the following observation to get around this problem. Notice that,

$$Y_t = y_{t+1} + \gamma y_{t+2} + \gamma^2 y_{t+3} + \cdots :$$
$$= y_{t+1} + \gamma \left[y_{t+2} + \gamma y_{t+3} + \gamma^2 y_{t+4} + \cdots \right] :$$
$$= y_{t+1} + \gamma Y_{t+1},$$

for $t = 0,1,2,\ldots$. Therefore, since $P_t(x_{t+1})$ is the estimate of Y_{t+1} available at step t (i.e., using the step-t table), one can estimate Y_t by the quantity $y_{t+1} + \gamma P_t(x_{t+1})$. That is, the current prediction function, $P_t,$ applied to the next input, x_{t+1}, multiplied by γ gives an estimate of the part of the prediction target that would otherwise require waiting forever (in this case) to obtain. The result in this lookup-table case is an algorithm that, upon receiving input (x_{t+1}, y_{t+1}), updates the table entry for x_t by changing its value from P_t to $p_t + \alpha[y_{t+1} + \gamma P_t(x_{t+1}) - p_t] = (1-\alpha)p_t + \alpha[y_{t+1} + \gamma P_t(x_{t+1})]$.

More concisely, define the following *temporal difference error* (or TD error):

$$\delta_{t+1} = y_{t+1} + \gamma P_t(x_{t+1}) - P_t(x_t).$$

Then the simplest TD algorithm updates a lookup-table as follows: for each $t = 0,1,2,\ldots$, upon observing (x_{t+1}, y_{t+1}):

$$P_{t+1}(x) = \begin{cases} P_t(x) + \alpha\delta_{t+1} & \text{if } x = x_t \\ P_t(x) & \text{otherwise,} \end{cases}$$

Where x denotes any possible input signal. Although the detailed behavior of this algorithm is complicated, an intuitive understanding is possible. The algorithm uses a prediction of a later quantity, $P_t(x_{t+1})$, to update a prediction of an earlier quantity, $P_t(x_t)$, where each prediction is computed via the same prediction function, P_t. This may seem like a futile process since neither prediction need be accurate, but in the course of the algorithm's operation, later predictions tend to become accurate sooner than earlier ones, so there tends to be an overall error reduction as learning proceeds. This depends on the learning system receiving an input sequence with sufficient regularity to make predicting possible. In formal treatments, the inputs x_t represent states of a Markov chain and the y values are given by a function of these states. This makes it possible to form accurate predictions of the expected values of the discounted sums Y_t.

Another view of the TD algorithm is that it operates to maintain a consistency condition that must be satisfied by correct predictions. Since $Y_t = y_{t+1} + \gamma Y_{t+1}$, for $t = 0,1,\ldots$ (Equation (1), the following relationship should hold between successive predictions:

$$P(x_t) = y_{t+1} + \gamma P(x_{t+1})$$

Or $t = 0,1,2,\ldots$. One can show, in fact, that within an appropriate mathematical framework any function that satisfies this condition for all t must actually give the correct predictions. TD algorithms adjust the prediction function with the goal of making its values always satisfy this condition. The TD error indicates how far the current prediction function deviates from this condition for the current input, and the algorithm acts to reduce this error. This view of TD learning is connected to the theory of Markov decision processes, where the prediction function corresponds to a value function and the update process is closely related to dynamic programming methods. Most of the theoretical results about TD learning derive from these connections.

TD with Function Approximation

Beyond lookup tables, TD learning can update prediction functions represented in a variety of ways. Consider, for example, the case in which each prediction is a linear function of the input signals, where each input signal x_t is now a vector of real numbers,

$$x_t = (x_t^1, x_t^2, \ldots, x_t^n).$$

Then the prediction function of step t applied to the signal at step t', where t' can be different from t, is defined by,

$$P_t(x_{t'}) = \sum_{i=1}^{n} v_t^i x_{t'}^i,$$

Where the $v_t^i, i = 1, \ldots, n,$ are the coefficients, or weights, of the linear prediction function of step t, and the $x_{t'}^i$ are components of the vector $x_{t'}$. Then TD learning adjusts the weights according to the following rule: for each $t = 0, 1, 2, \ldots$, upon observing (x_{t+1}, y_{t+1}):

$$v_{t+1}^i = v_t^i + \alpha[y_{t+1} + \gamma P_t(x_{t+1}) - P_t(x_t)]x_t^i :$$
$$= v_t^i + \alpha \delta_{t+1} x_t^i.$$

For $i = 1, \ldots, n$, where $\alpha > 0$ is a step-size parameter.

This learning rule adjusts each weight in a direction that tends to reduce the TD error. It is similar to the conventional Least Mean Square (LMS) or delta rule for supervised learning with the difference being the presence of $\gamma P_t(x_{t+1})$ in the error term. TD learning with linear function approximation is the best understood extension of the lookup-table version. It is widely used with input vectors consisting of the outputs of a possibly large number of sophisticated feature detectors, which is equivalent to employing representations involving sophisticated basis vectors. Note that lookup-tables correspond to linear function approximation using standard unit basis vectors (in which case Equation (3) reduces to Equation (2). TD learning with nonlinear function approximation is also possible. In general, any incremental function approximation, or regression, method can be adapted for use with TD learning. In all of these cases, it is important to recognize that TD learning does not entail specific assumptions about how stimuli are represented over time. There is a wide latitude in the alternatives that can be employed, and each has implications for the behavior of the algorithm.

Eligibility Traces

TD learning can often be accelerated by the addition of eligibility traces. When the lookup-table TD algorithm described above receives input (y_{t+1}, x_{t+1}), it updates the table entry only for the immediately preceding signal x_t. That is, it modifies only the immediately preceding prediction. But since y_{t+1} provides useful information for learning earlier predictions as well, one can extend TD learning so it updates a collection of many earlier predictions at each step. Eligibility traces do this by providing a short-term memory of many previous input signals so that each new observation can update the parameters related to these signals. Eligibility traces are usually implemented by an exponentially-decaying memory trace, with decay parameter λ. This generates a family of TD algorithms TD$(\lambda), 0 \leq \lambda \leq 1$, with TD(0) corresponding to updating only the immediately preceding prediction as described above, and TD(1) corresponding to equally updating all the preceding predictions. This also applies to non lookup-table versions of TD learning, where traces of the components of the input vectors are maintained. Eligibility traces do not have to be exponential-ly-decaying traces, but these are usually used since they are relatively easy to implement and to understand theoretically.

Action-conditional Prediction

Consider a setting in which the future values of inputs (x_t, y_t) are influenced by an agent's actions. The prediction at step t is often denoted $Q(x_t, a_t)$, where x_t is the input signal and at is the agent action at step t. The objective is to find a function that accurately predicts Y_t, the discounted sum of future values of y, on the basis of x_t and a_t. In the usual reinforcement learning setting of a Markov decision process, Y_t also depends on all the agent's actions taken after step t. Two differ-ent cases are considered for the actions taken after step t : (1) assume that after step t, the agent selects actions that generate the largest possible value of Y_t, or (2) assume that the agent follows a fixed rule, or policy, for selecting actions as a function of future inputs. In either case, the desired predictions are well-defined.

A TD learning process for case (1), known as Q-Learning, works as follows for a lookup-table rep-resentation. For each $t = 0,1,2,\dots$, upon generating action a_t and observing (x_{t+1}, y_{t+1}), the pre-diction function Q_t is updated to Q_{t+1} defined as follows:

$$Q_{t+1}(x,a) = \begin{cases} Q_t(x,a) + \alpha[y_{t+1} + \gamma \max_a Q_t(x_{t+1},a) - Q_t(x_t,a_t)] & \text{if } x = x_t \text{ and } a = a_t \\ Q_t(x,a) & \text{otherwise,} \end{cases}$$

Where x denotes any possible input signal and α denotes any of a finite number of possible ac-tions. For case (2), the update is the same except that $\max_a Q_t(x_{t+1}, \alpha)$ is replaced by $Q_t(x_{t+1}, a_{t+1})$, producing a TD learning rule called Sarsa (for state-action-reward-state-action). These learning rules can also be extended to allow function approximation.

Q-Learnng and Sarsa are useful in reinforcement learning where y_t is a reward signal. An agent selecting actions that maximize $Q(x,a)$ for each current $x|$ is fully exploiting the knowledge con-tained in Q in its attempt to maximize the measure of long-term reward, Y_t. Under appropriate conditions, both Q-Learning and Sarsa converge to prediction functions that allow an agent to make optimal action choices.

Other Prediction Problems and Update Rules

TD learning is not restricted to the infinite-horizon discounted problem. If the input sequence is divided up into finite-length episodes, and the predictions are not expected to extend beyond single episodes, then the discount factor γ can be set to one, resulting in the undiscounted case. TD algorithms also exist for problems requiring the prediction of the average value per-unit-time of the target variable. In reinforcement learning where the target variable is reward, this is called the average reward case. TD learning has also been generalized to TD Networks. Conventional TD learning is based on a consistency condition relating the prediction of a quantity to the prediction of the same quantity at a later time. TD Networks generalize this to conditions relating predictions of one quantity to a set of predictions of other quantities at a later time. More sophisticated update methods have been studied that use the basic TD idea but that often have better performance. Examples include least squares TD, an adaptation of a conventional recursive least squares regression method, and Gaussian Process TD, an adaptation of Gaussian Process methods.

Psychology and Neuroscience

Theories of animal learning as studied by psychologists were a major influence on the development of TD learning. In particular, TD learning can be viewed as an extension of the Rescorla-Wagner model of Pavlovian conditioning in which the timing of stimuli within learning trials plays a significant role in how associative strengths change. A slightly modified version of the TD algorithm given above accounts for a range of phenomena observed in Pavlovian conditioning experiments. Of particular significance is the ability of the algorithm to produce an analog of secondary reinforcement when used as a component of a reinforcement learning system. Predictions of future reward formed by TD learning can be treated as rewarding themselves, thereby acting as secondary reinforcers. This is most clearly demonstrated in reinforcement learning systems that use the TD error δ as a reward signal. TD learning is also related to the neuroscience of reward learning through the similarity of the behavior of δ in analogs of conditioning experiments and the behavior of midbrain dopamine neurons in the brain. This observation has stimulated both neuroscientific and computational research based on the computational theory of TD learning in efforts to improve understanding of the brain's dopamine system and its role in reward-related behavior and drug addiction.

TD Methods

TD methods bootstrap and sample:

- Bootstrapping: update uses an estimate of the successor state.
  - MC does not bootstrap.
  - DP bootstraps.
  - TD bootstraps.
- Sampling: update looks ahead for a sample successor state.
  - MC samples.
  - DP does not sample.
  - TD samples.

Example: Driving Home.

State	Elapsed Time (minutes)	Predicted Time to Go	Predicted Total Time
Leaving office	0	30	30
Reach car, raining	5	35	40
Exit highway	20	15	35
Behind truck	30	10	40
Home street	40	3	43
Arrive home	43	0	43

- The "rewards" are the elapsed times on each leg of the journey.

- We are not discounting (y=1), and thus the return for each state is the actual time to go from that state.

- The value of each state is the expected time to go.

Driving Home

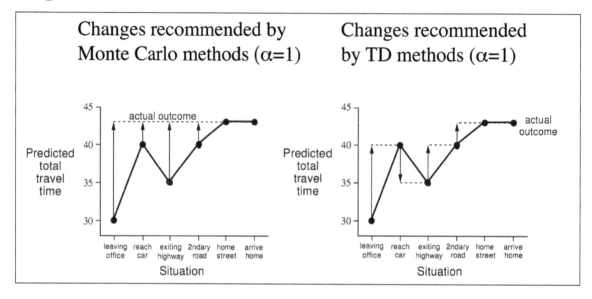

$$V(s_t) \leftarrow V(s_t) + \alpha \left[R_t - V(s_t) \right]$$

$$V(s_t) \leftarrow V(s_t) + \alpha \left[r_{t+1} + \gamma V(s_{t+1}) - V(s_t) \right]$$

MC must wait with the update until the final outcome.

Advantages of TD Prediction Methods

- TD methods do not require a model of the environment, only experience.

- TD, but not MC, methods can be fully incremental.

  ○ You can learn before knowing the final outcome.

    ▪ Less memory.

    ▪ Less peak computation.

  ○ You can learn without the final outcome.

    ▪ From incomplete sequences.

- Both MC and TD converge (under certain assumptions to be detailed later), but which is faster?

Random Walk Example

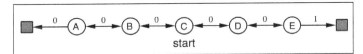

- All episodes start in the center state C.

- Proceed either left or right by one state on each step, with equal probability.

- Episodes terminate either on the extreme left or the extreme right.

- When an episode terminates on the right a reward of 1 occurs; all other rewards are zero.

- Because this task is undiscounted and episodic, the true value of each state is the probability of terminating on the right if starting from that state.

- The true values of all the states, A through E, are 1/6, 2/6, 3/6, 4/6, 5/6.

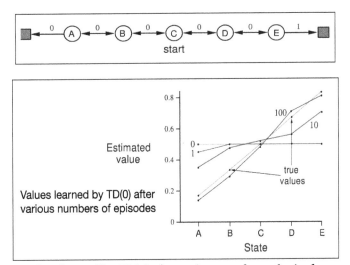

Values learned by TD(0) after various numbers of episodes.

TD and MC on the Random Walk

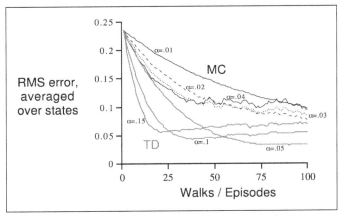

Data averaged over 100 sequences of episodes.

Optimality of TD(0)

Batch Updating: Train completely on a finite amount of data, e.g., train repeatedly on 10 episodes until convergence.

Compute updates according to TD(0), but only update estimates after each complete pass through the data.

For any finite Markov prediction task, under batch updating, TD(0) converges for sufficiently small α.

Constant-α MC also converges under these conditions, but to a difference answer.

Random Walk under Batch Updating

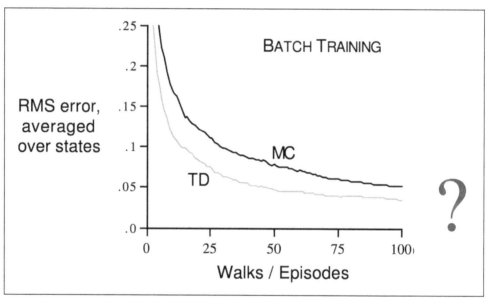

After each new episode, all previous episodes were treated as a batch, and algorithm was trained until convergence. All repeated 100 times.

TD vs. MC

You are the predictor:

Table: Suppose you observe the following 8 episodes:

A, 0, B, 0	
B, 1 B, 1 B, 1 B, 1	This means that the first episode started in state A, transitioned to B with a reward of 0, and then terminated from B with a reward of 0.
B, 1 B, 1 B, 1 B, 0	The other seven episodes were even shorter, starting from B and terminating immediately.
	What is the optimal value for the estimate V(A) given this data?

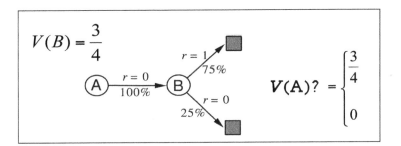

- The prediction that best matches the training data is V(A)=0.

  ◦ This minimizes the mean-square-error on the training set.

  ◦ This is what a batch Monte Carlo method gets.

- If we consider the sequentiality of the problem, then we would set V(A)=.75.

  ◦ This is correct for the maximum likelihood estimate of a Markov model generating the data.

  ◦ This is called the certainty-equivalence estimate, because it is equivalent to assuming that the estimate of the underlying process was known with certainty rather than being approximated.

  ◦ This is what TD(0) gets.

Sarsa: On-policy TD Control

Sarsa: Learning an action-value function.

Estimate Q^{π} for the current behavior policy π.

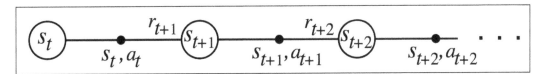

After every transition from a nonterminal state S_t, do:

$$Q(s_t,a_t) \leftarrow Q(s_t,a_t) + \alpha\left[r_{t+1} + \gamma Q(s_{t+1},a_{t+1}) - Q(s_t,a_t)\right]$$

If S_{t+1} is terminal, then $Q(s_{t+1},a_{t+1}) = 0$.

Turn this into a control method by always updating the policy to be greedy with respect to the current estimate:

Initialize $Q(s,a)$ arbitrarily
Repeat (for each episode):
    Initialize s
    Choose a from s using policy derived from Q (e.g., ε − greedy)

Repeat (for each step of episode) :

  Take action a, observe r, s'

  Choose a' from s' using policy derived from Q (e.g., ε – greedy)

  $Q(s,a) \leftarrow Q(s,a) + \alpha\left[r + \gamma Q(s',a') - Q(s,a)\right]$

  $s \leftarrow s'; a' \leftarrow a';$

  until s is terminal

$\left(s_t, a_t, r_{t+1}, s_{t+1}, a_{t+1}\right)$ Quintupal

Move from S to G, but consider the crosswind that moves you upward. For example, if you are one cell to the right of the goal, then the action left takes you to the cell just above the goal.

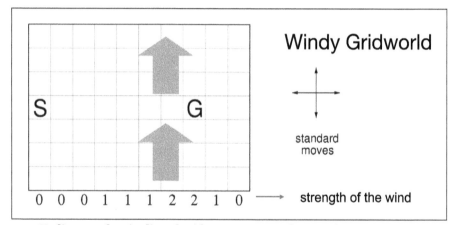

Undiscounted, episodic task with constant rewards reward = −1 until goal.

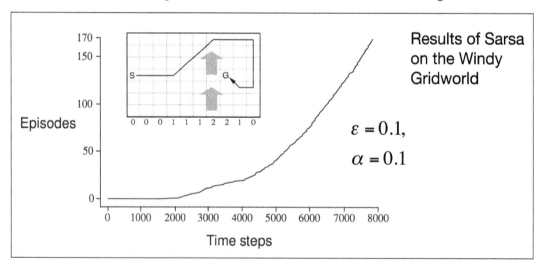

No, since termination is not guaranteed for all policies.

And Sarsa?

Step-by-step learning methods (e.g. Sarsa) do not have this problem. They quickly learn during the episode that such policies are poor, and switch to something else.

Q-learning: Off-policy TD Control

One -step Q - learning:

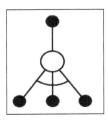

$$Q(s_t,a_t) \leftarrow Q(s_t,a_t) + \alpha \left[r_{t+1} + \gamma \max_a Q(s_{t+1},a) - Q(s_t,a_t) \right]$$

Initialize $Q(s,a)$ arbitrarily
Repeat(for each episode):
   Initialize s
   Repeat(for each step of episode):
      Choose a from s using policy derived from Q(e.g.,ε – greedy)
      Take action a, observe r,s'
      $Q(s,a) \leftarrow Q(s,a) + \alpha \left[r + \gamma \max_{a'} Q(s',a') - Q(s,a) \right]$
      $s \leftarrow s'$;
   until s is terminal

Example:

d	e	f
a	b	c

$\alpha = 0.9 \quad \gamma = 1$
Initialize $\quad Q(s,a) = 0$

d	e	f
a	b	c

$c \rightarrow f$
$Q(c,\uparrow) \leftarrow 0 + 0.9[100 + 0 - 0] = 90$

d	e	f
a	b	c

$e \rightarrow f$
$Q(e,\rightarrow) \leftarrow 0 + 0.9[100 + 0 - 0] = 90$

Example:

d	e	f
a	b	c

$b \rightarrow c$

$$Q(b,\rightarrow) \leftarrow 0 + 0.9[0 + 90 - 0] = 81$$

d	e	f
a	b	c

$b \rightarrow e$

$$Q(b,\uparrow) \leftarrow 0 + 0.9[0 + 90 - 0] = 81$$

d	e	f
a	b	c

$a \rightarrow b$

$$Q(a,\rightarrow) \leftarrow 0 + 0.9[0 + 81 - 0] \approx 73$$

Example:

d	e	f
a	b	c

$b \rightarrow a$

$$Q(b,\leftarrow) \leftarrow 0 + 0.9[0 + 73 - 0] \approx 66$$

d	e	f
a	b	c

Example:

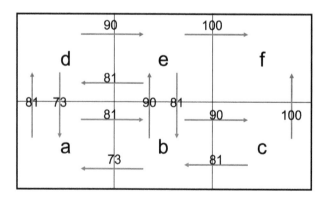

$$\gamma = 0.9$$

Cliffwalking

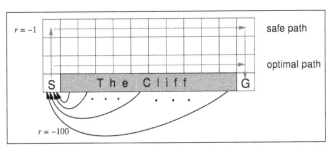

Reward is on all transitions -1 except those into the the region marked "The Cliff."

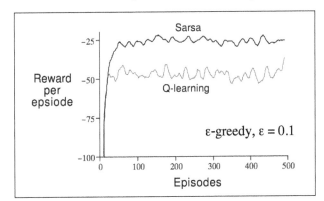

- Q-learning learns quickly values for the optimal policy, that which travels right along the edge of the cliff. Unfortunately, this results in its occasionally falling off the cliff because of the "-greedy action selection.

- Sarsa takes the action selection into account and learns the longer but safer path through the upper part of the grid.

- If ε were gradually reduced, then both methods would asymptotically converge to the optimal policy.

Actor-critic Methods

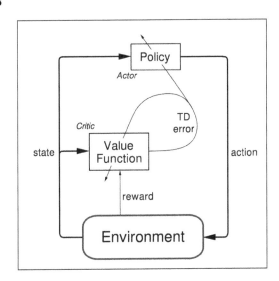

- Explicit representation of policy as well as value function.
- Critic drives all learning.
- On policy method.
- Appealing as psychological and neural models.

Actor-critic Details

Typically, the critic is a state-value function. After each action selection, the critic evaluates the new state to determine whether things have gone better or worse than expected. That evaluation is the TD error:

$$\delta_t = r_{t+1} + \gamma V\left(s_{t+1}\right) - V\left(s_t\right)$$

Let's assume actions are determined by preferences, $p(s,a)$, as follows:

$$\pi_t\left(s,a\right) = \Pr\left\{a_t = a \mid s_t = s\right\} = \frac{e^{p(s,a)}}{\sum_b e^{p(s,b)}},$$

Then strengthening or weakening the preferences, $p(s,a)$, depends on the TD error (β – step size parameter):

$$p\left(s_t,a_t\right) \leftarrow p\left(s_t,a_t\right) + \beta\delta_t$$

Advantages:

- Minimal computation to select actions, since it does not have to search through the action space – particularly important for large action spaces.
- Can learn an explicit stochastic policy.

R-learning for Undiscounted Continuing Tasks

- Off-policy control method.
- No discounts.
- No division of experience into distinct episodes with finite returns.
- One seeks to obtain the maximum reward per time step.

Average expected reward per time step under policy π :

$$\rho^\pi = \lim_{n \to \infty} \frac{1}{n} \sum_{t=1}^{n} E_\pi\left\{r_t\right\}$$

- The same for each state if ergodic.
- Nonzero probability of reaching any state from any other under any policy.

From any state, in the long run the average reward is the same, but there is a transient. From some states better-than-average rewards are received for a while, and from others worse-than-average rewards are received. It is this transient that defines the value of a state:

$$\tilde{V}^{\pi}(s) = \sum_{k=1}^{\infty} E_{\pi}\left\{r_{t=k} - \rho^{\pi} \middle| s_t = s\right\}$$

Value of the state action pair:

$$\tilde{Q}^{\pi}(s,a) = \sum_{k=1}^{\infty} E_{\pi}\left\{r_{t=k} - \rho^{\pi} \middle| s_t = s, a_t = a\right\}$$

relative values because they are relative to the average reward under the current policy.

R-learning

- Other than its use of relative values, R-learning is a standard TD method using off-policy Generalized Policy Iteration (GPI), much like Q-learning.

It maintains:

- A behavior policy to generate experience, e.g. ε-greedy policy

- Estimation policy, involved in GPI

- Action value function

- Estimated average reward

    Initialize ρ and $Q(s,a)$, for all s,a, arbitrarily
    Repeat forever :
        $s \leftarrow$ current state
        Choose action a in s using behavior policy $(e.g., \varepsilon - greedy)$
        Take action a, observe r,s'
        $Q(s,a) \leftarrow Q(s,a) + \alpha\left[r - \rho + \max_{a'} Q(s',a') - Q(s,a)\right]$
        If $Q(s,a) = \max_a Q(s,a)$, then :
            $\rho \leftarrow \rho + \beta\left[r + \rho + \max_{a'} Q(s',a') - \max_a Q(s,a)\right]$

Access-control Queuing Task

- n servers.

- Customers have four different priorities, which pay reward of 1, 2, 4, or 8, if served.

- At each time step, customer at head of queue is accepted (assigned to a server) or removed from the queue.

- Proportion of randomly distributed high priority customers in queue is h.

- Busy server becomes free with probability p on each time step.

- Statistics of arrivals and departures are unknown.

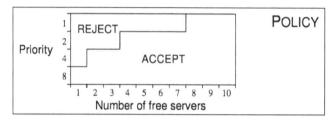

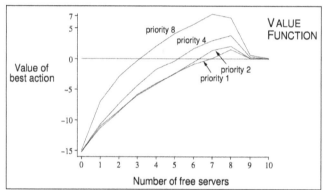

Apply R- learning

$$n = 10, h = 5, p = .06$$

References

- 5-things-reinforcement-learning: kdnuggets.com, Retrieved 28 April, 2019

- Kroese, D. P.; Brereton, T.; Taimre, T.; Botev, Z. I. (2014). "Why the Monte Carlo method is so important to-day". WIREs Comput Stat. 6 (6): 386–392. doi:10.1002/wics.1314

- Kamalapurkar, Rushikesh; Walters, Patrick; Rosenfeld, Joel; Dixon, Warren (2018). "Optimal Control and Lyapunov Stability". Reinforcement Learning for Optimal Feedback Control: A Lyapunov-Based Approach. Berlin: Springer. pp. 26–27. ISBN 978-3-319-78383-3

- Temporal-difference-learning: scholarpedia.org, Retrieved 17 May, 2019

Applications

There are a wide range of applications of machine learning which include price optimization and dynamic pricing, heart disease diagnosis, diabetes and liver disease prediction, robotic surgery, cancer detection, drug discovery, etc. All these applications of machine learning have been carefully analyzed in this chapter.

MACHINE LEARNING IN IMAGE RECOGNITION

When it comes to identifying images, we humans can clearly recognize and distinguish different features of objects. This is because our brains have been trained unconsciously with the same set of images that has resulted in the development of capabilities to differentiate between things effortlessly.

We are hardly conscious when we interpret the real world. Encountering different entities of the visual world and distinguishing with ease is a no challenge to us. Our subconscious mind carries out all the processes without any hassle.

Contrary to human brains, computer views visuals as an array of numerical values and looks for patterns in the digital image, be it a still, video, graphic, or even live, to recognize and distinguish key features of the image.

The manner in which a system interprets an image is completely different from humans. Computer vision uses image processing algorithms to analyze and understand visuals from a single image or a sequence of images. An example of computer vision is identifying pedestrians and vehicles on the road by, categorizing and filtering millions of user-uploaded pictures with accuracy.

A digital image represents a matrix of numerical values. These values represent the data associated with the pixel of the image. The intensity of the different pixels, averages to a single value, representing itself in a matrix format.

The information fed to the recognition systems is the intensities and the location of different pixels in the image. With the help of this information, the systems learn to map out a relationship or pattern in the subsequent images supplied to it as a part of the learning process.

After the completion of the training process, the system performance on test data is validated.

In order to improve the accuracy of the system to recognize images, intermittent weights to the neural networks are modified to improve the accuracy of the systems.

Some of the algorithms used in image recognition (Object Recognition, Face Recognition) are SIFT (Scale-invariant Feature Transform), SURF (Speeded Up Robust Features), PCA (Principal Component Analysis), and LDA (Linear Discriminant Analysis).

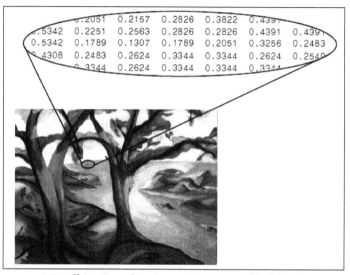

A Small Section of An Image Represented In Matrix
Format Note Values Of The Pixel Average To A Single Value.

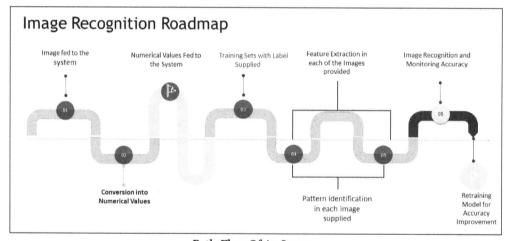

Path-Flow Of An Image.

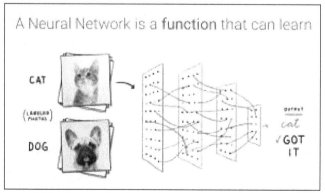

Output Of An Image: Cat. Input Image – Formulation Of Values –
Identification Of Pattern – Training Of The Images- Test Data Validation.

Challenges of Image Recognition

Viewpoint Variation: In a real world, the entities within the image are aligned in different directions and when such images are fed to the system, the system predicts inaccurate values. In short, the system fails to understand that changing the alignment of the image (left, right, bottom, top) will not make it different and that is why it creates challenges in image recognition.

Scale Variation: Variations in size affect the classification of the object. The closer you view the object the bigger it looks in size and vice-versa.

Deformation: Objects do not change even if they are deformed. The system learns from the perfect image and forms a perception that a particular object can be in specific shape only. We know that in the real world, shape changes and as a result, there are inaccuracies when the system encounters a deformed image of an object.

Inter-class Variation: Certain object varies within the class. They can be of different shape, size, but still represents the same class. For example, buttons, chairs, bottles, bags come in different sizes and appearances.

Occlusion: Certain objects obstruct the full view of an image and result in incomplete information being fed to the system. It is necessary to devise an algorithm that is sensitive to these variations and consist of a wide range of samples of the data.

To train the neural network models, the training set should have varieties pertaining to single class and multiple class. The varieties available in the training set ensure that the model predicts accurately when tested on test data. However, since most of the samples are in random order, ensuring whether there is enough data requires manual work, which is tedious.

Limitations of Regular Neural Networks for Image Recognition

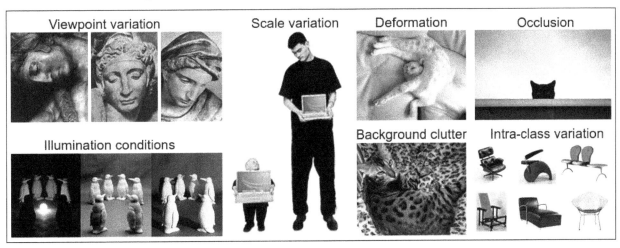

- The huge availability of data makes it difficult to process it due to the limited hardware availability.

- Difficulty in interpreting the model since the vague nature of the models prohibits its application in a number of areas.

• Development takes longer time and hence, the flexibility is compromised with the development time. Although the availability of libraries like Keras makes the development simple, it lacks flexibility in its usage. Also, the Tensorflow provides more control, but it is complicated in nature and requires more time in development.

Role of Convolutional Neural Networks in Image Recognition

Convolutional Neural Networks play a crucial role in solving the problems stated above. Its basic principles have taken the inspiration from our visual cortex.

CNN incorporates changes in its mode of operations. The inputs of CNN are not fed with the complete numerical values of the image. Instead, the complete image is divided into a number of small sets with each set itself acting as an image. A small size of filter divides the complete image into small sections. Each set of neurons is connected to a small section of the image.

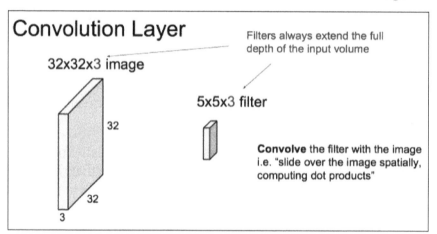

Filter Of Size 5*5*3 Dividing The Image.

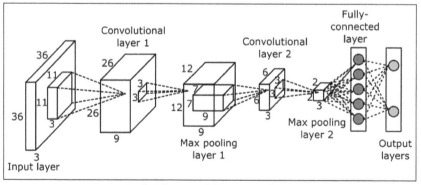

Path Of CNN With Max Pooling.

These images are then treated similar to the regular neural network process. The computer collects patterns with respect to the image and the results are saved in the matrix format.

This process repeats until the complete image in bits size is shared with the system. The result is a large Matrix, representing different patterns the system has captured from the input image.

This Matrix is again downsampled (reduced in size) with a method known as Max-Pooling. It extracts maximum values from each sub-matrix and results in a matrix of much smaller size.

These values are representative of the pattern in the image. This matrix formed is supplied to the neural networks as the input and the output determines the probability of the classes in an image.

During its training phase, the different levels of features are identified and labeled as low level, mid-level, and high level. The low-level features include color, lines, and contrast. Mid-level features identify edges and corners, whereas the high-level features identify the class and specific forms or sections.

Thus, CNN reduces the computation power requirement and allows treatment of large size images. It is sensitive to variations of an image, which can provide results with higher accuracy than regular neural networks.

MACHINE LEARNING IN PHARMA AND MEDICINE

Heart Disease Diagnosis

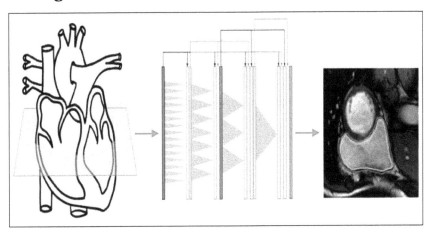

The heart is one of the principal organs of our body. We often suffer a variety of heart diseases like Coronary Artery Disease (CAD), Coronary Heart Disease (CHD), and so forth. Many researchers are working on machine learning algorithms for heart disease diagnosis. It is a very hot research issue all over the world. An automated heart disease diagnosis system is one of the most remarkable benefits of machine learning in healthcare.

Researchers are working several supervised machine learning algorithms like Support Vector Machine (SVM) or Naive Bayes to use as a learning algorithm for heart disease detection.

The Heart disease dataset from UCI can be used as a training or testing dataset or both. The WEKA data mining tool can be used for data analysis. Alternatively, if you want, you can use an Artificial Neural Network (ANN) approach to develop the heart disease diagnosis system.

Predicting Diabetes

Diabetes is one of the common and dangerous diseases. Also, this disease is one of the leading causes to create any other severe illness and towards death. This disease can damage our various body parts like kidney, heart, and nerves. The objective of using a machine learning approach in this field is to detect diabetes at an early stage and save patients.

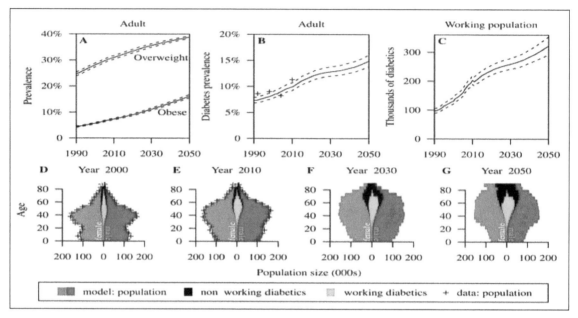

As a classification algorithm, Random forest, KNN, Decision Tree, or Naive Bayes can be used to develop the diabetes prediction system. Among these, Naive Bayes outperforms the other algorithms in terms of accuracy. Because its performance is excellent and takes less computation time. You can download the diabetes dataset from here. It contains 768 data points with nine features each.

Prediction of Liver Disease

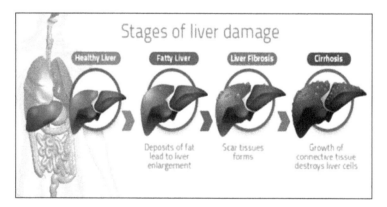

The liver is the second most significant internal organ in our body. It plays a vital role in metabolism. One can attack several liver diseases like Cirrhosis, Chronic Hepatitis, Liver Cancer, and so on.

Recently, machine learning and data mining concepts have been used dramatically to predict liver disease. It is very much challenging task to predict disease using voluminous medical data. However, researchers are trying their best to overcome such issues using machine learning concepts like classification, clustering, and many more.

Robotic Surgery

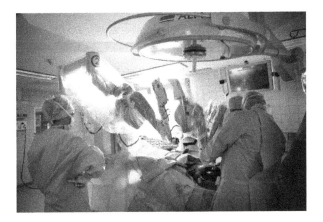

Robotic surgery is one of the benchmark machine learning applications in healthcare. This application will become a promising area soon. This application can be divided into four subcategories such as automatic suturing, surgical skill evaluation, improvement of robotic surgical materials, and surgical workflow modeling.

Suturing is the process of sewing up an open wound. Automation of suturing may reduce the surgical procedure length and surgeon fatigue. As an instance, The Raven Surgical Robot. Researchers are trying to apply a machine learning approach to evaluate surgeon performance in robot-assisted minimally invasive surgery.

As, in the case of neurosurgery, robots are not able to operate effectively. The manual surgical workflow is time-consuming, and it can not provide automatic feedback. Using a machine learning approach, it can speed up the system.

Cancer Detection and Prediction

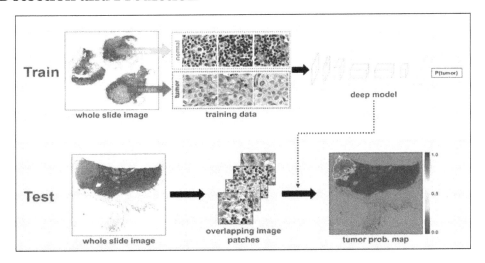

At present, machine learning approaches are being used to detect and classify tumors extensively. Also, deep learning plays a significant role in cancer detection. As deep learning is accessible and data sources are available. A study showed that deep learning reduces the percentage of error for breast cancer diagnosis.

Machine learning has proven its capabilities to detect cancer successfully. China researchers explored DeepGene: a cancer type classifier using deep learning and somatic point mutations. Using a deep learning approach, cancer can also be detected by extracting features from gene expression data. Moreover, the Convolution Neural Network (CNN) is being applied in cancer classification.

Personalized Treatment

Machine learning for personalized treatment is a hot research issue. The goal of this area is to provide better service based on individual health data with predictive analysis. Machine learning computational and statistical tools are used to develop a personalized treatment system based on patients' symptoms and genetic information.

To develop the personalized treatment system, a supervised machine learning algorithm is used. This system is developed using patient medical information. SkinVision app is the example of personalized treatment. By using this app, one can check his/her skin for skin cancer on his/her phone. The personalized treatment system can reduce the cost of healthcare.

Drug Discovery

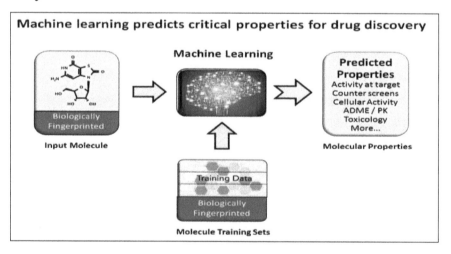

The use of machine learning in drug discovery is a benchmark application of machine learning in medicine. Microsoft Project Hanover is working to bring machine learning technologies in precision medicine. At present, several companies are applying machine learning technique in drug discovery. As an instance, BenevolentAI. Their objective is to use Artificial Intelligence (AI) in drug discovery.

There are several benefits of applying machine learning in this field, such as it will speed up the process and reduce the failure rate. Also, machine learning optimizes the manufacturing process and cost of drug discovery.

Smart Electronic Health Recorder

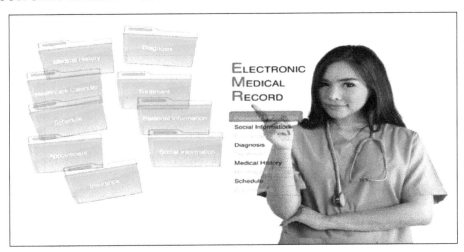

Machine learning scope such as document classification and optical character recognition can be used to develop a smart electronic health record system. The task of this application is to develop a system which can sort patient queries via email or transform a manual record system into an automated system. This objective of this application is to build a safe and easily accessible system.

The rapid growth of electronic health records has enriched the store of medical data about patients, which can be used for improving healthcare. It reduces data errors, for example, duplicate data.

To develop the electronic health recorder system supervised machine learning algorithm like Support Vector Machine (SVM) can be used as a classifier or Artificial Neural Network (ANN) can also be applied.

Machine Learning in Radiology

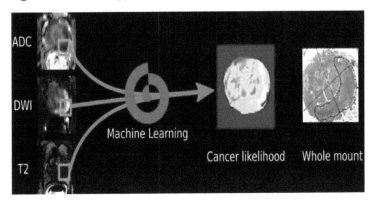

Recently, researchers have been working to integrate machine learning and artificial intelligence in radiology. Aidoc provides software for the radiologist to speed up the process of detection using machine learning approaches.

Their task is to analyze the medical image to offer the intelligible solution for detecting abnormalities across the body. The Supervised machine learning algorithm is used mostly in this field.

For medical image segmentation, machine learning technique is used. Segmentation is the process of identifying structures in an image. For image segmentation, the graph cut segmentation method is used mostly. Natural Language Processing is used for analysis for radiology text reports. Therefore, applying machine learning in radiology can improve the service of patient care.

Clinical Trial and Research

The clinical trial may be a set of queries that require answers to obtain the efficiency and safety of an individual biomedical or pharmaceutical. The purpose of this trial is to focus on the new development of treatments.

This clinical trial costs a lot of money and time. Applying machine learning in this field has a significant impact. An ML-based system can provide real-time monitoring and robust service.

A Practical Application of Machine Learning in Medicine

One application of machine learning in a healthcare context is digital diagnosis. ML can detect patterns of certain diseases within patient electronic healthcare records and inform clinicians of any anomalies. In this sense, the artificial intelligence technique can be compared to a second pair of eyes that can evaluate patient health based on the knowledge extracted from big data sets by summarizing millions of observations of diseases that a patient could possibly have.

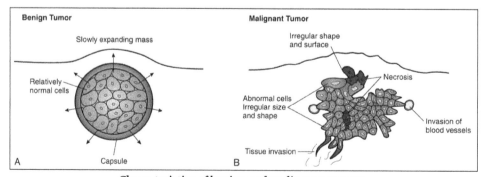

Characteristics of benign and malignant tumors.

This data set consists of several instances of tumors. Tumors can either be benign (non-cancerous) or malignant (cancerous). Benign tumors grow locally and do not spread. As a result, they are not considered cancerous. However, they can still pose a danger, especially if they press against vital organs like the brain. Malignant tumors, in contrast, have the ability to spread and invade other tissues. This process, known as metastasis, is a key feature of cancer. There are many different types of malignancy-based tumors as well as locations that this type of cancer tumor can originate.

The breast cancer data set consists of 699 tumor samples where 458 (65.5%) are benign (non-cancer) tumors and 241 (34.5%) malignant (cancer) tumors. Instances in the data set have the following attributes:

	Attribute	Domain
1	Sample code number	ID number
2	Clump Thickness	1-10
3	Uniformity of Cell Shape	1-10
4	Marginal Adhesion	1-10
5	Single Epithelial Cell Size	1-10
6	Single Epithelial Cell Size	1-10
7	Bare Nuclei	1-10
8	Bland Chromatin	1-10
9	Normal Nucleoli	1-10
10	Mitoses	1-10
11	Class	2 for benign, 4 for malignant

Solving a problem with machine learning often involves many iterative experiments meant to find the best model for solving the problem by further tuning the model. Given that there are many machine learning algorithms and different neural network architectures, a researcher (based on his/her experience, knowledge and trusting his/her intuition) will select the most promising model to set up the first experiment.

In our example, given the relatively small sizes of data sets, my intuition was to start modeling using traditional machine learning algorithms (e.g. SVM, KNN etc.) and shallow neural networks. To demonstrate some initial results using machine learning to diagnose breast cancer, the following set of metrics are used: ROC curve $\approx$ 0.99, Precision-Recall curve $\approx$ 0.99, and F1 $\approx$ 0.97.

Setting up the Diagnosis Model

Step: Dividing the Data Set

In order to get started modeling, the data set was split into two parts:

- Train set (70%), for choosing and validating models.

- Test set (30%), hold out data on which we will see how well models are able to generalize on unseen data.

Step: Defining the Metrics

Next, we need to define the key metrics to measure the efficiency of the models. In order to describe the classifiers' performance in the digital diagnoses problem, we have four basic characteristics (numbers) based on which we can define derivative measurement metrics. These four numbers are:

- TP (True Positive): Number of correctly classified patients who have the disease.

- TN (True Negative): Number of correctly classified patients who are healthy.

- FP (False Positive): Number of misclassified patients who are healthy.

- FN (False Negative): Number of misclassified patients who have the disease.

Based on these numbers we define the metrics as follows:

- Accuracy: Ratio of correctly classified patients to the total number of patients (Accuracy = (TP+TN)/(TP+FP+FN+TN)).

- Precision: Ratio of correctly classified patients with the disease to the total patients classified as having the disease. The intuition behind precision is how many patients classified as having disease truly have the disease (Precision = TP/TP+FP).

- Recall: Ratio of correctly classified diseased patients to patients who have the disease. The intuition behind recall is how many patients who have disease classified as having the disease. (Recall = TP/TP+FN).

Step: Evaluating the Models

The next step involves using precision and recall metrics to evaluate the models. For the sake of simplifying the comparison of various models, we will use the harmonic mean of precision and recall which is called an F1 score (F1 Score = 2*(Recall * Precision) / (Recall + Precision)).

After experimenting with different algorithms, the mean F1 scores, in cross-validation, gained by each classifier is presented below. Given that accuracy is considered the most intuitive measure, it has also been plotted on the graph.

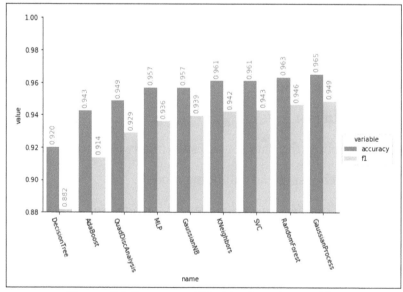

Cross-validation scores of Machine Learning models.

As you can see from the graph, the classifiers are showing pretty good results in terms of being able to better distinguish patients who have cancer versus those who are healthy by reaching 0.94 F1 scores. Where the best value for F1 is 1, and the worst value is 0. In order to gain higher scores, ensembles of these models were created by using bagging techniques.

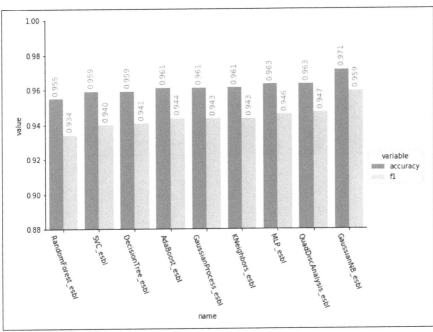

Cross-validation scores of the ensemble Machine Learning models.

As shown in the graph, the ensembles of models performed even better by reaching 0.95 F1 scores.

Step: Creating a Neural Network Model

In addition to the aforementioned diagnostic models, a Neural Network model was created and tuned using the architecture shown below.

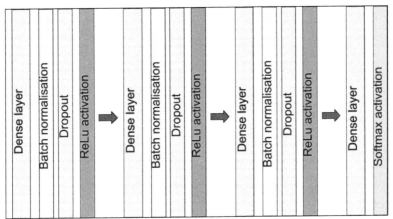

Neural Network model architecture.

This neural network classifier has resulted in 0.97 F1 mean scores on cross-validation. This new neural network model's F1 score is better compared to the best model's score gained in Step 3. Here are the top three models results so far.

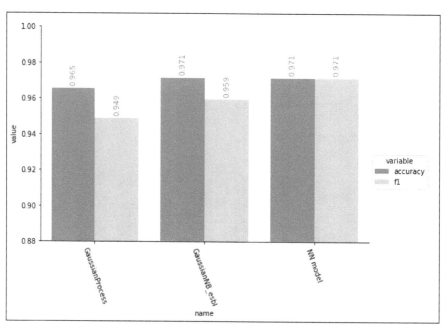

Cross-validation results of the top three models.

Now let's evaluate these models on the test data set which previously was not shown to classifiers imitating new data. Below are the results demonstrating just how well these models performed on the test data set.

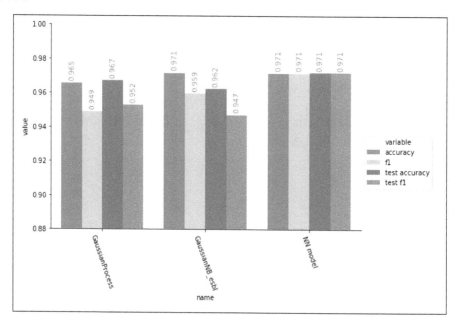

As it's shown in the graph, neural network classifier have performed better by gaining 0.97 F1 scores on the test set.

Step: Evaluating Output Quality through Receiver Operating Curves

In order to further evaluate classifiers' output quality, let's view their receiver operating characteristic (ROC) curves.

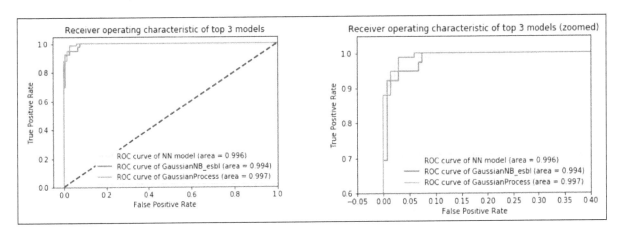

The ROC graph efficiency is measured by the area under the curve. An area of 1 represents a perfect classifier, an area of 0.5 represents a worthless classifier (navy color, dashed line in the graph). Here is the academic point system for judging classifiers efficiency given to area under the curve.

0.90-1 = excellent (A)

0.80-0.90 = good (B)

0.70-0.80 = fair (C)

0.60-0.70 = poor (D)

0.50-0.60 = fail (F)

As it's shown in the graph, all of three classifiers have above 0.99 area under the curve which is considered excellent.

Step: Evaluating Output Quality through Precision-recall Curves

Let's also look at the precision-recall curves associated with these classifiers.

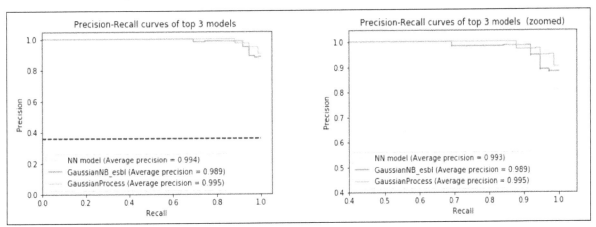

The navy dashed line represents the baseline, where the perfect model is the one with 1 average precision. As you can see, all three models' average precision is close to 1, which are excellent scores.

Step: Visualizing the Decision Boundaries

Lastly, an additional note about the models' decision boundaries:

In order to gain some visual intuition about the data set and the algorithms decision boundaries, we will reduce the dimensionality of 9D feature space to 2D using PCA techniques and visualize the decision boundaries.

PRICE OPTIMISATION AND DYNAMIC PRICING

Briefly, price optimization uses data analysis techniques to pursue two main objectives:

- Understanding how customers will react to different pricing strategies for products and services.

- Finding the best prices for a given company, considering its goals.

Pricing systems have evolved since the early 1970s until now, from applying very simple strategies, such as a standard markup to base cost, to being capable of predicting the demand of products or services and finding the best price to achieve the set KPI.

Price optimization techniques can help retailers evaluate the potential impact of sales promotions or estimate the right price for each product if they want to sell it in a certain period of time.

Current state-of-the-art techniques in price optimization allow retailers to consider factors such as:

- Competition.

- Weather.

- Season.

- Operating costs.

- Local demand.

- Company objectives.

To determine:

- The initial price.

- The best price.

- The discount price.

- The promotional price.

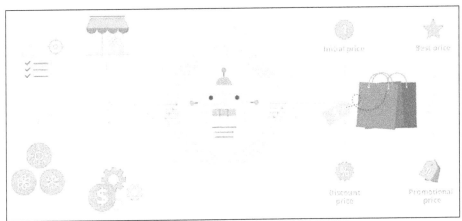

Using different kind and sources of data to find the prices that improve profits.

Price Optimization vs. Dynamic Pricing

It is important to differentiate price optimization from dynamic pricing, given that these terms are sometimes used as synonyms. The main difference is that dynamic pricing is a particular pricing strategy, while price optimization can use any kind of pricing strategy to reach its goals. Despite having many advantages and being quite used, dynamic pricing has some disadvantages when used in an extreme way.

Simply put, using a dynamic pricing strategy, retailers can dynamically alter the prices of their products based on current market demand. In contrast, price optimization techniques consider many more factors to suggest a price or a price range for different scenarios (e.g. initial price, best price, discount price, etc.).

We all know and somehow accept because it seems reasonable, that the price of a hotel room or a plane ticket varies according to the season, the day of the week or the anticipation with which we booked. However, when prices change too fast – sometimes in the course of a few hours – some customers might have the feeling that prices are unfair or that the company is practicing price gouging. Dynamic pricing is, therefore, a strategy to be used with caution.

Machine Learning for Retail Price Optimization

The pricing strategies used in the retail world have some peculiarities. For example, retailers can determine the prices of their items by accepting the price suggested by the manufacturer (commonly known as MSRP). This is particularly true in the case of mainstream products. Another simple strategy is keystone, which consists in defining the sale price as the double of the wholesale price or cost of the product.

While these and other strategies are widely used, ML enables retailers to develop more complex strategies that work far better to achieve their KPIs. ML techniques can be used it in many ways to optimize prices.

A Typical Scenario

Imagine an online or brick-and-mortar retailer who wants to estimate the best prices for new products for the next season. The competition is hard, so their prices and promotions need to be taken into consideration. Therefore, the retailer adopts a widely used strategy: competitive pricing. Simply put, this strategy defines the price of a product or service based on the prices of the competition.

Let's see the steps needed to develop a ML solution for this use case.

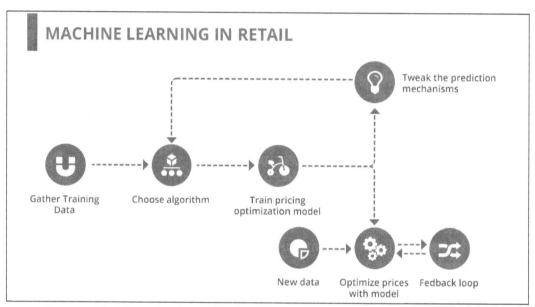

Process of defining prices in retail with price optimization using Machine Learning.

Gather Input Data

First of all, we need data. To train Machine Learning models, it is necessary to have different kinds of information:

- Transactional: A sales history that includes the list of the products purchased and, eventually, the customers who purchased them.

- Description of the products: A catalog with relevant information about each product such as category, size, brand, style, color, photos and manufacturing or purchase cost.

- Data on past promotions and past marketing campaigns.

- Customer Reviews: Reviews and feedback given by customers about the products.

- Data on the competition: Prices applied to identical or similar products.

- Inventory and supply data.

- In the case of physical stores: Information about their geographical location and that of the competitors.

Depending on the set KPIs and the way of modeling the solution, some of this data may not be necessary. For example, if there is little or no information about customers, which is sometimes the case for brick-and-mortar retailers, the model can nonetheless be trained.

In contrast, information about the competition is crucial for a competitive pricing strategy. In many cases, it is even possible to connect via APIs to this information or monitor it online.

Define Goals and Constraints

The next step is to define the strategic goals and constraints.

Retailers may pursue a unique, clear objective of profit maximization. However, they may also be interested in customer loyalty (e.g. increasing the net promoter score or the conversion rate) or in attracting a new segment (e.g. young people).

Restrictions may be of legal nature (e.g. if some type of control of sale prices is carried out), they may have to do with the reputation of the company (e.g. fearing a bad image for applying favorable prices only to a certain segment of customers) or be related to physical aspects such as the capacity of a store or the average time of supply.

Each particular scenario will impact the way the problem is modeled. It is possible, and usually very interesting, to test different scenarios for the same retailer, which implies using different models.

Modeling and Training

In this step, the data previously gathered is used to train the ML models. There is a wide variety of models that can be used in price optimization. Historically, Generalized Linear Models (GLMs) have been used (in particular, logistic regression. However, for a few years, more complex and powerful methods have been developed. For instance, depending on the volume of data available, it could be possible to use Deep Learning methods.

In this case, in which we are dealing with new products for the next season, there is an additional difficulty since there is no previous product data. The interesting thing is that the ML models will know how to find similar products and be effective despite not having specific prior data. The same happens in the case of retailers that sell rare or exotic products.

Execute and Adjust Prices

Once the model is trained, prices can be estimated for the new products. Depending on the modeling, the estimate may be an exact price or a range. The prices obtained by the model can be subsequently adjusted manually by the retailer.

More Opportunities of using Machine Learning for Price Optimization

Machine Learning can be used for other tasks related to pricing in retail. For example, given a new product, clustering algorithm can quickly associate it with similar products to obtain a probable price segment. Another compelling possibility is to jointly predict prices and demands for items that were never sold.

More generally, ML can be a tremendous tool for insights:

- In what way is the sale of pants impacted when shirts' prices are drastically cut?
- When efforts are made to sell more pens, are the related products, such as ink, notebooks or work agendas, impacted?

- Are customers who buy a certain computer more or less likely to buy monitors the following month?

- Are inactive clients in the last year sensitive to a promotion campaign?

These are just some examples of the questions that ML models can help answer.

Advantages of Price Optimization with Machine Learning

In addition to automation and speed, there are several advantages to using ML to optimize prices.

First, ML models can consider a huge number of products and optimize prices globally. The number and nature of parameters and their multiple sources and channels allow them to make decisions using fine criteria. This is a daunting task if retailers try to do it manually, or even using basic software.

For example, it is known that changing the price of a product often impacts the sales of other products in ways that are very hard to predict for a human. In most cases, the accuracy of a ML solution will be significantly higher than that of a human. In addition, retailers can modify the KPI and immediately see how the models recalculate prices for the new goals.

Second, by analyzing a large amount of past and current data, a ML can anticipate trends early enough. This is a key issue that allows retailers to make appropriate decisions to adjust prices.

Finally, in the case of a competitive pricing strategy, ML solutions can continuously crawl the web and social media to gather valuable information about prices of competitors for the same or similar products, what customers say about products and competitors, considering hot deals, as well as the price history over the last number of days or weeks.

A system that can learn most of what is happening in the market allows retailers to have more information than their competitors in order to make better decisions.

Online vs. Brick-and-mortar Retailers

While it may seem more natural to apply ML in the case of online retailers, brick-and-mortar retailers can perfectly take advantage from this technology. For this type of retailers there are restrictions of physical order, which can be integrated into the models.

For example, it is possible to jointly optimize the sale price, the way in which the products are displayed, the place they occupy on the shelves and their location in the store.

Variables such as the dimensions of the product or the distance from the entrance of the store to the shelves play an important role in how the problem is modeled. This is not a problem of optimizing the space on the shelves, which can also be addressed with ML, but of building a model that captures the way in which the disposition of the products in the store influences the demand.

Companies using Machine Learning for Price Optimization

Price optimization has been used, with significant success, in industries such as hospitality, airline, car rental, and online retail. In some cases, it is more about dynamic prices than price optimization, and we saw above that these terms are sometimes confused.

One of the first success stories occurred in the early 2000s, when Hilton Hotels Corp and Inter-Continental Hotels Group decided to eliminate fixed rates in favor of a fluid scheme, including dynamic pricing strategies. In those years the prices of the rooms were modified once or twice a day. The current computational power allows prices to change practically in real time.

The hotel industry continues to employ dynamic pricing strategies, based entirely on ML. Currently, Airbnb proposes a dynamic price tool that recommends prices to its hosts, considering parameters such as seasonality, the day of the week or special events, and also more sophisticated factors such as photos of the property to be rented or the prices applied in the neighborhood. Other companies such as eBay and Uber have adopted similar approaches.

In the retail world, the most popular examples have been in e-commerce, but brick-and-mortar retailers have not been left behind. Although it is difficult to know precisely all the retail companies using ML to optimize their prices and operating processes, there are nevertheless some known success stories.

Companies like Ralph Lauren and Michael Kors use ML to offer fewer markdowns and better manage their inventory, seeking to increase profit margins, even at the risk of losing a little revenue. Another well-known case is that of Zara, which uses ML to minimize promotions and adapt quickly to the changing trends. There are many other success stories, such as Morrisons —one of the largest supermarket chains in the United Kingdom–, bonprix –an international fashion company based in Germany– or Monoprice –an American B2B and B2C electronics retailer–, among others. While there is no information available on the exact modeling of the problems, it is known that these companies are taking advantage of the power of ML to increase their revenues and improve operations.

References

- Understanding-image-recognition-and-its-uses: einfochips.com, Retrieved 19 August, 2019

- Top-10-potential-applications-of-machine-learning-in-healthcare: ubuntupit.com, Re-trieved 15 April, 2019

- A-practical-application-of-machine-learning-in-medicine: macadamian.com, Retrieved 10 March, 2019

- Price-optimization-machine-learning: tryolabs.com, Retrieved 24 February, 2019

PERMISSIONS

We would like to thank the editorial team for lending their expertise to make the book truly unique. They have played a crucial role in the development of this book. Without their invaluable contributions this book wouldn't have been possible. They have made vital efforts to compile up to date information on the varied aspects of this subject to make this book a valuable addition to the collection of many professionals and students.

This book was conceptualized with the vision of imparting up-to-date and integrated information in this field. To ensure the same, a matchless editorial board was set up. Every individual on the board went through rigorous rounds of assessment to prove their worth. After which they invested a large part of their time researching and compiling the most relevant data for our readers.

The editorial board has been involved in producing this book since its inception. They have spent rigorous hours researching and exploring the diverse topics which have resulted in the successful publishing of this book. They have passed on their knowledge of decades through this book. To expedite this challenging task, the publisher supported the team at every step. A small team of assistant editors was also appointed to further simplify the editing procedure and attain best results for the readers.

Apart from the editorial board, the designing team has also invested a significant amount of their time in understanding the subject and creating the most relevant covers. They scrutinized every image to scout for the most suitable representation of the subject and create an appropriate cover for the book.

The publishing team has been an ardent support to the editorial, designing and production team. Their endless efforts to recruit the best for this project, has resulted in the accomplishment of this book. They are a veteran in the field of academics and their pool of knowledge is as vast as their experience in printing. Their expertise and guidance has proved useful at every step. Their uncompromising quality standards have made this book an exceptional effort. Their encouragement from time to time has been an inspiration for everyone.

The publisher and the editorial board hope that this book will prove to be a valuable piece of knowledge for students, practitioners and scholars across the globe.

INDEX